John L. Tomkinson comes from Stoke-on-Trent in the English Midlands. He was educated at the University of Wales (Lampeter) and the University of Keele in Staffordshire. He holds an MA in History and an MA and a PhD in Philosophy from the University of Keele.

A British qualified and trained teacher, he has thirty-five years experience teaching History to students from primary to undergraduate level, the latter for the University of Maryland, and has experience of the British and US systems of education, and of teaching in international schools. He has taught IB History for fifteen years and has been an assessor for the International Baccalaureate since 1995.

Today he teaches at the Moraitis School in Athens, and writes on various subjects.

Themes in Twentieth Century World History for the International Baccalaureate

In the same series and by the same author:

Single-Party States

The Cold War

Susie Shih

Wars and Warfare

John L. Tomkinson

Anagnosis
Athens, Greece

Anagnosis
Harilaou Trikoupi 130
145 63 Kifissia
Athens, Greece
Website: www.anagnosis.gr

First published 2003
Reprinted 2005
Second edition 2006
Reprinted 2006
Reprinted 2007

ISBN 978-960-88087-2-3
Third Edition
© Anagnosis 2008

Photoset and printed by:
K. Pletsas - Z. Karadri O.E.
Harilaou Trikoupi 107
Athens
www.typografio.gr

Teachers' Preface

The teacher of history for the course of the International Baccalaureate has a very difficult task. Some problems are shared with teachers of other subjects, while some are unique to history.

The IB course is a short one: two academic years means considerably less time than two calendar years, when the final examinations are held in May or November. In addition, many of the students are studying in a language which is not their mother tongue.

Unlike the "newer" Group Three subjects, where it is assumed that students enter the course knowing nothing about the subject at all, and where the standards of examination are based entirely upon what can reasonably be accomplished in such a short time, it is assumed that history students will already have a long background in the subject when they enter on the course, and the standard of the examination is necessarily set high, because the grades awarded have to be comparable with those of long-established university entrance examinations, which are themselves the final stage in a long period of education and training in the discipline.

Yet in practice IB History students, particularly those in international schools, come to the subject from very different backgrounds. Their experience of history in their previous schools may not provide any useful foundation for their IB studies at all; and it may even be counterproductive. In his book *Lies My Teacher Told Me: Everything Your American History Textbook Got Wrong*, James W. Loewen quotes a colleague teaching history in college as saying that he sees his first job as disabusing his charges of what they learned in high school. "In no other field does this happen. Mathematics professors, for instance, know that non-Euclidian geometry is rarely taught in high school, but they don't assume that Euclidian geometry was *mistaught*. Professors of English literature don't presume that *Romeo and Juliet* was misunderstood in high school. Indeed, history is the only field in which the more courses students take, the stupider they become." In many countries, the study of history in schools has been reduced to the rote learning of selective "basic facts" and stories, or it is so imbued with nationalist ideology as to be worse than useless.

The history teacher is thus pulled from both ends. On the one hand his/her pupils may have no useful background in the subject at all, or one which is actually counterproductive, and they may not be working in their mother tongue. On the other hand, he/she has to prepare students in a very short period of time for examinations which are marked to a standard which matches those of students who have usefully studied history in their mother tongue over many years. This means that the history teacher has very speedily to instill in his/her students a new way of looking at the subject, teach new skills and provide basic facts, yet at the same time provide a level of analysis which will enable the students to obtain the best grades of which they are capable.

There is no shortage of excellent texts for school history, but few are designed to provide for the wide range of levels and backgrounds which the IB course needs to encompass. Either they are designed for lower level examinations, and provide basic facts and an elementary introduction to analysis, or they provide adequate analysis, but assume knowledge of basic facts.

This small series of books is an attempt to fill that void, by providing both basic facts and a range of analysis, which will enable the students to make the transition to an appropriate level as quickly as possible.

They may usefully be employed as an accompaniment to a course taught in class, the numbered paragraphs providing ready references. Students may use the text as a model upon which to construct their own notes. The texts may also function as revision notes for examinations. Each individual note usually contains a single idea which can be identified by a key word or phrase. If the student identifies these key words by highlighting or underlining them, then the very mental process of making the decision about which word(s) to highlight will ensure that he/she will have actively considered the points, and the process of committing facts and theories to memory will have already taken place. Running the eye over the highlighted words will then quickly enable recall of the entire set of ideas. As examples, the key words in the notes have sometimes been highlighted in bold; but most have been left for the students themselves to do.

The unusual format of these texts is an attempt to combine the condensation of notes with the readability of a text, giving the student some idea both of the depth of knowledge which needs to be acquired and the level of analysis which needs to be aimed at.

Like many books designed for use in schools, these do not have detailed footnotes. Students should be warned that this makes them unsuitable for use as sources for internally assessed studies or extended essays; although used as initial reading they may provide the student with some initial idea of the background to be mastered, and the issues to be confronted, in approaching a particular topic.

A lot of attention has been paid to the development of the students' vocabulary, with the needs of those not working in their mother tongue in mind. Science students spend much of their time becoming acquainted with the technical vocabulary of their subject. By contrast, students of history are frequently quite unaware of the need to assimilate a special vocabulary at all, because history books do not have the immediate opacity that science texts present to the uninitiated. Teachers are sometimes unaware of the burden of new vocabulary required of their students because they themselves assimilated it imperceptibly over many years, and fail to realise how unfamiliar it may be to their students.

A good grade in one of today's university entrance examinations such as the IB, requires that the student demonstrate evidence of wide reading. Without an adequate command of the terminology of history, such reading may be superficial, ill-assimilated, and of limited use. Even those students who understand such terms in context may be unable to use them confidently, if at all, in their own essays and examinations, without some explicit focus upon their meaning. Dictionaries have their uses as works of reference, but there are few students so highly motivated, or so Spartan in character, as to work their way through a dictionary of relevant terms. I have tried to focus upon the meaning of key terms which dominate the study of the themes covered in each volume. This should make the students more aware of the complex conceptual issues at stake in the subjects they are studying, and might also go some way towards dragging students away from narrative, and focusing their attention upon ideas and issues.

Finally, History should never be a "dead subject" concerned entirely with the past, with no relevance to the burning issues of the day. These books are offered to help students see the relevance of what they study to understanding today's world, to be more intelligent and critical in their reading of contemporary situations, and so come to grips with the living issues of the day in a confident and thoughtful manner.

John L. Tomkinson
Athens 2005

Contents

Acknowledgements

My thanks are due to Aris Karey of *Anagnosis Books* for encouraging and fostering the project, Christine Lacroix for reading and correcting the manuscript, and Aliki Kotsikou for the cover design.

Every effort has been made to trace all copyright-holders, but if any have been inadvertently overlooked, the publishers will be pleased to make the necessary arrangements at the first opportunity.

Author's Note

IB teachers will be aware that the various options on the History course overlap considerably. For this reason, a considerable amount of material directly relevant to the study of wars and warfare may be found in the other volumes in this series: for example, on the Vietnam War(s) and the Afghan War in *The Cold War*.

1. Wars and Warfare

Peace and War

The Balance of Power

1. Warfare is a state of armed conflict involving different states; although **civil war** is war fought principally between different forces within the *same* state.
2. It was once generally considered that the chief function of statesmen was to avoid wars and to maintain the peace.
3. During the eighteenth century the maintenance of the peace among the Great Powers of Europe (France, Austria, Prussia, Russia and Britain), was accomplished by the creation and maintenance of a **balance of power**. This was achieved when the great powers were grouped into defensive alliances which were so evenly balanced that neither alliance could be sure of winning a war against the other. Under those conditions neither side could rationally contemplate going to war, since to do so would be to risk the genuine possibility of defeat, with all the loss, for the leaders themselves and for their countries, which this entailed. (The assumption was that the statesmen who made decisions of war and peace were motivated by rational calculations - by **reason**.)
4. Thus wars would only break out in Europe if an unnoticed, or unprepared for, increase or decrease in the military power of one or more states took place, which would disturb the balance of power.
   The wars at the end of the eighteenth century were caused by the disproportionate power of France, which upset the balance of power in Europe. They were fought to decide whether or not France would come to dominate the continent of Europe, and hence the world. This was settled finally with the defeat of Napoleon in 1815.
5. After the disruptions of the French Revolution and the Revolutionary Wars, the practice was adopted whereby the leaders of the great powers would meet together to settle possible sources of conflict or disturbance between themselves. Known as the **Concert of Europe**, this lasted into the latter part of the century.
6. After 1815 Britain was the dominant world power, but Britain was:
   (a) isolated from the continental mainland by the English Channel;
   (b) preoccupied with maintaining and extending her overseas empire.
   Thus this did not upset the balance of power in Europe.
7. With the creation of the German Empire in 1871, bringing together the military power of Prussia and the manpower, intellectual, agricultural and industrial resources of the other German states, the balance of power was once more destabilized.
   The great wars of the twentieth century (the First and Second World Wars) were fought, in large part, to determine whether or not Germany would come to dominate Europe and the world.

The Purposes of Waging War

1. Wars may be classified according to the chief reasons for which they are fought.
   For each side, any particular war will have an **offensive** or a **defensive** character. A war in which one side simply attacks the other is a **war of aggression**. A **punitive** war, or war of **revenge**, is fought to punish the other side for some real or imagined aggression in the past. A **pre-emptive** war is one which is actually offensive, but for which defensive reasons are claimed. A attacks B because A believes, or claims to believe, that B was about to attack A, and A wants to get in first so as not to lose the initiative.

2. An **ideological** war is one in which the two sides are divided by ideology, and this difference is a major factor in the character of the war. A **holy war** is a special type of ideological war. The Christian crusades of the Middle Ages were fought as holy wars, and the term **crusade** is now used as a synonym for a holy war. Islamic nations sometimes claim that their wars have a religious character. The term *jihad* is used to denote such a conflict.

3. **Imperial** wars, or **colonial** wars, are wars fought by imperial powers to acquire or safeguard colonies or client states (disguised colonies). When subject peoples struggle to obtain their independence they are said to fight wars of **national liberation**, or wars of **decolonization**.

4. **Post-colonial conflicts** arise when newly-independent countries go to war with each other to resolve some problem between them which is an inheritance of the colonial era. This is usually because the former colonial boundaries, imposed upon them by the conquerors, were drawn with rulers on maps in European palaces during conferences, and represent no realities on the ground, such as mountain barriers or tribal boundaries.

5. A **proxy** war is one fought between states on behalf of other states. Many wars during the Cold War period were proxy wars, fought by small nominally independent client states on behalf of their **hegemonic powers**. In this way the two **superpowers** jockeyed for advantage without the risks involved in a direct confrontation with each other.

International Relations

1. Representatives of one state who are officially accredited to another are collectively known as diplomats, and their work of managing inter-state relations is called **diplomacy**.

2. The chief representative of one government to another is usually known as an **ambassador**. His office, the embassy, is reckoned to be under the law of the country represented in it, and not the law of the country in which it is situated.

3. A special representative of a government who is empowered to make decisions on his own, either in talks with another government or at a conference, is known as a **plenipotentiary**.

4. Today modern methods of transport allow such representatives to move around the world from capital city to capital city at great speed. This is known as "**shuttle diplomacy.**"

5. War is usually an indication of a severe failure of diplomacy.

The Causes of War

1. Wars bring death and destruction, sometimes on a massive scale, therefore statesmen rarely lead their countries into a war without claiming to have adequate justification. To do this, they usually cite a **pretext**. This is a reason, or set of reasons, designed to make their actions appear justifiable to their own people, to world public opinion, and to the judgement of history. A pretext is not merely claimed as the main *cause(s)* for launching a war, it is an attempted *justification* for going to war. Such a pretext is sometimes called a ***casus belli***.

2. The pretext for going to war is frequently fictitious. This can be seen when the initial pretext is changed, during the course of the war, when it has generally come to be seen as false. Thus the pretext for the USA going to war against Saddam Hussein in 2004 was originally the danger posed by his stockpiles of weapons of mass destruction: chemical, biological and nuclear, which could swiftly be deployed against the USA, and his links to Al-Quaida, the terrorist organisation supposedly responsible for the attack of 11th September 2002 on the centres of US power. These were not very convincing pretexts, since not only was there no evidence that Saddam Hussein had any weapons of mass destruction, but it was known that the facilities for creating and maintaining them did not exist, and since the secularist Saddam Hussein was hated by the religious extremists who were supposed to comprise Al-Quaida. When it became obvious that Saddam did not have any weapons of mass destruction, and that there had never been any good evidence available to those launching the war that he had, and that there was no connection between Saddam Hussein and Al-Quaida, the pretext for going to war was changed to: "pre-empting someone who in the future might develop weapons of mass destruction" (which country might not?); to "deposing an evil dictator" (why this one?); and then "bringing democracy to Iraq" (why Iraq of all places?).

Historians have to look behind the various unconvincing pretexts offered by politicians for their aggression to seek the genuine causes: in the case of the example above: the possibilities include: to dominate the region; to secure the Iraqi oil-fields under US military control; to provide lucrative business contracts for powerful cronies of the administration; to create "war fever" in order to suppress criticism of the administration and secure its re-election; to pursue a family vendetta; etc., etc. The real causes of a war are usually complex.

3. Paradoxically, a pretext can be false in one sense, even though it is true in another. The pretext for Hitler's invasion of the USSR in 1941 was that Stalin was preparing to double cross him and attack Germany. This was false, since the real reason for Hitler's invasion of the USSR was his desire to destroy Bolshevism, to expand into Eastern Europe and to enslave the Slavs; and he found that in the summer of 1941 he was able at last to turn to this long awaited and long-planned-for task outlined years beforehand in *Mein Kampf*, and mentioned in the *Hossbach Memorandum*. However, the pretext also happened to be true, in the sense that Stalin *was* undoubtedly planning to double-cross Hitler by invading Germany when he was ready to do so in order to pre-empt the threat that Hitler posed to the USSR. However, in any objective analysis of *causes* of Hitler's invasion of the USSR, it is important only to take into account those factors which genuinely determined Hitler's decision.

The Classification of Genuine Causes

1. When people first start learning history at school, it is frequently seen as a collection of facts about the past, for example, that World War I broke out in 1914. But history would hardly be worth doing, if all that it consisted of was in amassing collections of facts: ''A mere collector of supposed facts is as useful as a collector of matchboxes'' (Febvre.) In addition to gathering factual information about past events, historians seek to *understand* and *explain* these events. In order to do this, they seek causes.

2. Causes in history are different from the causes dealt with in physics, chemistry or biology. Those causes are almost always general. They are of the form "events of type a regularly follow events of type b." By contrast, causes in history are usually particular. In this, they are more like the causes we seek in everyday life.

3. Establishing the causes of an event such as the outbreak of a war can be a complex business.

The factors which help bring about a state of affairs are of several kinds. This may be best seen by considering a fictional situation:

4. In the land of X there had long been a struggle for power between two parties, the Browns, who favoured eating brown eggs, and the Whites, who preferred white eggs. Over the years, the struggle between the two had grown very bitter, particularly between the extremists on both sides.

   When, one year, the whites won the elections by a narrow margin, the party was dominated by White extremists. These immediately laid onerous legal penalties upon the Browns. While moderate Browns suffered passively or protested vocally, the extremists determined to overthrow the whites by force. Despising both their White foes and their Brown allies, they determined to strike decisively at the leaders of both groups by blowing up the parliament building.

   Now it so happened that in order to raise money, the cellars beneath the parliament building were advertised for rent as storage space. Fawkes, a Brown leader, saw his chance. He rented out the cellars and filled them with barrels of gunpowder. Then, he left a pile of gunpowder at the foot of the barrels, with a trail of powder leading up the stairs to the inside of the door of the cellar.

   When parliament met he took a flaming torch to the cellars and lit the end of the trail of gunpowder. The flame passed along the trail of powder to the barrels, which exploded with great force, destroying the leadership of the Whites and the moderate Browns at the same time. This went down in the history books of X as "the Great Gunpowder Assassination."

   What was the cause of the Great Gunpowder Assassination?

5. Clearly there were many causal factors to take into account in any explanation of this event:
   - (a) Fawkes' lighting the trail of gunpowder;
   - (b) Fawkes' bravery and ruthlessness;
   - (c) The leasing of the cellars for storage;
   - (d) The opposition of the Browns and Whites;
   - (e) The oppression of the Browns by the Whites;
   - (f) The resentment by the Browns of this situation;
   - (g) The fact that above a certain temperature gunpowder explodes.

   The most obvious candidate for the most important factor is (a), since it was this which actually set off the explosion. But by itself, (a) explains little. It does not explain why anyone would *want* to blow up the parliament.

   More important causal factors are (d), (e), and (f). These are required to explain *why* the Great Gunpowder Assassination happened. These are called **long term causes,** using the metaphor of distance, or **deep causes** or **underlying causes**, using the metaphor of depth; while factors (a) (b) and (c) may be referred to as a **short term causes** or **shallow causes**.

   These are relative terms. One cause may be more long term, or deeper, than another.

   Factor (g) is a **standing condition**. It is always true. Yet if it were not true, the explosion would not have occurred. It is usually taken for granted, and is of no real interest to the investigator concerned with this particular event.

   At the other extreme, factor (a) seems to be the shortest term cause of all. It is sometimes called the **immediate cause**.

The Nature of Warfare

1. In Europe the religious wars of the sixteenth century were very bloody affairs. The enemy were considered wicked and damned to hell simply for holding the "wrong" religious beliefs. All the "righteous," i.e. those who held the "right" religious beliefs, had a duty to participate, and to

show the enemy no mercy. The defeated would be treated with inhuman cruelty, being routinely tortured and executed in various vile ways, e.g. by hanging and disembowelling.

2. As a reaction, by the eighteenth century, known as the "Age of Reason," warfare was considered as an unfortunate breakdown in normal civilised relations.

3. It was almost exclusively the business of rulers and the professional armies which they paid to fight them. The duty of the citizen was simply to pay his taxes and to let the rulers get on with their business of diplomacy, and the armies with their business of fighting wars. Warfare was not the business of civilians. Indeed, it was not unusual for citizens of a country to visit another country with which their king was at war, either for business or pleasure, and to suffer no ill consequences.

4. By the eighteenth century, war in Europe was highly **conventionalized**.

Conventions are accepted ways of doing things. There are many possible ways of eating food, but in China people often use chopsticks, while in the West they usually use knives and forks. In Britain, the knife must be held in the right hand and the fork in the left. In some countries the traffic keeps to the right of the road, and in others to the left.

Regiments of soldiers in distinctive brightly coloured uniforms, designed for instant recognition, lined up and faced each other on reasonably level ground, while their generals, on horseback on rising ground behind, sent down orders moving them about like chess-pieces on a board.

The Manner in which Wars are Fought

1. Wars may also be classified according to the manner in which they are fought.

2. The standard pattern is that wars are fought between **regular armies**. If one side fights with irregular soldiers, that is, soldiers who do not wear uniform and engage in ambush and hit-and-run tactics, it is said to be fighting a **guerrilla war**. During an armed occupation of one country by the army of another, resistance may take the form of **irregular warfare,** while fighting may be conducted by fighters called **partisans**, or freedom fighters, by the people of the occupied country, and terrorists by the occupiers. Wars which display great difference between the levels of military development of the weaponry and resources of the two sides are examples of **asymmetrical warfare**. Such wars are sometimes **low-intensity wars**, i.e. violence may be sporadic, but carried out over a long period of time.

3. Most wars have been **wars of movement**, when armies manoeuvre and counter-manoeuvre as each army tries to gain some tactical advantage over the other. By contrast, in static warfare, both sides face each other for some time without movement, as in the Westerb Front in the First World War. **Mechanised warfare** refers to the use of mechanised transport to gain advantage in a war or movement.

4. A **limited war** is one fought with limited aims and within a restricted area, and/or with limited resort to weapons. By contrast, total war is war fought to destroy the enemy, without any such limitations on the areas of activity or weapons employed.

Strategy, Tactics and Logistics

In the process of fighting wars, it is normal to distinguish strategy from tactics.

Strategy is the means by which the commanders dispose of the forces which are under their command in such a way that they impose upon the enemy the necessity to fight at a disadvantage.

Tactics are the means adopted to achieve victory when actually in contact with the enemy on the battlefield.

Logistics refers to the necessary and complex art of moving troops about and quartering (or lodging) them, and of keeping them adequately supplied with food, equipment, arms, fuel, etc.

The Conclusions of Wars

1. Wars usually end with the surrender or defeat of one of the parties. This may be **conditional surrender**, i.e. one side may offer to surrender under certain conditions, or it may be **unconditional surrender.** In either case the side surrendering has been defeated, and the other side can claim a victory.

2. Both sides may initially agree only to an **armistice**, **cease-fire** or **truce**. This is simply an agreement to stop the actual fighting, and, technically, it may not lead to an end to the war; although in general, the side requesting the armistice is usually reckoned to have lost, since the other side may impose terms as a condition for agreeing to an armistice.

3. A **peace settlement** usually follows. This may be negotiated with the defeated side or it may simply be imposed upon them, when the victors reward themselves at the expense of the defeated.

4. The victorious side may demand **war reparations** from their opponents. This is a fine to cover the cost of fighting the war, and is levied upon the assumption that the defeated side was responsible for the war, and therefore should be required to pay its costs. The victorious side may also hold trials of members of the defeated governments or armies for **war crimes** they may have committed.

5. The victors are never held responsible, either for the outbreak of the war, or for their own war crimes.

Glossary

armistice: a cease-fire, an agreement to stop the fighting

asymmetrical warfare: warfare between very unequally balanced forces of different levels of military sophistication, in which the more sophisticated usually call the less sophisticated "terrorists" and use this as a pretext themselves to evade the rules of war.

balance of power: a situation in which it would not be rational for either side to resort to war.

blockade: an attempt to prevent supplies from reaching a country or port

cease-fire: an agreement to stop the fighting

civil war: war chiefly fought between citizens of the same country

conditional surrender: a negotiated surrender whereby both sides agree to certain limitations on their actions

casus belli: a pretext for war

declaration of war: a formal note sent from one government to another expressing the intention of going to war

diplomacy: the management of international relations

diplomats: government officials charged with managing relations with other countries

economic warfare: the attempt to sabotage the economy of another country

international law: law which governs the relations between nations

limited war: a war between countries limited to only one area

logistics: the art of moving, lodging and supplying troops with all that is necessary for them to fight

occupation: the forces of one country enter and dominate another

partisans: freedom fighters who are resisting foreign occupation

peace conference: a meeting of the victors, perhaps with the vanquished, to arrange their affairs after a war

peace treaty: an agreement among the victors to arrange their affairs in a certain way

plenipotentiary: a representative with full powers to conclude negotiations on his own authority

pretext: a professed reason (as opposed to the real reason), or excuse

psychological warfare: an attempt to mislead or undermine the morale of an enemy

reparations: a fine or penalty imposed by the victors of a war upon the defeated parties to recompense them for the cost of the war, on the assumption that the war was the fault of the losers

shuttle diplomacy: travel from capital city to capital city to arrange matters between nations, usually in a crisis, possibly due to the speed of modern communications and travel

strategy: the management of war

tactics: the art of disposing military forces, especially in the presence of the enemy

total war: war without restraint or limits

truce: an armistice or cease-fire

unconditional surrender: surrender without any conditions

war crimes: crimes committed in the process of waging war, e.g. launching a war of aggression, ill-treatment of POWs, depriving people in occupied territories of their basic civil rights

weapons of mass destruction (WMDs): name given at the beginning of the twenty-first century to chemical, biological and nuclear weapons when not in the hands of the USA and its allies.

Bibliography

Blainey, Geoffrey, *The Causes of War, 3rd ed.,* Free Press (New York, 1988)

Bond, Brian, *War and Society in Europe, 1870-1970,* Fontana (London, 1984)

Brodie, Bernard & Fawn, M., *From Crossbow to H-Bomb,* Indiana University Press (Bloomington, 1973)

Brown, Seyom, *The Causes and Prevention of War, 2nd ed.,* St. Martin's Press, (New York, 1994)

Buchan, Alastair, *War in Modern Society,* Watts (London, 1966)

Calvocoressi, Peter & Wint, Guy, *Total War, 2nd ed.,* Pantheon (London, 1989)

Cashman, Greg, *What Causes War? An Introduction to Theories of International Conflict,* Lexington Books, (New York, 1993)

Copeland, Dale C., *The Origins of Major War,* Cornell University Press (Ithaca, NY., 2000)

Ellis, John A., *A Short History of Guerrilla Warfare,* Ian Allan, (London, 1975)

Fuller, J. F. C., *The Conduct of War, 1789-1961: A Study of the Impact of the French, Industrial, and Russian Revolutions on War and Its Conduct,* Da Capo Press (New York, 1992)

Glossop, Ronald J., *Confronting War: An Examination of Humanity's Most Pressing Problem, 3rd ed.,* McFarland, (Jefferson, NC., 1994)

Howard, Michael, *The Causes of War, and Other Essays,* Harvard University Press (Cambridge, Mass., 1983)

Howard, Michael, *War in European History*, Oxford University Press (Oxford & New York, 1976)

Kagan, John, *On the Origins of War and the Preservation of Peace*, Doubleday (New York, 1995)

Knapp, Wilfrid, *A History of War and Peace, 1939-1965,* Oxford University Press (Oxford, 1967)

Laqueur, Walter, *Guerilla a Historical and Critical Study,* Little, Brown, (London & Boston, Mass., 1977)

Leiden, Carl, & Schmitt, Karl M., *The Politics of Violence: Revolution in the Modern World,* (Engelwood Cliffs, NJ., 1968)

Marwick, Arthur, *War and Social Change in the Twentieth Century,* (London, 1974)

Nelson, Keith L. & Olin, Spencer C. Jr., *Why War? Ideology, Theory, and History,* University of California Press (Berkeley, 1979)

Stoessinger, John G., *Why Nations Go to War. 8th ed.,* St. Martin's Press, (Boston, 2001)

Taber, Robert, *The War of the Flea: a study of guerrilla warfare: theory and practice,* Lyle Stuart, (New York, 2002)

Van Evera, Stephen, *Causes of War: Power and the Roots of Conflict.* Ithaca, Cornell University Press (New York, 1999)

Watt, D. C., *Too Serious a Business: European Armed Forces and the Approach to the Second World War*, Temple Smith (London, 1975)

Otto von Bismarck

2. The First World War

"The next war will start because of some damn fool thing in the Balkans." (Otto von Bismarck)

Background

1. At the beginning of the twentieth century, Europeans, or people of European descent, dominated the world. Vast areas of Africa and Asia were ruled directly from Europe by imperial powers. Most of the rest of the world, although nominally independent, was indirectly under European or US control, or dominated by the descendants of European settlers.

2. In the eighteenth century Europe itself had been dominated by five Great Powers: Britain, France, Prussia, Austria and Russia.

3. Traditionally, peace between the Great Powers had been secured by creating and preserving a balance of power. Since losing a war would be so damaging, statesmen thought that reasonable leaders would not start one unless there was a high probability of winning. Therefore responsible statesmen sought to arrange international relations in such a way that each of the great powers was enrolled in one of two more or less equally balanced alliances. In that way one side would never be tempted to launch a war, because no alliance would have such an advantage over the other that its leaders could be reasonably certain of winning. This was known as the **balance of power**.

4. Only when conditions changed, and one state became so powerful that its leaders were tempted to believe that they could disturb the peace with impunity, was this balance of power lost. This happened at the end of the eighteenth century, when France was much more powerful than the other states, and produced an extended period of warfare (The Revolutionary and Napoleonic Wars), until France was decisively defeated in 1815.

5. Afterwards, Britain was probably the greatest of the Powers, but since she was isolated from the continent by the English Channel, and was preoccupied with her overseas empire, this did not disturb the peace of Europe.

6. In 1871, following the Franco-Prussian War, the union of all of Germany under the Prussian monarchy once more threatened the balance of power, because it brought together the greatest

concentration of industrial, economic and military power on the continent. Thus the main issue for the statesmen of Europe after 1871 was how to prevent Germany from dominating Europe. This was to last until 1945.

The Alliance System

During much of the third quarter of the nineteenth century, European (and world) politics was dominated by the Minister-President of Prussia and Imperial German Chancellor, Otto von Bismarck. By a ruthless policy of alternating diplomacy and war, he had created the new German Empire in 1871. After this success, his main purpose was to safeguard his new creation. In doing this, he founded the alliance system.

The Dual Alliance

1. After the Franco-Prussian War (1870-1) Bismarck's policy was:
    (a) To isolate the French, so as to prevent them from forming an alliance to place themselves in such a position that they might consider a war to recover Alsace-Lorraine;
    (b) In particular, to prevent an alliance between France and Russia, which might result in Germany having to fight a war on two fronts;
    (c) To ensure that in a Europe of five great powers, Germany would be in an alliance of three against two.
2. It was necessary for Germany to remain on good terms with both Russia and Austria-Hungary, but this was difficult, since these powers had conflicting interests in the Balkans. *[See below: The Eastern Question]* This problem came to a head in the Balkan Crisis of 1878. At the Berlin Conference Bismarck pretended impartiality, hoping to get Russo-Austrian agreement.
3. Forced to take sides, he leaned more towards Austria-Hungary because:
    (a) Austria-Hungary was a partly German empire, under German leadership;
    (b) As a partner, Austria-Hungary would be more easy to dominate than Russia;
    (c) An alliance with Austria Hungary would open up the Danube Basin into economic association with Germany.
    (d) Control of the Danube Basin would in turn open up a path to the Middle East.
4. In 1879, the **Dual Alliance** was agreed between Germany and Austria-Hungary. By the terms of this originally secret treaty, each state was to help the other against an attack by any state other than Russia (i.e. France or Britain).
    The reason for excluding Russia was that Bismarck did not wish Germany to become entangled in a war with Russia in support of Austrian ambitions in the Balkans.

The Triple Alliance

1. Although Italy was not itself a powerful state, because of its location in the event of a European war :
    (a) It would tie down divisions of French troops in the event of a war between France and Germany;
    (b) It would release Austrian troops in the event of a war between Austria-Hungary and Russia.
2. The Italians hoped to take Tunisia as a colony:
    (a) It was just across the sea from Sicily;
    (b) There were a lot of Italians living in Tunis at that time.
    They were just about to take it when the French seized it in 1881. The Italians were angered.

3. The Italians then wanted:
    (a) an ally against France;
    (b) an alliance to prevent Austria-Hungary from being persuaded to intervene in Italy to restore his ancient dominions to the Pope.
4. In 1882 Italy joined the alliance with Germany and Austria-Hungary in the Triple Alliance. Italy would join the other states if they were to be attacked, and the others would similarly assist Italy. In no case would Italy be obliged to assist against Britain. This last clause was due to:
    (a) Italy's vulnerability to naval attack;
    (b) gratitude for the small but key role played by Britain in the unification of Italy.
5. Bismarck intended the Triple Alliance to:
    (a) strengthen Germany against France;
    (b) strengthen Austria-Hungary against Russia.
6. When the treaty came up for renewal in 1887 Bismarck had to make concessions to Italy, as he was afraid of a Franco-Russian *rapprochement.**
    (a) Italy was promised German support if France occupied Morocco or Tripoli;
    (b) Italy was to be informed of all Austro-Hungarian moves in the Balkans;
    (c) If Austria-Hungary took more land in the Balkans Italy was to receive "compensation."
7. The treaty was renewed periodically until the outbreak of the First World War.

The Dual Entente

1. The main fear of the French was of having to fight another war alone against Germany. Their natural ally against Germany was Russia.
2. When Bismarck closed the German money markets to Russian loans in 1885 in order to discourage their engaging in an adventure in the Balkans, the French moved in to replace them, and during 1888-9 made a series of loans to Russia.
3. In 1891 Russia and France agreed to consult together on common action to be taken in the event of a threat to peace.
4. In 1892 the Russian and French general staffs drew up a draft convention for mutual military aid.
5. The **Dual Entente*** was agreed only by the end of 1893, since:
    (a) the Russians did not want to become involved with France in a war against Germany to recover Alsace-Lorraine;
    (b) The French disliked Russian autocracy, and did not want to be involved in a war against Austria-Hungary because of Russian ambitions in the Balkans.
6. For the first three years, this agreement was mostly directed at Britain, since both powers had interests which could only be satisfied at British expense:
    (a) France had ambitions in Africa and the Eastern Mediterranean;
    (b) Russia had ambitions in Asia and the Eastern Mediterranean.
    Against Germany, the entente was only defensive.
7. It provided that in the event of an attack on France by Germany or by Italy supported by Germany, Russia would field 700,000 to 800,000 men to fight Germany; in the event of an attack on Russia by Germany or by Austria-Hungary supported by Germany, France would field 1,300,000 men to fight Germany. Provisions for specific military plans and organisations were also made.
8. The alliance was renewed and strengthened in 1899, when its terms were extended to cover the balance of power in Europe, and in 1912.
9. This alliance was bound to create among the Germans the sense of being "boxed in" and

frustrated. This may have been a major factor in 1914 in the freedom Germany gave to Austria-Hungary to deal with the Assassination Crisis.

The Anglo-French Entente

1. The Germans thought that Britain's long term interests lay with Germany, and that it was only a matter of time before Britain joined the Triple Alliance They felt that they could afford to wait to exact whatever price they chose when Britain decided to end its policy of "splendid isolation."
2. By 1898, Britain found itself under pressure and without allies:
   (a) The Kaiser supported the Boers in the Boer War with the Kruger Telegram, 1895;
   (b) Russian influence was extending into China with the Russian occupation of Manchuria.
3. Initially, the British approached the Germans with a view to an alliance against Russia in Asia. The Germans wanted instead a strengthening of the Triple Alliance in Europe.
4. As a measure to soften their isolation, the British concluded the **Anglo-Japanese Entente** in 1902, by which:
   (a) Japanese interests in Korea were recognised by Britain;
   (b) Each side would assist the other if either were to be attacked by two powers or more.
5. Later in 1902, the British and French began discussions to settle outstanding matters of difference between them. This led in 1904 to the **Anglo-French Entente**. This did not commit either party to help the other in the event of a European war, but by removing differences between them it made war between Britain and France unlikely:
   (a) The French recognised British interests in Egypt;
   (b) The British recognised French interests in Morocco.
6. The Kaiser decided to convince the French that the Anglo-French Entente was useless to them. He went to Tangiers in Morocco, ignoring French claims, and promised the Sultan his support if any power tried to take away his sovereignty. A conference of the powers was organised to protect the commercial interests of all the powers in Morocco in 1905.
7. The effect of all this was to panic the French, who asked the British for military staff conferences on arrangements for co-operation in the event of a war.
   Thus the effect of the Kaiser's actions was the opposite of that intended. The Anglo-French Entente was:
   (a) given a military character;
   (b) given a defensive character for France against Germany;
   neither of which it had had before, and which the British had not intended.
8. In 1906, the Dreadnought battleship was introduced. Britain proposed talks to prevent a naval arms race. The Kaiser believed this to be a trick to preserve British naval superiority. He proposed talks in return for a British promise not to intervene in a Franco-German war. The British, regarding this as a plot to split the allies in the Anglo-French Entente, refused to agree.

The Anglo-Russian Entente

1. The period of Russian expansion in the Far East came to an end with the Russo-Japanese War in 1905. The Russian fleet was destroyed and the Japanese won victories in Manchuria. This relieved Russian pressure on the British in that region.
2. The Balkan crisis of 1908 made the Russians more fearful of a war with the Triple Alliance.
3. In 1899 the Sultan of Turkey had agreed to a German plan to build a railway from Berlin to Baghdad. The company would get mining rights in the areas it passed through. This threatened both British and Russian interests in the Middle East.
4. In 1907, the British and Russians concluded the **Anglo-Russian Entente**, an agreement to settle

matters of outstanding difference between them. There were no secret military protocols.*

5. The Kaiser saw this as a plot by the British King, Edward VII, against Germany.

Results

By 1914 the Great Powers were divided into two rival alliances:

(a) The Central Powers: Germany, Austria-Hungary and Italy;

(b) The Allies: France, Russia and Britain.

The treaties which bound the Central Powers are called alliances, while those which bound the Allies are called ententes in order to distinguish them. Ententes are vaguer and less specific than alliances. Thus the arrangements which united the Allies were weaker, in their terms, than those which bound the Central Powers.

Economic Rivalries

1. Advances in military technology made military strength dependent upon economic and industrial strength for the production of war materials: guns, shells, warships, etc.
2. By the end of the nineteenth century Germany had become the world's leading economic and industrial power.
3. Potentially, because of their resources, the USA and Russia would overtake Germany during the mid-twentieth century.
4. Much economic rivalry was fought out in the scramble for colonies, known as imperialism.

Imperialism

1. Between 1870 and 1900 there was a burst of imperial expansion during which most areas of the world not colonised by Europeans or their descendants were taken under European rule. This was partly caused by the invention of the steamboat, quinine and the machine gun.
2. The reasons for desiring colonies were:

(a) economic. The economist J. A. Hobson at the time in *Imperialism: a Study* and V. I. Lenin argued in *Imperialism: The Highest Stage of Capitalism*, that imperialism was nothing more than finance capitalism on the international stage. In capitalist states great concentration of wealth in the hands of a few creates a surplus of capital which can only be used for investment overseas. This led inevitably to political expansion and imperialism. Production costs were lower at home than abroad. But:

(i) Colonies incurred costs as well as benefits;

(ii) Most European investment went to places which were not colonised, like the USA, and Latin America.

(b) Fear of protectionism led to a desire for autarchy (economic self-sufficiency). Colonies provided:

(i) sources of raw materials for factories;

(ii) foreign markets for manufactured goods.

(c) Political: D. K. Fieldhouse argued that imperialism was an extension of Great Power rivalry out of Europe: "Imperialism may be seen as the extension into the periphery of the political struggle in Europe." There were military reasons for acquiring colonies:

(i) Strategic: Many colonies were strategically located for the defence of the homeland or for the defence of its interests abroad, e.g. the British colonies which were of naval strategic interest such as Gibraltar, Malta and Cyprus in the Mediterranean, Cape Colony in South Africa and the Falklands off South America.

(ii) Manpower: Colonies provided sources of manpower for the new mass armies which the great powers were building up. The race for colonies was part of an arms race.

(d) Imperialism could be seen as an extension of chauvinistic nationalism. Colonies provided prestige for the country which obtained them (as well as popularity for the politicians who obtained them). For the French, imperialism was a way of recovering national prestige after the defeat of 1871.

(e) Social: They provided opportunities for adventurers and the discontented (especially younger sons) to make their fortunes abroad.

3. This led to colonial rivalries. Between 1898 and 1912 there was a series of crises which might have led to war between the imperial powers:

(a) The Fashoda Incident (1898) Armed British and French expeditions in the Sudan met at Fashoda on the Nile. In 1899 a convention was signed to prevent conflict between them.

(b) Morocco (1905) By the Entente Cordiale France was to recognise Britain's interests in Egypt, while Britain would recognise French interests in Morocco. When the French demanded to control Moroccan banks and police, the Kaiser sailed to Tangier to promise to preserve the independence of the Sultan of Morocco and demanded an international conference to ratify this. Russia, Britain and Italy supported France. The only effect of the pressure upon France was to drive her to open Anglo-French military talks.

(c) Morocco (1911) When French troops put down a rebellion in Morocco and the annexation of the country seemed imminent, the Kaiser sent the gunboat *Panther* to Agadir to warn off the French. Its main effect was to drive the French and British closer together, although an agreement was reached whereby Germany gave France a free hand in Morocco while France made concessions to Germany in the Congo.

Chauvinism and Belligerence

1. Before the First World War there were many trends which seemed to lead towards a peaceful future:

(a) The **Concert of Europe** still settled problems peacefully, such as the partition of Africa.

(b) International disputes were increasingly settled by arbitration. In 1899 the Permanent Court of Arbitration had been set up at the Hague.

(c) International agreements were made to limit some of the horrors of warfare made possible by technological developments, such as poison gas and dum-dum (soft expanding) bullets.

(d) Institutions had been set up to promote peace, such as the Nobel Committee.

(e) International agencies had been set up to regulate matters of common interest between nations, e.g. telegraph, railways, postage. They were very successful.

However, there were many other factors which militated against a peaceful future.

2. **Nationalism** was the dominant ideology in Europe during the nineteenth century.

[For a fuller account of nationalism see the companion volume "Single-Party States]

Populations fervently supported their own nation, and this support was often chauvinistic.* Franz Fischer revealed documentary evidence for German chauvinism at the highest levels, which led German Chancellor Bethmann-Hollweg to produce, in September 1914, a plan for German domination of Europe after a German victory.

3. War was popular. It was romanticised and idealised. People knew little about it because:

(a) There had been no general war in Europe for ninety-nine years.

(b) There was little reporting from the battlefield. What there was, was heavily censored.

(c) Belief in the virtue of war was a consequence of widespread **Social Darwinism**.

[For a fuller account of Social Darwinism see the companion volume "Single-Party States]
Some writers in Germany suggested that war was a panacea* for social ills. Von der Goltz argued that a long and bitter war was necessary for the sake of Germany's "health." In the UK Lord Roberts argued that a war was necessary to clear away "the mass of human rottenness that threads the thoroughfares of any of our large industrial cities."

4. The right-wing press in all countries encouraged national rivalries and belligerent* chauvinism. Populations were enthusiastic for war.
Colonel House, who was in Europe during 1914 shortly before the outbreak of war reported to US President Woodrow Wilson: "The situation is extraordinary. It is militarism run mad."

5. Civil society became militarised:
    (a) Most countries introduced compulsory military service (conscription).
    (b) The values of the military (obedience and discipline) were regarded as desirable for everyone.
    (c) Boys' books were full of information about military regiments, ships of the navy, etc.
    (d) Children were regimented into quasi-military organisations. E.g. In the UK the Boy Scouts, Sea Scouts, Church Lads' Brigade, the British Girls' Patriotic League, and Cadet Corps of various kinds. They would drill in uniform and engage in quasi-military training. Baden-Powell exhorted boy scouts to "Be prepared to die for your country...so that when the time comes you may charge home with confidence, not caring whether you are to be killed or not." In Germany there was the *Jungdeutschlandbund*. In Jan. 1913 the *Jungdeutschlandbund Post* declared that: "It will be more beautiful and wonderful to live for ever among the heroes on a war memorial in a church than to die an empty death in bed, nameless..."
    (e) Military leaders were popular heroes in their own countries. Children collected their idealized portraits on cigarette cards.

6. Patriotic pressure groups were formed at the turn of the century to ensure the military strength and preparedness of their own country:
    (i) the Pan-German League in Germany;
    (ii) the *Wehrverein* in Germany;
    (iii) the National Service League in the UK.

7. There were periodic war scares and invasion fears, e.g. belief in "fifth columnists."* These fears surfaced in literature: e.g. Le Queue, *The Invasion of 1910* (1906).

8. Peace movements were isolated. They consisted of unpopular minorities of intellectuals, zealots and idealists.

Arms Races

1. The lesson of 1870-1 was that it is necessary to prepare for war during peacetime. This led to:
    (a) arms races (acquiring more and better weapons of war, and more and better trained soldiers and sailors);
    (b) the drawing up of war plans during peacetime.

2. There was a Franco-German arms race between 1871 and 1914, with a lull during the late 1890s and early 1900s.

3. Arms races were made possible by:
    (a) Increased communications, and so increased ability to obtain information about the forces and weapons of other powers;
    (b) Increased industrial capacity to produce weapons with the Second Industrial Revolution;
    (c) Technological advances in weapons design, e.g. the development of:

(i) More efficient explosives, e.g. nitro-glycerine;

(ii) accurate rifles which could kill at 2,000 yards;

(iii) efficient self-loading machine guns;

(iv) more powerful artillery made of steel with recoil absorbing carriages, some with ranges greater than 10 km;

(v) ships which had abandoned wood for iron and sail for steam power;

(vi) naval guns made of steel, and housed in revolving turrets;

(vii) ships with thicker armour;

(viii) primitive submarines or U-boats;

(ix) primitive aeroplanes and airships, available for use over the battlefield.

4. Fortresses were built of concrete and steel and made part of generally fortified areas containing guns in revolving turrets set in pits. Trenches and tunnels linked gun emplacements and contained magazines and barracks, e.g. at Verdun.

5. Arms manufacturers expanded production and became major capitalist enterprises, e.g. Nobel in Sweden, Creusot in France, Skoda in Austria-Hungary and Krupp in Germany. The arms race benefited the armaments manufacturers and, to a much less extent, workers in areas where ships and armaments were produced. These had a vested interest in the fear and expectation of war.

6. In 1898 the Kaiser declared: "The future of Germany lies on the water." The **Anglo-German naval arms race** began. Admiral Von Tirpitz' Naval Programme threatened British naval supremacy and alienated the British from Germany. (The British always wished to maintain a war fleet which was larger than the second and third largest fleets in the world combined.)

   In 1905 rivalry increased with the building by Britain of the first *Dreadnought*, since Germany could begin competing on equal terms. By 1912 Tirpitz accepted failure to overtake Britain, and the need for investment in the German army. German socialists saw the naval programme as a means of diverting public attention from the need for social and political reforms.

   Although the naval arms race greatly contributed to the deterioration of relations between Germany and Great Britain, Churchill said that it was not a major problem by 1914, since by that time it was clear that Germany had lost the race.

7. Military plans tended to become "fossilized" because of increasing reliance on the use of railways to move troops quickly. Military plans became dependent upon railway timetables.

8. Most military leaders believed in a short war, and therefore in a strategy of attack, which must be initiated quickly.

   German plans for coping with fighting a war on two fronts were drawn up by Count Schlieffen. Since Russia was thought to be slow to mobilise but almost impossible to defeat quickly, the German plan was to invade France immediately war was declared, deliver a knock-out blow to that country as swiftly as possible, secure its surrender, and then deal with Russia afterwards at leisure. Since the French had built fortified defences along their borders, which would hold up a German invasion for some time, the German plan was to invade France through neutral Belgium, since there were no defences on the Franco-Belgian border. This was known as the **Schlieffen Plan**. The violation of Belgian neutrality might bring Britain into the war, but the speedy defeat of France would render this irrelevant by allowing the British no toehold in Europe.

9. Military planning was beginning to lose touch with reality:

   (a) As the experience of the wars of 1866 and 1870-1 faded into the past;

   (b) Because of a failure of the generals to see the significance of new technological developments, particularly their failure to appreciate the importance of the machine gun and the trench when used in combination;

   (c) Because of a reluctance to discard old ways of thinking, e.g. the importance of cavalry, brightly coloured uniforms;

(d) Because war planning was carried out by military experts in isolation from diplomats.

The Eastern Question

1. This problem was created by the power vacuum caused by the decline of the Ottoman Empire "the sick man of Europe", which was seen to have begun with Greek independence.
2. Rival interests in the region were a permanent threat to European peace:
   (a) The Russians wanted to:
   (i) expand into the Slav lands;
   (ii) secure the Straits as a warm water port for its fleet with access to the Mediterranean;
   (iii) recover Constantinople for Orthodoxy;
   (iv) prevent Austrian expansion along their south-western boundaries.
   (b) The Austrians wanted to:
   (i) expand into Serbian lands to counter Slav nationalism, which was a threat to the multi-national empire;
   (ii) protect their trade route down the Danube;
   (iii) prevent Russian expansion along their south-eastern boundaries.
   (c) The British wanted to:
   (i) secure the Mediterranean by preventing free access to it by the Russian fleet;
   (ii) prevent the Russians from controlling the overland route to India.
3. To complicate matters, the various Christian peoples of the Balkans wanted to:
   (i) win their freedom from Turkish oppression;
   (ii) achieve their own national ambitions, often focused upon winning the territory which their ancestors held when at its widest extent in history.
   This led to chronic instability in the region and to successive crises.
4. Because of the Great Power rivalries, each crisis of the nineteenth century raised the possibility of a general war between the powers, e.g. 1840, 1878 and 1886.
5. In 1908 intellectuals and army officers in Macedonia revolted under Enver Pasha:
   (a) Bulgaria declared itself independent under Tsar Ferdinand.
   (b) Austria-Hungary formally annexed Bosnia-Herzegovina. Serbia resented this, since the Serbs had been hoping to annex it themselves. They appealed to the Russians. The Russians called a conference, expecting British and French support. When it became clear that Germany would support Austria-Hungary, the French drew back, unwilling to be involved in a war for the Balkans. The British were anxious to avoid a war with Germany also. The Russians had recently been defeated by the Japanese, and could not stand alone. No conference took place and Austria-Hungary kept Bosnia. As a result:
   (i) The Serbs became hostile to Austria-Hungary.
   (ii) The Russians were determined to avoid any further humiliation in the Balkans, and embarked upon a programme of rearmament.
   (iii) They resolved that no further Serbian appeal for aid against Austria-Hungary would go unheeded.
6. The Christian states of the Balkans went to war against the Ottoman Empire in 1912, and in the **First Balkan War** eliminated Turkish rule in Europe outside the area of Constantinople. The powers settled the map of the Balkans by the **Treaty of London** (May 1912). The Austrians insisted upon the creation of an independent Albania to limit Serbian expansion, and to deprive Serbia of access to the Adriatic Sea.
7. Unsatisfied with their spoils, the Bulgarians then attacked the Serbs in Macedonia. The Serbs

repelled the attack, and the Greeks and Rumanians and Turks turned upon the Bulgarians. During this **Second Balkan War** the Austrians were intent upon attacking Serbia, but they were restrained by the Germans and the British.

The Assassination Crisis (1914)

1. Austrian statesmen had debated for 50 years the question how the Habsburg Empire could possibly survive the rise of nationalism in Eastern Europe, One possibility was to introduce some form of federalism, permitting political autonomy to the various nationalities. Such reforms were vetoed by the Hungarians, who would lose their own privileged position in their half of the empire. The two extremes are represented by:
   (a) Conrad Franz, Graf von Hotzendorf, chief of the general staff: who favoured preventive war against Serbia to stifle nationalist agitation for good and reinforce the old order.
   (b) Archduke Franz Ferdinand: who wrote "I live and shall die for federalism; it is the sole salvation for the monarchy, if anything can save it."
2. Archduke Franz Ferdinand was out of favour:
   (a) with the court, for his marriage to a woman of merely low aristocratic rank;
   (b) resented by the Hungarians and by conservatives for his support of federalism;
   (c) feared by Slavic radicals as the one man who might really satisfy the nationalities within the empire, and so frustrate their dreams of a Greater Serbia. Hence the archduke was a marked man among the secret societies which were formed to liberate Bosnia.
3. The National Defence (*Narodna Odbrana*) was formed in Serbia in 1908 to carry on pro-Serbian and anti-Austrian agitation across the border. Its non-violent methods were seen as insufficient by some, who in 1911 formed the secret society "Union or Death", also known as the **Black Hand**, led by the head of Serbian military intelligence, Colonel Dragutin Dimitrijevic.
4. With his support, if not on his direct orders, a band of youths conspired to assassinate Franz Ferdinand during a state visit to Sarajevo, the capital Bosnia-Herzegovina, on June 28, 1914, the Serbian national holiday.
5. As the Archduke and his wife rode in an open car through the streets, a bomb was thrown, but missed. The Archduke completed his official duties, after which the governor of Bosnia suggested they take a detour from the planned route on the return trip for to avoid the narrow streets of the inner city. But the lead driver in the procession took a wrong turn, the cars had to stop for a moment, and Gavrilo Princip shot both royal visitors.

Glossary

belligerent: warlike, aggressive

chauvinistic: aggressive patriotism

panacea: a cure-all

protocols: additions to a treaty

rapprochement: a reconciliation between nations

Franz-Joseph

The Causes of the First World War

"Oh - if only I knew!" (German Chancellor Bethmann-Hollweg, when asked how the First World War came about)

The Slide into War

1. Reaction in Vienna, and Europe was remarkably low-key, but Conrad von Hotzendorf and Austrian Foreign Minister Leopold, Graf von Berchtold saw the assassination as providing a pretext for the preventive war he sought against Serbia. Berchtold proposed a firm policy toward Serbia lest:
   (a) Austria's prestige deteriorate further;
   (b) the Balkan states unite behind Russia.
2. The prime minister of Hungary insisted that diplomatic and legal justifications precede any war: Austria must present a list of demands for redress. Should Serbia accept, the empire would win a "brilliant diplomatic success"; should Serbia refuse, war could be launched with Austria-Hungary posing as the aggrieved party.
3. In his **"blank check"** memo the Kaiser promised to support whatever action Austria might take against Serbia. Although Bethmann warned that a move against Serbia could lead to a world war, the Germans expected Russia to back down, since its military reforms were incomplete.
4. The president and prime minister of France, were visiting St. Petersburg. Poincaré assured the Russians that France would stand by her alliance commitments.
5. On July 23rd, Austria presented an ultimatum to Belgrade, demanding:
   (a) the dissolution of the secret societies,
   (b) a cessation of anti-Austrian propaganda,
   (c) Austrian participation in the investigation of the Sarajevo crime.
   Serbia was given forty-eight hours to respond.
6. The Russian foreign minister, Sergey Dmitriyevich Sazonov, insisted on military measures. He was supported by the French ambassador. On July 25 the Russian Council of Ministers decided that if Austrian forces entered Serbia, Russia would mobilise its army.
7. On July 25th, Serbia accepted all the Austro-Hungarian conditions save two that it claimed undermined its sovereignty.

8. The Kaiser, returned from a yachting trip, and at this late date tried to restrain the Austrians.
9. On July 28th Austria Hungary declared war on Serbia and bombarded Belgrade.
10. In St. Petersburg on the afternoon of July 30th, the generals insisted on the mobilisation of the Russian army. The Tsar approved the mobilisation against Austria Hungary, but the generals told him that they could only mobilise against both Austria Hungary and Germany.
11. Alarm now began to spread across Europe. Sir Edward Grey, Kaiser William, and the Italian government all proposed negotiations.
12. On the 31st, Germany delivered ultimata to Russia, demanding an end to mobilisation, and to France, demanding a declaration of French neutrality in case of war in the East.
13. When the ultimata expired, the German Army hastnd to put into effect the Schlieffen Plan. Thus Germany declared war against Russia on August 1st.
14. War was declared on France on August 3rd, and at the same time a demand for safe passage for its troops through Belgium made. When this was refused, Germany invaded Belgium.
15. On August 3rd, Italy argued that Austria-Hungary had not been attacked, and announced its neutrality.
16. Britain was faced with the possibility of German domination of the Channel ports, and on the same day, demanded that German forces withdraw from Belgium. When they did not, on August 4th, Britain declared war on Germany. This was immediately followed by declarations of war by the self-governing dominions of the British Empire.

Timetable for the Outbreak of The War

1914	JUN	28th	Assassination of Archduke Franz Ferdinand in Sarajevo
	JUL	23rd	Austrian ultimatum to Serbia
		25th	Serbian acceptance of most points of the ultimatum
		28th	Austria declares war on Serbia
		29th	General mobilisation ordered in Russia
		31st	German demand to Russia to end mobilisation
			Austria-Hungary orders mobilisation
			Russian failure to comply with German ultimatum
			British issue statement of intention to support France
	AUG.	1st	Germany declares war on Russia
		2nd	German gives ultimatum to Belgium
		3rd	Italy declares its neutrality
			Germany declares war on France
			Germany invades Belgium and Luxembourg
			British ultimatum to Germany
		4th	Great Britain declares war on Germany
		6th	Austria-Hungary declares war on Russia

Causal Analysis

Standing Conditions

Economic rivalries
   esp. Russo-German rivalry
Colonial rivalries
   esp. Franco-German rivalry in Morocco

The alliance system
The arms race
      esp. The Schlieffen Plan
The climate of chauvinism and belligerence

Long-Term Causes

Austrian-Russian rivalry in the Balkans
Franco-German rivalry over Alsace-Lorraine
The perceived fragility of the Austro-Hungarian empire in an age of nation states

Short-Term Causes

Austrian desire to destroy Serbian independence
German desire to provoke a war for world domination? (Fritz Fischer)
German desire for a war before Russia became too powerful?
German desire to warn Russia not to intervene in the Balkans against Austria-Hungary
The Kaiser's promise of unqualified support to the Austrians - a tragic miscalculation?
Mobilisation plans based upon a strategy of attack increased the pace of the crisis, suggesting that initiative passed from the politicians to the generals.

The **Immediate Cause** - The "trigger" which set off the war:
The assassination of the Archduke Franz Ferdinand in Sarajevo

Negative Factors

Leaders and diplomats failed to prevent this crisis from developing into a major war.

Economic Rivalries

Economic rivalries and fears underlay and aggravated international tensions.

1. The British resented the rise of German economic power;
2. The USA and Russia were long term threats to German economic supremacy; Russia, because nearer, being the most immediate. Referring to the Russian threat, in 1914 Bethmann-Hollweg said: "It grows and hangs over us ever more heavily like a nightmare."

The Alliance System

1. Some historians held that the existence of the rival armed alliances itself made war at some point inevitable.
2. However:
   (a) The alliances were primarily defensive, and this should have lead to greater restraint, rather than aggression.
   (b) The situation leading up to war was at odds with the terms of the alliances:
       (i) Russia had no actual alliance obligation to go to the aid of Serbia;
       (ii) Despite the Dual Alliance Germany had no treaty obligation to give Austria a "blank cheque";
       (iii) France should have declared war on Germany as soon as Germany declared war on Russia, but did not;
       (iv) Britain only intervened after the German ultimatum to Belgium, a matter not covered by the entente;
       (v) Italy remained neutral.
   Thus the Alliance System was not, by itself, a major cause of the war.
3. However, the Alliance System did contribute to the outbreak of the war in that:
   (a) It helped generate the arms race, and war plans, such as the Schlieffen Plan.
   (b) Germany needed to preserve the Dual Alliance to prevent its being alone in a hostile

Europe in 1914
Norway
Sweden
Great Britain
and Ireland
Denmark
Holland
Belgium
Germany
Russia
France
Austria-Hungary
Switzerland
Rumania
Portugal
Serbia
Montenegro
Bulgaria
Spain
Italy
Albania
Greece

continent, and that may have led to it being overly supportive of Austrian actions in 1914.
(c) The alliance with Germany probably made Austria-Hungary less cautious than it would otherwise have been in confronting Serbia.
(d) The alliance system provided the mechanism by which the Assassination Crisis, initially a purely Balkan affair, became a general European crisis.

The Climate of Chauvinism and Belligerence

1. War was particularly attractive to some governments:

    (a) For Austria-Hungary the destruction of Serbia may have seemed necessary to keep the multi-national Habsburg Dual Monarchy together after the coming death of the aged emperor, Franz Joseph II.

    (b) For Germany:

    (i) The shadow of Russia's future status as a superpower was already altering the balance of power. By 1917 the Russians would have completed the Great Programme of rearmament and railway building begun in 1912. If there was going to be a war, this development dictated that the sooner it happened, the better for Germany.

    (ii) The weakness of the Habsburg monarchy made its saving by war attractive to Germany.

    (c) The French were afraid of the relative decline in the French population, compared with that of Germany. This would be their last chance to destroy Germany.

    (d) If Germany won a general European war, Britain would be faced with a danger on the continent unprecedented since the days of Napoleon.

2. There was a feeling among many of fatalism,* that war was inevitable. This increased after the Agadir (Morocco) Crisis of 1911.

    (a) General von Moltke said in 1912, "I hold war to be inevitable, and the sooner the better."

    (b) The UK Govt. gave its blessing to plan to send the British Expeditionary Force (BEF) to Europe. Churchill was sent to Admiralty to prepare the Navy for war.

    (c) In Russia mobilisation procedures were speeded up and Great Programme accelerated.

3. As a long war would be expensive, and destructive of the fabric of society, General Staffs regarded the best policy to be one of attack to keep the war short. Therefore if there was a danger of war it would be necessary to move fast. The Schlieffen Plan was a special case of planning on this basis.

4. There was a general belief that modern warfare would be deadly but short. "It will all be over by Christmas." This was based upon recent European wars, e.g. the Seven Weeks War, the Franco-Prussian War, etc. No country had war plans which extended beyond the deployment of existing forces and supplies.

    (a) National leaders were not so optimistic.

    (i) Bethmann Hollweg warned the Bavarian minister that war "would topple many a throne."

    (ii) The French were doubtful of their ability to enforce conscription and were prepared immediately to arrest left-wing leaders.

    (iii) The Germans were reluctant to enforce military service upon industrial populations considered unreliable. Count Schlieffen argued, in an article in 1909, that a war involving millions of men could not be sustained because of the cost.

    (iv) The Russo-Japanese war had ended in revolution, and the Russian authorities did not want another war which might have similar consequences.

    (b) Some writers also foresaw the implications of modern weapons:

    (i) A. J. A. Morris, in *The Scaremongers*, attempts to show that the social consequences of a temporary blockade on Britain would have been bread riots and revolution.

    (ii) Ivan Bloch, in *La Guerre future*, (1898) argued that the accuracy and power of modern weapons would produce deadlock on the battlefield and a war of attrition which would destroy the fabric of the societies involved in the war.

Imperialism

1. Colonial rivalries did increase tension between the powers:
    (a) The Moroccan crises aggravated bad relations between France and Germany.
    (b) The German plan for a railway from Berlin to Baghdad, opening up Turkey and the Middle East to German influence:
        (i) threatened the southern flank of the Russian Empire;
        (ii) threatened the land route to the British Empire of India.
2. Despite this, it could be argued that colonial rivalries were not a major factor in causing the First World War.
    (a) The main conflicts of interests were between Britain and France in Africa and Britain and Russia in Asia. Yet Britain, France and Russia fought on the same side in the war.
    (b) The main crises over colonial rivalries during the years 1898-1914, namely: Fashoda (1898), Morocco (1905) and Morocco (1911), were settled without going to war.
    (c) The colonies may actually have functioned as a safety-valve, keeping conflict between the European powers outside the continent itself.

The Arms Race

1. Lord Grey, British Foreign secretary, was clear abour this: "The moral is obvious: it is that greater armaments lead to war... The enormous growth of armaments in Europe, the sense of insecurity and fear caused by them - it was these that made war inevitable."
2. Projections of future arms levels based upon economic potential suggested a need for Germany to strike against Russia before the balance inevitably tipped against Germany, which it would do in the mid twentieth century.
3. The main arms races were the Franco-German Arms Race and the Anglo-German Naval Arms Race. But the war arose out of a Russo-Austrian confrontation. In any case, the Anglo-German Naval Arms Race could not have been a significant cause of war, since Britain and Germany were two of the last countries to go to war.
4. The Russian Government was surprised to discover that there were no war plans for an attack on Austria-Hungary alone, only for a war against Austria-Hungary and its ally Germany. Therefore there were no plans for mobilization* against Austria-Hungary alone. Any "warning mobilization" had to be directed against both Austria-Hungary and Germany.
5. The Schlieffen Plan determined that if there were to be a war, France must be defeated within six weeks before facing Russia, and once the Russians mobilised, the six weeks began ticking away, forcing the Germans to back down or launch a general war.

The Eastern Question

In the events of the Balkans during the early twentieth century:
1. The small Balkan powers had showed themselves capable of acting without Great Power prompting and support. Their successes generated a feeling that decisive action could reap enormous rewards, and that their various national goals were achievable.
2. In particular, Serbia had been strengthened, was resentful of the creation of Albania, and was determined to stir up trouble among the Serbs and Croats inside Austria-Hungary, so as to create a South Slav empire.
3. The Russians were determined to avoid any further humiliation in the Balkans, like that of 1908, and had:
    (a) embarked upon a programme of rearmament;
    (b) resolved that no further Serbian appeal for aid against Austria-Hungary should go unheeded.

4. The Austrians felt that *they* had stood back in the Balkan Wars, allowing developments which had not been to their advantage, and that they must not let this happen again.
5. The Germans took British co-operation during the Balkan Wars to mean that Britain could be detached from its ententes with France and Russia, and might even tempted to join the Central Powers.

Internal Stresses
1. Franz Fischer challenged the idea that foreign policy was made with reference only to inter-state relations, and argued that it could be affected by internal factors. War can be launched for domestic reasons.
2. Internal divisions generally lead to a prudent foreign policy:
     (a) the social divisions in the UK and the Irish problem,
     (b) the political and social divisions in France,
   led to a reluctance to commit to war.
3. The threat of revolution in Russia, together with memories of the near-revolution during the Russo-Japanese War of 1904-5, suggested caution, while the Pan-Slavs argued that if Russia let Serbia down again, as it had in 1908 when Austria annexed Bosnia Herzegovina, then Russian influence in the Balkans must inevitably decline.
4. It was long held that the nationalities problem in the Austro-Hungarian Empire led to a desperate desire in some quarters to tame Serbian separatism by destroying independent Serbia, lest the multi-national empire be torn apart. This fear was behind the Austrian attack upon Serbia in 1914, using the assassination of Franz Ferdinand as a pretext.
5. Franz Fischer argued that internal stresses in German society impelled Germany into war. The privileged classes of Junkers and capitalists were threatened by the strongest and best organized Social Democrat (Marxist) Party in Europe and by powerful trades unions. The party was:
     (a) Anti-militarist,
     (b) Against the privileges of the upper classes as written into the constitution.
   The ruling classes had long seen expansion abroad as a means of staving off revolution and preserving the privileges of the upper classes by either:
       (i) uniting the nation against a common external threat,
       (ii) providing a justification for the crushing of socialism.
6. Since Austria-Hungary and Germany were the states most active in bringing about the war, these factors must be taken into account.

The Failure of Diplomacy
1. There had been war crises in 1886, 1905 and 1911. These had not led to war. Therefore it needs to be asked why in 1914 the crisis was allowed to develop into war.
2. None of the responsible leaders or ministers of Summer 1914 recognised early enough the importance of the crisis.
     (a) The Kaiser promised to support Austria-Hungary without qualification in the telegram known as the Blank Cheque. This may be contrasted with Bismarck's restraining of the Austrians during the crisis of 1886. German leaders simply assumed that Britain would remain neutral.
     (b) The French President was travelling en route from St. Petersburg to Paris at the height of the crisis.
     (c) Austrian leaders assumed that Russia would not intervene.
     (d) Russian leaders assumed that Germany would not respond to Russian mobilisation.

(e) British leaders assumed that the crisis would resolve itself before they got involved.

3. When it finally did become clear that this crisis was a danger to peace, and that nobody was doing anything effective to defuse it, the leaders at first floundered ineffectively, and then resorted to fatalism.

(a) The German Chancellor, Bethmann-Hollweg, briefly tried to restrain the Austrians. Then he moaned: "We have lost control and the landslide has begun."

(b) On his return to Paris, the French President tried to restrain the Russians without success, after which he concentrated upon blaming Germany, so as to ensure that the British would enter the war against the Germans.

(c) British leaders seem only gradually to have realised how committed to France they were by the Anglo-French Entente. As war approached, Prime Minister Lloyd George said that they must simply "face it".

4. This all suggests a significant lack of talent, foresight and initiative among the leaders of the time. Had Bismarck been alive, he would surely not have let things slide! Yet the statesmen could point to all the previous crises as evidence that they could be settled peacefully, and usually were. Each seems to have been expecting someone else to do something about it.

The German Foreign Minister, Von Jagow, wrote: "When war did break out, unexpectedly and not desired by us, Moltke was very nervous and obviously suffering from strong depression." This suggests that in his view the outbreak of the war was an accident.

5. Anxiety about the causes of the war was immediately evident since all belligerent governments sought to present the war to their people as an essentially defensive struggle.

Historiography

1. Each of the belligerent nations published collections of documents carefully selected to:

(a) blame the other side

(b) show that it was fighting in self-defence.

(i) Serbia was defending itself against Austrian bullying.

(ii) Austria-Hungary was defending itself against Serbian terrorists.

(iii) Russia was defending Serbia and all the Slavs against German imperialism.

(iv) Germany was defending Austria from attack, and the Central Powers from encirclement.

(v) France was defending itself against an unprovoked attack by Germany.

(vi) Britain was defending Belgium.

2. In the treaty signed during the Peace of Paris, the victors blamed Germany and its allies.

3. Revisionist* historians soon challenged the view of the victors. The German government had:

(a) issued the "blank check";

(b) allowed diplomacy to be subordinated to the requirements of the Schlieffen Plan.

However:

(c) Serbia dabbled dangerously in terrorism for nationalist ambitions;

(d) Austria-Hungary was too quick to crush its enemies;

(e) Russia's mobilization expanded the crisis beyond the Balkans and put immense pressure on the Germans;

(f) France failed to restrain Russia;

(g) The British did not make their intentions clear, something which could have deterred the Germans.

Many historians concluded that no single country was to blame for the war.

4. Other historians sought for long-term causes. Surely, they reasoned, such profound events must

have had profound origins.

(a) Marxists, following Lenin in his *Imperialism, the Highest Stage of Capitalism,* blamed capitalism.

(b) The American Sidney B. Fay cited the alliance systems, militarism, imperialism, nationalism, and the power of the press.

(c) In 1961, the German historian Fritz Fischer argued that:

(i) Germany's government and elites had consciously pursued a drive towards world supremacy during the years before World War I;

(ii) The German government had deliberately provoked the crisis of 1914 in an attempt to preserving the German social order.

(d) Opponents argued that much of the evidence for this: imperialism, social Darwinism, and militarism, was common throughout Europe.

(e) Left wing historians argued for the "primacy of domestic policy": that all the European powers had chosen war as a means of controlling or weakening the working classes.

(f) A German historian, Wolfgang J. Mommsen, argued that Germany's rapid industrialization and the backwardness of Austria-Hungary and Russia created instabilities in central and eastern Europe that were compensated for by aggressiveness.

(g) Paul Schroeder thought that the key to European stability was Austria-Hungary. But the other powers gradually undermined the Habsburg monarchy. Austria-Hungary was threatened with collapse because of its multi-national composition, when confronted by Serbia. It could better have met that threat if the Great Powers had worked to relieve pressures on it. The ambitions of Russia, France, and Britain pushed Austria-Hungary over the brink. Germany, unable to develop an overseas empire, despite her strength, was left with the choice of watching her only ally collapse or risking a war against the rest of Europe.

(h) L.C.F. Turner, argued that the outbreak of war was the result of incompetence and tragic miscalculations. The Austrians and Germans thought that Russia would not support Serbia. The Russians thought that mobilization would not lead to war. They were wrong.

Glossary

belligerents: the countries at war

chauvinism: aggressive and belligerent patriotism

conscription: compulsory service in the armed forces

fatalism: the inclination to accept one's fate without exercising any initiative to change circumstances

imperialism: the system whereby Great Powers build empires

mobilization: preparing the armed forces of a country for war, sometimes used as a warning to rival nations to change their policies

nationalism: ideology which holds that everyone must belong to a nation, and that all nations must hold territory as independent nation states.

revisionist: a historian who contradicts a well-established explanation of some important event with a radically different theory

Bibliography

Abrams, Lynn, *Bismarck and the German Empire, 1871-1918,* Lancaster Pamphlets, Routledge (London & New York, 1995)

Bell, Philip, "Origins of the War of 1914," in *Themes in Modern European History*, ed. Paul Hayes, Routledge (London & New York, 1992)

Berghahn, V. R., *Germany and the Approach of War in 1914*, Macmillan (London, 1973)

Bridge, F. R., *From Sadowa to Sarajevo*, Routledge (London, 1972)

Fischer, F., *Germany's Aims in the First World War*, Chatto & Windus (London, 1967)

Henig, Ruth, *The Origins of the First World, War*, Lancester Pamphlets, Routledge (London & New York, 1993)

Joll, J., *The Origins of the First World War,* Longman (London, 1992)

Kennedy, P., *The Rise of Anglo-German Antagonism, 1860-1914*, Allen & Unwin (London, 1980)

Mason, John W., *The Dissolution of the Austro-Hungarian Empire, 1867-1918,* Seminar Studies in History, Longman (London & New York, 1985)

Stevenson, D., *First World War and International Politics*, Oxford University Press (Oxford & New York, 1987)

Tuchman, B., *The Guns of August: August 1914*, Macmillan (London & New York, 1972)

Turner, L., C. F., *The Origins of the First World War*, Arnold (London, 1970)

Kaiser Wilhelm II

The Course and Character of the Great War

"It would all have been quite simple had there been some solid reason for the war, had Austria bluntly demanded a Protectorate in Serbia, or Germany claimed some concrete prerogative, some strong-point or slice of territory either in Europe or abroad... Such demands would have been a matter of dispute ... and therefore a matter for discussion... But there was absolutely no definable area of disagreement and therefore no problems to be solved, the solution of which would mean peace. It was this that turned the First World War into an insane orgy of destruction. With the lack of any rational declaration of intentions, the formulation of the whole conflict was left to the apocalyptic imagination. Blind hatred reached the level of delirium, because there was nothing, no handhold, to which articulate thought might cling." (Herbert Lüthy)

"The outbreak of World War I signaled the end of a peaceful and unsuspecting era, unleashing an age of warfare, totalitarian oppression, mechanistic barbarism and bureaucratic mass murder. " (Jurgen Habermas)

Popularity

1. When war broke out it was almost universally welcomed.
    (a) Austrian statesmen welcomed the chance to solve the nationalities problem by defeating and annexing* Serbia; while some of their subjects welcomed war as hastening the break up of the empire and their own independence.
    (b) The French welcomed the opportunity to:
        (i) reverse the dishonour of 1871;
        (ii) recover Alsace-Lorraine.
    (c) The Germans welcomed the opportunity:
        (i) to solve the Austrian nationalities problem;
        (ii) to destroy the rising power of Russia while there was still a chance to do so.
    (d) The Russians welcomed the chance to assert themselves in the Balkans once more.
    (e) The British welcomed the chance to destroy German naval power.
2. The populations of Europe flocked to the fight enthusiastically.

Timetable of the First World War

1914

Aug 4	Germany invades Belgium
Aug 7	British Expeditionary Force (BEF) arrives in France
Aug 17	Russia invades East Prussia
Aug 23	Japan declares war on Germany
Aug 23	Austria-Hungary invades Galicia
Aug 26-30	Battle of Tannenberg, Russian advance in the East checked
Sept 5-10	First Battle of Marne begins, halts German advance
Sept 9	First Battle of Masurian Lakes begins
Sept 14	First Battle of Aisne begins
Oct 14	First Battle of Ypres begins
Oct 15	Trench digging and the "race to the sea" begin
Oct 29	Ottoman Empire declares war on the Allies
Dec 8	Anglo-German naval battle off the Falkland Islands

1915

Jan	Battles of Artois and Champagne begin
Jan 15	Japan issues "Twenty-one Demands" to China
Feb 4	German U-boats attack shipping, blockade of UK
Feb 7	Second Battle of Masurian Lakes begins
Feb 19	Dardanelles campaign begins
Mar 11	British begin blockade of German ports
Apr 22	Second Battle of Ypres begins; First use of poison gas
Apr 25	Anzac landing at Gallipoli
Apr 26	Italy and the Allies conclude secret Treaty of London
May 2	Austro-Hungarian/German offensive in Galicia begins
May 7	German U-boat sinks British liner *Lusitania*
May 9	Second Battle of Artois begins
May 23	Italy declares war on Austria-Hungary
Jun	First official death marches begin in Armenian genocide
Jun 29	Italy attempts invasion of Austria-Hungary
Sept 5	Tsar Nicholas II takes command of Russian armies
Sept 22	Second Battle of Champagne begins
Oct 3	Anglo-French force lands at Thessaloniki
Oct	Central Powers invade Serbia
Nov	Flight of Serbian Army to Corfu begins
Dec 28	Evacuation of Anzac troops from Gallipoli begins

1916

Feb 21	German attack at Verdun begins
Apr	British forces in Mesopotamia begin expedition to Baghdad
Mar 9	Pancho Villa raids Columbus, New Mexico, USA
May 19	Sykes-Picot agreement concluded
May 31	Battle of Jutland inconclusive
Jun - Aug	Russian victories against the Turks in the Caucasus
Jun 4	Brusilov's offensive against Austria-Hungary begins
Jun 5	Arab revolt launched against the Turks
Jul 1	Battle of the Somme begins

Jul 29	US siezes Haiti
Aug	Romania declares war on Austria-Hungary and Germany
Aug 31	Germany suspends U-Boat war
Sept 15	Tanks used for the first time in the battle of the Somme
Nov 29	US siezes Santa Domingo
Dec 12	Germany issues note suggesting compromise peace
Dec 18	Battle of Verdun ends

1917

Jan 10	Allies state their war objectives
Feb 1	Germany resumes unrestricted submarine warfare
Feb 23	German forces begin withdrawal to Hindenburg Line
Feb 24	Zimmermann Telegram passed to the US by Britain
Mar 11	British take Baghdad
Mar 15	Tsar Nicholas II abdicates
Apr 6	USA declares war on Germany
Apr 9	Battle of Vimy Ridge; Nivelle Offensive begins
Apr 29	Major mutiny in French army
Jun 27	Greece declares war on Central Powers
Jul 6	The Arabs capture Aquaba
Jul 16	Battle of Passchendaele begins
Oct 24	Austro-Hungarian/German breakthrough on Italian front
Nov 2	Balfour Declaration issued
Dec 9	British Army under General Allenby enters Jerusalem
Dec 22	Russia opens peace negotiations with Germany

1918

Mar 3	Soviet Russia concludes Treaty of Brest-Litovsk
Mar 21	Germany launches Spring offensive: Battle of Picardy
Apr 9	Battle of Lys, German attack on Flanders, begins
Apr 14	Foch Commander-in-Chief of Allied forces on Western Front
Jul 15	Second Battle of the Marne begins
Aug 8	Amiens Offensive forces Germans back to Hindenburg Line
Sept 19	British offensive launched in Palestine, Battle of Megiddo
Sept 26	Allied forces attack Bulgaria, Battle of the Vardar
Sept 28	Ludendorff and Hindenburg recommend an armistice.
Sept 29	Bulgaria concludes an armistice
Oct 6	Yugoslavia declares independence from Austria-Hungary.
Oct 7	Poland declares its independence
Oct 27	Resignation of General Ludendorff
Oct 28	Czechoslovakia declares independence from Austria-Hungary
	German sailors mutiny at Kiel
Oct 30	Ottoman Empire concludes armistice with Allies
Nov 1	Hungary declares separation from Austria
Nov 3	Austria/Hungary conclude armistice with Allies
Nov 7	Germany begins armistice negotiations
Nov 9	Kaiser Wilhelm II abdicates
Nov 10	Kaiser Wilhelm II goes into exile in Holland
	Germany becomes a republic
Nov 11	Armistice comes into force at 11am

This enthusiasm and national unity was due to:

   (a) The prevalence of chauvinistic nationalism;

   (b) The relief felt at the end of a long period of tension, arms race and war scares;

   (d) People's idea of what war was like was romantic and unrealistic;

   (c) It provided a glamorous and romantic escape for young men from the constraints of everyday life, particularly those in unpleasant, repetitive and unrewarding jobs, or those in debt or at odds with their parents, the community or the police.

   (e) People were too unsophisticated to resist government propaganda.

   (f) People were swept along by mass psychology.

3. Almost everywhere there was a cessation of internal conflict.

   (a) In Germany a state of *Burgfrieden* or 'fortress truce' was declared whereby employers and employees ended all conflict in the interest of victory. The Social Democrats, in theory committed to internationalism, supported the war almost to a man.

   (b) In Austria-Hungary the various nationalities of the empire obediently took up arms.

   (c) In France the Union Sacrée was founded to unite socialists and anarchists in a patriotic movement to support the war.

   (d) Only in Italy did the socialist deputies oppose the war and people were generally unenthusiastic.

The War on the Western Front

The War of Manoeuvre

1. The Schlieffen Plan envisaged that German forces would sweep through Belgium and Luxembourg into Northern France in a wide arc, enfolding Paris from the West. This would bring about the surrender of France within six weeks. German forces would then be rushed across Germany by rail to the Eastern Front in time to meet the advancing Russians.

2. The German attack came to a halt before its objectives had been achieved, because:

   (a) The Belgian forts offered unexpectedly strong resistance, slowing down the German advance a little.

   (b) The Russians attacked Germany sooner than expected, forcing Moltke to move two army corps to the Eastern Front.

   (c) The German advance was foreshortened, failing to encircle Paris. After five weeks the men were exhausted and outrunning their supplies.

2. Meanwhile, the French attack into Alsace-Lorraine (Plan XVII), also failed, being repulsed with 300,000 French casualties, by the German 7th Army.

3. The French Government left for Bordeaux, leaving Paris under the control of General Galieni.

4. When it was realised that the main German army presented the Allies with its flank on the Marne. General Joffre ordered a counter-attack with the **First Battle of the Marne** (5th-12th September).

5. The Germans were forced to retreat, and both armies, seeking to avoid being outflanked, fanned out and "dug in." Lines of trenches stretching from the English Channel to the Swiss border were created. This was the **Western Front**.

The Stalemate

1. Under these conditions, the instruments of defence: trenches, artillery, barbed wire, magazine rifle and machine gun, proved more effective than the instruments of attack: artillery, rifle and bayonet. As a result, no attack could succeed. Cavalry and unsupported infantry attacks became

suicidal. This had been foreseen by Ivan Bloch in *La Guerre Future* (1898), but not by any of the military establishments of the great powers.

Surprise attacks were impossible as aerial observation of troop movements and the preliminary artillery barrage signalled intentions to the enemy. Lengths of enemy trench, when captured, formed salients (or bulges) in the front which had vulnerable flanks and were difficult to hold.

2. The Germans were in all parts of the Front on Allied territory, therefore the greater onus was upon the Allied side to drive the Germans back.

3. Since an attack could not succeed the war became a contest of endurance, with each side trying to wear out the other by exhausting its supplies of men, guns and ammunition or its will to continue. The war became a **war of attrition** directed against the enemy's economy and will to continue. This involved the total mobilisation of all the resources of society, and led to **total war**.*

4. The French war effort was undermined by the loss of its industrial north-eastern provinces. France had to depend upon war supplies and financial aid from Britain and the USA.

5. In Germany, the British naval blockade prompted scientific research to produce *ersatz*,* or substitute materials for those rendered unavailable.

6. Both sides hastily developed new methods of warfare in order to break the stalemate. In April 1915 the Germans used poison gas for the first time at Ypres. Its value was limited as:
    (a) With a change in the wind, it could blow back over the lines of the side using it;
    (b) Gas masks were quickly developed.

7. Thus both sides resorted to attacks using greater and greater resources of manpower to overcome the defence by sheer weight of numbers.
    (a) Thus in 1916 there was a huge German attack at **Verdun.** General Falkenhayne argued that if the Germans launched a massive attack on the heavily fortified fortress of Verdun, then the French would use up their manpower to retain it, while German casualties could be kept at a lower rate by the use of artillery. The French defended the fortress under Marshal Pétain at a cost of 362,000 men. But the Germans lost a third of a million men, i.e. almost as many.
    (b) The British and French launched massive attacks on the **Somme**. This merely caused vastly increased casualties.

8. The Germans improved their defences with the construction of the **Hindenburg Line** in early 1917.

9. Allied attacks during 1917 were unsuccessful.

10. The imminent arrival of fresh American forces made a German breakthrough early in 1918 imperative. The Entente reorganised its command and placed Marshall Foch as overall commander. Successive German attacks failed to break through the Allied lines.

11. In August the British counter-attacked. By the end of September the Front was beginning to move.

The Eastern Front

1. Fighting on the Eastern Front remained more mobile than in the West. Large areas of territory changed hands.

2. In 1914 the Russians prepared for war more quickly than expected and advanced into East Prussia before von Hindenburg and von Ludendorff defeated them at **Tannenberg** and the **Masaurian Lakes**.

3. The Russians also advanced into Galicia in Austria-Hungary before the Germans attacked in Poland to take the pressure off them

4. During summer 1915 the Germans focused their main efforts on the Eastern Front. They drove

back the Russians and advanced into Poland and Galicia, capturing Warsaw.

5. In order to keep the Russians in the war, the Allies offered her Constantinople and the Straits after the war.

6. In 1916, Russian General Brusilov invaded Galicia. Rumania joined the Allies, but was overrun by the Germans in December. Her grain and oil became available to the Central Powers.

7. With the Revolution of February/March 1917, there was considerable debate in Russia about whether to continue the war. It was decided to do so, and Brussilov led another offensive in Galicia in July which failed. With the coup of the Bolsheviks in October/November talks were instituted on ending the war. This allowed the movement of German resources from the East to the Western Front.

The Italian Front

1. After long negotiations which resulted in the secret **Treaty of London**, in May 1915, Italy joined the Allies

2. The main purpose of the Italians was to complete the process of achieving independence and unity by taking the last Italian speaking areas from Austria-Hungary. A front was opened in the Alps against the Austrians.

3. A massive Austrian attack in May 1915 in the Trentino ultimately failed.

4. Another was launched in 1917, which was only held with British and French help.

5. Late in 1918, when the nationalities began to defect from Austria-Hungary, the Italians launched their own offensive, which led to an Austrian request for an armistice.

6. By the end of the war, the Italians had lost one million men to gain twelve miles of territory.

The Balkan Front

1. The Entente Powers followed the policy of offering everything to everybody to gain allies.
    (a) Bulgaria was offered land in Thrace and Macedonia (held by Greece);
    (b) Greece was offered Smyrna and its hinterland.

2. Since the Central Powers seemed likely to win the war, the Bulgarians joined them in September 1915. In October, in concert with the Austrians and Germans, they attacked Serbia.

3. In Greece the King thought that his brother-in-law and friend the Kaiser would win the war, and sought to keep Greece neutral, while his prime minister, Eleftherios Venizelos favoured joining the Allies. British and French troops landed at Thessaloniki to assist the Serbs, but were pushed back into Greece. Paradoxically, the British, who had claimed to have entered the war because the Germans had violated the neutrality and independence of Belgium were themselves doing the same in Greece.

4. After a major defeat, the remnants of the Serbian Army escaped to Corfu.

5. In September 1918, General Franchet d'Esperey led an Allied force from Macedonia into Bulgaria, which almost immediately sought an armistice.*

The Ottoman Empire and the War

In October 1914, Turkey entered the War on the side of the central Powers.

The Gallipoli Campaign

1. The stalemate on the Western Front encouraged many to seek to open another front in the Balkans.

2. On January 2nd 1915 the Russians appealed for assistance in their war with Turkey in the Caucasus.

3. It was decided to launch an attempt to break through, and seize, the Dardanelles in order to:
    (a) open up the supply route to Russia;
    (b) close a supply route to Central Europe.
4. On 19th February 1915 the British navy bombarded Turkish shore batteries and occupied Lemnos.
5. Admiral de Robeck led eighteen ships into the Straits, but abandoned the attempt after four ships had been struck by mines.
6. On 25th April, British, Australian and New Zealand troops landed. They had no detailed maps, or hospital ships. General Liman von Sanders had prepared over 100,000 defenders in well-prepared positions. The Allied troops became trapped between the Turkish positions and the sea.
7. A second landing at Suda in August also failed.
8. The troops were evacuated during December and January. Some 150,000 were killed.

The Armenian Genocide*

1. The Christian Armenians of Anatolia had been periodically subjected to massacres by the Muslim Turkish majority, for example in 1894-1896 and in 1909. Between 100,000 to 300,000 were killed, mostly men.
2. The Young Turks, who took power in 1908 decided to Turkify the multinational Ottoman Empire in order to preserve it from disintegration.
3. When the First World War broke out, they saw an opportunity to eliminate the Armenian population of the Empire.
4. The Armenian men conscripted into the Ottoman army were killed first in 1915. Then rest of the adult population was arrested, sometimes massacred in the towns, but more usually driven out of towns on forced marches or transported in trains, and killed in remote places. The army and local gendarmerie, assisted by units of convicts specially released from prisons for the purpose, carried out the deportations. The majority in the caravans were murdered by groups of local people or died from exposure or starvation. Most of those who survived the marches died in the concentration camps set up in the Syrian desert. About one and a half million people were killed.
5. Some were spared during deportation by being taken as slaves, especially women and children.
6. A special agency was set up to distribute the homes, land, and personal property of the Armenians to the Turks.
7. The Turks systematically destroyed all trace of the Armenians: desecrating their churches, burning their libraries, destroying their schools, monasteries, artistic monuments and historical sites.
8. The flight of many Armenians across the border into Russian held territory pushed much of the surviving Armenian population into the small area Armenia ruled by the Russians. Out of that region was created the present country of Armenia. Many others became scattered about the world.
9. The extremist nationalists who came to rule over Turkey began to deny that the genocide had ever taken place, and to this day publishes propaganda to deny it or to explain it away. This set a precedent for Hitler, who, when discussing his own plans for "racial cleansing" in the East, remarked: "Who, after all, speaks today of the annihilation of the Armenians?"

The Arab Revolt

1. British and Indian troops landed at Basra to safeguard Allied oil supplies in December 1914.

2. In summer 1915 they advanced on Baghdad, where they were defeated by the Turkish Army.
3. The British engineered an Arab revolt, assisted by Lawrence of Arabia. To do so they promised the Arabs a united, independent Arab Empire. At the same time:
    (a) In the **Sykes-Picot Agreement** they conceded to the French that they would control Syria;
    (b) Promised a national homeland for the Jews in Palestine, in the **Balfour Declaration**.
4. General Allenby led a British Army into Palestine, which defeated the Turks at Megiddo on 18th September 1918, and moved on to Damascus.
5. At the end of October Sultan Mohammed VI negotiated an armistice with the British.

The USA

1. In 1914, US President Woodrow Wilson proclaimed US neutrality.
2. Wilson took advantage of the preoccupation of the European powers to consolidate the hold of the US over the Western hemisphere. He sent troops to maintain US dominance in Mexico, Nicaragua, Haiti and Santo Domingo.
3. The USA also took full advantage of the economic opportunities offered by the war, by:
    (a) taking over European markets;
    (b) increasing its trade with the belligerents on both sides.
4. US trade with the belligerents was impeded by naval blockades. From the beginning his administration adopted a stand biased towards the British, that:
    (a) German U-boat attacks threatened lives and goods;
    (b) British mines somehow only threatened goods.
5. With the sinking of the *Lusitania* (June 6th 1915), in which US citizens were killed. Germany was pressured into calling off the U-boat blockade. Several times this was reimposed and then called off again.
6. At the beginning of 1917 the German High Command concluded that a blockade would bring the Allies to their knees very quickly. It may also bring the Americans into the war, but before they would have the time to make a difference on the Western Front, the war would have been won.
7. At the same time, the Germans sent a telegram to the Mexican Government, the **Zimmernann Telegram**, proposing an alliance to recover New Mexico, Texas and Arizona. The British intercepted it and handed it over to the Americans at the same time that several US ships were sunk by U-boats. The USA declared war on the Central Powers on April 6th 1917.
8. The entry of the USA into the war had little immediate effect. Their resources would prove decisive, but they would take some time to become available.
9. By summer 1918 American troops began appearing in significant numbers on the Western Front.

The War on other Fronts

1. In fighting in Africa and the Pacific, the Allies seized all German colonies.
2. The Japanese took over all Germany's rights in China, and sought to secure their position there by making the **Twenty-One Demands**.

The War at Sea

In the war at sea, both Britain and Germany sought to impose an economic blockade on the other, to starve each other of supplies. The British did this with mines and Germans with U-boats.* This was an example of economic warfare.

The Surface War

1. Before the war, both Germany and Britain had built up large surface fleets, including the formidable *Dreadnoughts*. Britain had twenty and Germany thirteen. Both sides believed that a single dramatic battle between these fleets would probably decide the war, and so the admirals were inclined to be cautious, so as not to risk a major defeat.
2. The British Grand Fleet was able to keep the German High Seas Fleet bottled up in harbour for the duration of the war.
3. On 31st May 1916 the Germans sailed out of harbour in what was to be called the **Battle of Jutland**, and retired again after an inconclusive engagement. This:
    (a) preserved the supply routes to Britain
    (b) allowed the Allies to blockade the Central Powers
4. Several skirmishes took place off South America.
5. Surface vessels played so small a role because:
    (a) The admirals were inclined to be cautious, so as not to risk a major defeat;
    (b) Mines, torpedoes and submarines proved such a threat to the security of surface vessels.

The U-Boat War

Although Germany only had thirty U-boats (*Unterseebooten*) at the beginning of the war, and one hundred and thirty at the end, they played the major role in the war at sea because they were most useful in the economic blockade.

The War in the Air

1. Aeroplanes were used by both sides for reconnaissance.
2. The Germans and British conducted small scale bombing raids on each others countries.
3. There was direct combat in the air between fighter planes.

Total War

The Concept of Total War

1. Arthur Marwick popularised this concept as that of a form of war which might be contrasted with the limited wars of the eighteenth century:
    (a) which were largely the business of the rulers and their armies;
    (b) in which armies were relatively small in size and would manoeuvre to avoid battle rather than engaging in it.
    (c) Societies would be largely untouched by the impact of war, e.g. trade would continue.
    By contrast, total war envelops the whole of society, and refers to:
    (i) Its all-encompassing character;
    (ii) Its severity;
    (iii) Total mobilization of the nation's resources for victory;
    (iv) The undermining of existing social and political structures and institutions;
    (v) colossal psychological trauma.
    The usefulness of the concept is not unchallenged. Ian Beckett points out the gradually increasing intensity and magnitude of war during the eighteenth, nineteenth and twentieth centuries.

All-Encompassing Character

1. By early September 1914 all the great European powers were at war. Other states were later drawn in. e.g. Turkey in 1914, Italy in 1915, Rumania in 1916 and the USA in 1917.

2. The war was fought across the world. There were campaigns in the colonies in Africa and in the Middle East.
3. The war was fought on land, on the sea, under the sea and in the air. Aircraft were used for reconnaissance and bombing missions.
4. All the European powers except Britain introduced conscription by 1914, and Britain introduced it during 1916.
5. The First World War was a war between nations, not rulers. Consequently civilians became targets. The German gun *Big Bertha* shelled Paris from a distance of 70 miles. Unrestricted submarine warfare by the Germans against shipping in the Atlantic ensured the sinking of the *Lusitania*. Night bombing raids were carried out by the Germans and the British on each others' territories. Civilians in occupied countries were sometimes ill-treated by the occupying power. e.g. The sack of Liege by the Germans.

Severity

1. The casualties of war were appalling:
    (a) About 10 million men were killed and about 20 million wounded. There were 5 million widows left and 9 million orphans.
    (b) Large numbers of the wounded were permanently blind or disabled.
    (c) New forms of killing had been used, e.g. poison gas.
2. Ill-treatment of prisoners-of-war was occasionally resorted to. The Turks had the reputation of being cruellest to prisoners.
3. There was a new bitterness between the populations of the powers. Churchill said: "This is no ordinary war, but a struggle between nations for life and death. It raises passions between nations of the most terrible kind."
    (a) National/racial hatred had been stirred up by the press:
        (i) In Germany there was an anti-British campaign.
        (ii) In the UK, the Daily Mail advised: "Refuse to be served by an Austrian or German waiter. If your waiter says he is Swiss ask to see his passport."
4. This had some results. Germans were interned in Britain, termed "Hun" and believed to be guilty of barbarities, particularly against the Belgian populace, e.g. bayoneting babies. German businesses were attacked. Prince Louis of Battenberg was forced to resign as First Sea Lord. Even the royal family changed its German family name, Saxe-Coburg Gotha, to Windsor.
5. Most of the atrocity stories turned out to have been false.
6. In 1916, some 60,000 Belgians were deported to Germany to work in factories there. But when the Social democrats in the *Reichstag* protested, this was stopped, and by summer 1917, all the deportees were home again.
7. By far the worst atrocities were committed by the Turks against the Armenian population of the empire. Some one and a half million were massacred in a deliberate act of genocide. The Turkish Government ordered the wholesale deportation of the Armenians near the battlefront with the Russians to the Syrian Desert. Most never reached the desert. They were killed by Kurds and Turks on the way, or died of starvation or cold or ill-treatment. Many were taken as slaves by the people in the villages through which they passed. In many places there was not even a pretence at deportation. The Armenians were simply massacred or taken as slaves.
    This was the last of a series of massacres of the Christian population of the Ottoman Empire over the preceding centuries, and it was the first genocide of the twentieth century. The Turkish Government sought to deny that the genocide ever took place, and has always refused to admit its guilt.

8. The areas of fighting along the Western Front were uniquely devastated by the methods of fighting.

Government Intrusion into Everyday Life

Throughout the nineteenth century governments had increasingly interfered more in the details of everyday life as public life became more organised, e.g. by regulating maximum working hours, eradicating child labour, building sewage systems, providing for compulsory education for children. As the nations geared up for a war of attrition, this interference suddenly increased dramatically, both in intensity and in detail.

1. Britain was the home of liberalism, and yet the government:
   (a) took over the running of the railways;
   (b) the purchasing and supply of raw materials for the armaments factories.
   (c) Some materials were simply requisitioned.
   (d) Food rationing was introduced.
   (e) Conscription into necessary industries, such as coal mining, and to work on the land supplemented conscription into the armed forces. Conscription into factories and farms was extended to cover women.
   (f) The government interfered in the public perception of time by introducing "daylight saving time" during the summer in order to extend the working day.
   (g) Strikes were made illegal.
   (h) Many country houses were taken over for government use.
   (i) "The official Secrets Act" impoed penalties on anyone giving away any information whatsoever about the operations of government.
2. Similar government intrusion into everyday life occurred throughout Europe.

The Undermining of Institutions

1. On the outbreak of war most governments handed over massive powers to military leaders, anticipating a short war.
   (a) In France the National Assembly placed Joffre in command of a "war zone" and then dissolved itself. The government fled to Bordeaux.
   (b) In Britain no politician dared criticise Lord Kitchener, who headed the War Office, in the conduct of the war.
   (c) In Germany the High Command dominated the government, and during the later years of the war Hindenberg and Ludendorff were virtually joint dictators.
   (d) In Vienna the *Reichsrat* was dissolved in 1916.
   When it became clear that the military could not ensure success, political leaders often found difficulties in recovering the powers they had surrendered.
2. By the end of the war, the Empires of Russia, Austria Hungary and Germany had collapsed. The Romanov, Habsburg and Hohenzollern dynasties were dethroned. The Austro-Hungarian, and to a lesser extent the Russian Empires were broken up.
3. There were social revolutions: the communist take-over in Russia and loss of power to the traditional aristocracies in central Europe. Five hundred years of hegemony were lost within five years. War taxation levelled out the existing differences in the levels of wealth. The masses came more and more to share in government. Trades unions were taken into partnership by governments. In Britain women were given the vote after the war as a consequence of their mobilisation.
4. Organised religion never recovered its previous level of popular support in the belligerent countries.

Psychological Trauma

1. The state of shock is manifest in the literature of the time. In Britain the "war Poets", e.g. Wilfred Owen, Siegfried Sassoon, Charles Sorley and Edward Thomas, chronicled the move from enthusiasm to despair, and from romantic idealism to cynicism. Some seventy British poets wrote about the war, some fifty actively engaged in it, and many were killed. Rupert Brook did the same in his autobiography. In Germany Erich Maria Remarque wrote All Quiet on the Western Front, which was later made into a classic film.
2. Pacifism gained adherents and became almost a respectable creed in some parts of Europe after the war.
3. Cynicism and fatalism became widespread. In the UK church attendance declined dramatically.

There has been some resistance to defining the difference between the First World War and other wars on this basis, by pointing out that during the late eighteenth and nineteenth Century wars gradually came to involve more people and more theatres of war, and to take on a national character. E.g. The French Revolutionary Wars and the Franco-Prussian War.

War Aims

During the war, each country drew up statements of war aims. The normal time to decide upon war aims would be *before* going to war. The fact that these were not issued until later is an indication of:

(a) The unpreparedness of governments for the outbreak of war;

(b) To justify to populations traumatized by the losses of the war what was basically an irrational war;

(c) To remove attention from the catastrophic failure of the European ruling class, whose sheer incompetence at government had led to the disaster which was the Great War.

German War Aims

These were drawn up in September 1914 by German Chancellor Bethmann-Hollweg

1. France and Russia must be so weakened that they would never again be a danger to Germany.
2. Most of central Europe, including Scandinavia, to be included in a customs union under German control called *Mitteleuropa*.
3. Germany to annexe Belgium and some French territory.
4. The west of the Russian empire to be dismantled and states dependent upon Germany set up there. (This was to happen in the Treaty of Brest-Litovsk.)
5. German, French, British and Belgian colonies in Central Africa to form *Mittelafrika* under German control.

French War Aims

In an agreement between France and the Russian Provisional Government:

1. Germany was to return to France Alsace-Lorraine.
2. The Saar and all land west of the Rhine were to be severed from Germany.
3. Heavy indemnities were to be paid by Germany to restore the economic imbalance between Germany and France.

Russian War Aims

Sazanov made Russian aims clear to the French Ambassador to Russia.

1. Russia wished to annex East Prussia, Posen and Galicia.

2. Hanover was to be independent.
3. Schleswig would be returned to Denmark.
4. Constantinople and the Straits would to go to Russia.
5. Russia was to be the dominant power in the Balkans.

British War Aims

Announced by Prime Minister Lloyd George in January 1918.

1. Belgian independence was to be restored.
2. Alsace-Lorraine was to be restored to France.
3. All other occupied lands of the Allies were to be restored.
4. "Russia can only be saved by her own people," i.e. non-interference in the affairs of Russia.
5. An independent Poland would be set up.
6. The various nationalities of Austria-Hungary would be granted self-determination.
7. All Italians would be united in Italy.
8. All Rumanians would be accorded justice.
9. There would be separate national conditions for the various subjects of the Turkish Empire.
10. Self-determination would be accorded to the German colonies; i.e. All Germany's overseas colonies were to be forfeit.
11. Reparations would be awarded for injuries received in violation of international law..
12. All treaties would be honoured.
13. An international organization would be created to limit armaments and reduce the risk of war.

US War Aims

These were expressed in President Wilson's **Fourteen Points** in January 1918.

President Wilson had the problem of showing why, if the war was fought to defend freedom and civilization from slavery and barbarism, as was being claimed in 1917, they had stood by and done nothing except make a profit out of it during the previous three years.

1. There was to be no more secret diplomacy (a reference to the incompatible Allied promises made to get other countries to join the war).
2. There would be freedom of navigation on the high seas.
3. All economic barriers would be removed, (free trade always favours the healthiest economy).
4. Armaments would be reduced.
5. Colonial problems would be settled with reference to the interests of colonial peoples;
6. Russia would be evacuated by the German and Austro-Hungarian armies;
7. Belgian independence was to be restored.
8. Alsace-Lorraine was to be restored to France.
9. Italian frontiers would be redrawn along lines of nationality.
10. There would be autonomous development for the peoples of Austria-Hungary.
11. The territorial integrity of the Balkan states would be respected.
12. Free passage through the Dardanelles and autonomous development for the peoples of the Turkish Empire would be guaranteed.
13. An independent Poland would be set up.
14. An association of nations would be created to prevent future wars (the League of Nations).

The End of the War

1. By 1917 enthusiasm was almost dead except among some civilians. Russia was on the verge of collapse. Many regiments in the Austro-Hungarian Army were showing signs of resentment and indiscipline. During 1917 there were mutinies in the French Army. Soldiers on both sides began

to feel a common brotherhood and a resentment of their own civilians. Individual desertions became more frequent.

2. Peace proposals were laid out during that year by:
    (a) the new emperor Charles of Austria-Hungary;
    (b) Lenin;
    (c) Pope Benedict XV.
3. In February/March 1917 the first Russian Revolution took place. The army was near collapse. In October/November the Bolsheviks seized control and within weeks withdrew from the war. They were forced to sign the humiliating **Treaty of Brest-Litovsk** (3rd March 1918), by which:
    (a) Russian lost Estonia, Latvia, Lithuania, Poland and the Ukraine (which became independent under German influence) and Kars and Batoum (to Turkey);
    (b) renounced influence over newly-independent Finland;
    (c) was to pay 3,000 million roubles to Germany.
4. With the entry of the USA into the war, it became clear to the German High Command that unless they broke through on the Western Front before fresh supplies of US troops appeared, they would never be able to win. Since US forces were very slow in appearing, a Spring Offensive was launched which failed to break through the French and British lines. By late summer, significant numbers of US forces began to appear.
5. By September 1918 it had become clear to Ludendorff and Hindenberg that Germany could not win the war:
    (a) With the arrival of US forces on the Western Front, the last chance to break through had passed, and the war of attrition had become unwinable.
    (b) The Austro-Hungarian Empire was disintegrating.
    (c) The Bulgarians were on the point of surrender.
    (d) The Turkish Army in Palestine had been defeated.
    (e) A deadly influenza epidemic hit Germany very hard. It was to kill more people than died on the Western Front in that year.
    The German High Command sought terms for an armistice before the German Army disintegrated.* This came into effect at 11.00 on 11th November, 1918.

Reasons for the Allied Victory

1. The Central Powers had some advantages in the war:
    (a) Internal lines of communication between Germany and Austria-Hungary. (By contrast, Russia was virtually cut off from the West.) This assisted:
        (i) the supply of the army;
        (ii) the movement of troops from one front to another.
    (b) Germany had a more developed industry and technology than any other European power.
    (c) The German Army was considered the best in the world, while German U-boats could challenge Britain's naval supremacy in surface vessels.
2. Despite this, the Allies commanded greater material resources. In 1913:
    (a) Germany and Austria-Hungary had approx. 19% world production;
    (b) Russia, Britain and France had approx. 28%.
    With the entry of the USA into the war, this imbalance was much more pronounced.
3. Once the Schlieffen Plan had failed the Central Powers were faced with a war on two fronts.
4. The Allies could call upon the vast resources of their overseas empires, including colonial troops and food.

5. Allied sea power ensured a more effective blockade in the war of attrition.
6. Germany had less useful allies.
7. The resources of manpower and supplies the USA, when these became available, could provide ensured that the Central Powers could not win the war of attrition.

Consequences of the War

1. Germany was defeated and had to withdraw from France and Belgium.
2. There were over eight million dead in Europe alone.
3. The human casualties were enormous. Almost two in three French soldiers had suffered some form of injury. Many suffered from "shell shock" and were mentally disabled.
4. Some men left the war convinced pacifists; others gloried in war and would become fascists.
5. The physical devastation in the battle areas, particularly on the Western Front, was spectacular.
6. All European belligerents ended the war with huge debts. Their economies had been ruined because they had waged a war beyond their means.
7. The European markets had been taken by peripheral belligerents:
    (a) Japan had taken European markets in Asia.
    (b) The USA had taken European markets in South America, became a creditor nation, built up a merchant fleet, and had become an economic superpower. Probably the major achievement was in Venezuela, where in 1920 Woodrow Wilson succeeded in excluding the British. Venezuela was an important source of oil, and had other resources, such as iron. US corporations grew rich in Venezuela, while the US supported a series of repressive dictators to keep the population amenable.
8. The USA emerged as the world superpower.
9. Belief in the superiority of the traditional governing classes of Europe had been destroyed.
    (a) Revolution was in the air: Russia 1917; Bavaria 1919; Hungary 1919.
    (b) Three autocratic empires had collapsed: Russia, Germany and Austria-Hungary.
    (c) The class which had ruled Europe for 500 years was swept away.
10. New (and unstable) states emerged in Central and Eastern Europe, imbued with nationalism and indignant that their borders did not coincide with what they saw as their national rights.
11. Belief in the superiority of the white races was undermined in the eyes of the Third World intelligentsia, particularly in Japan.
12. The savagery of the war on the Western Front made it difficult for the French and British to accept involvement in a similar war in 1940.
13. Promises had been made by the Allies which were not to be kept, which would cause problems in later years: e.g. to Italy, to the Kurds, to the Arabs. In particular, incompatible promises had been made to the Arabs and Jews concerning the future of Palestine.
14. Genocide had been tolerated in Armenia, setting a bad precedent for the future.
15. The vanquished, particularly the Germans, were left with the sense that:
    (a) they had been unfairly blamed for the outbreak of the war;
    (b) had somehow been cheated of victory by internal traitors, the "November Criminals", who destroyed the unity of the country (Communists, liberals, Jews);
    (c) were being made, unfairly, to pay for it.
Out of this feeling arose Hitler and the Nazi Party, and, ultimately, the Second World War.

Glossary

disintegrated: came apart

ersatz: substitute

genocide: the organized and systematic killing of an entire people in order to put an end to their separate and distinctive existence

U-boats: submarines

Zionist: a supporter of the colonization of Palestine by the Jews and the setting up of the state of Israel

Bibliography

Bell, Philip, "The Great War and its Impact," in *Themes in Modern European History*, ed. Paul Hayes, Routledge (London & New York, 1992)

Fischer, F., *Germany's Aims in the First World War*, Chatto & Windus (London, 1967)

Grayzel, Susan, *Women and the First World War*, Seminar Studies in History, Longman (London, 2002)

Marwick, Arthur, *The Deluge: British Society and the First World War*, Macmillan (London, 1973)

Robbin, K., *The First World War,* Oxford University Press (Oxford, 1984)

Sachar, Howard M., *The Emergence of the Middle East 1914-1924*, Alfred A. Knopf (New York, 1969)

Stone, Norman, *The Eastern Front*, Hodder & Stoughton (London, 1975)

Taylor, A. J. P., *The First World War: An Illustrated History*, Penguin (London, 1966)

The Armenian Genocide in Perspective, ed. Richard G. Hovannisian, Transaction Books (New Brunswick, NJ, 1986)

Winter, J. M., *The Experience of World War 1*, Macmillan (London & New York, 1989)

Wilson, Trevor, *The Myriad Faces of War : Britain and the Great War, 1914-1918*, Polity (Cambridge Mass., 1986)

Georges Clemenceau

The Peace of Paris

"If we suppose a sufficient righteousness and intelligence in men to produce presently, from the tremendous lessons of history, an effective will for a world peace--that is to say, an effective will for a world law under a world government--for in no other fashion is a secure world peace conceivable--in what manner may we expect things to move towards this end? . . . It is an educational task, and its very essence is to bring to the minds of all men everywhere, as a necessary basis for world cooperation, a new telling and interpretation, a common interpretation, of history." (H. G. Wells)

"When I gave utterance to those words [that all nations had a right to self-determination] I said them without the knowledge that nationalities existed which are coming to us day after day." (US President Woodrow Wilson)

It was the human spirit itself that failed at Paris. It is no use passing judgments and making scapegoats of this or that individual statesman or group of statesmen. Idealists make a great mistake in not facing the real facts sincerely and resolutely. They believe in the power of the spirit, in the goodness which is at the heart of things, in the triumph which is in store for the great moral ideals of the race. But this great faith only too often leads to an optimism which is sadly and fatally at variance with actual results. It is the realist and not the idealist who is generally justified by events. We forget that the human spirit, the spirit of goodness and truth in the world, is still only an infant crying in the night, and that the struggle with darkness is as yet mostly an unequal struggle. . . . Paris proved this terrible truth once more. It was not Wilson who failed there, but humanity itself. It was not the statesmen that failed, so much as the spirit of the peoples behind them." (Jan Christiaan Smuts)

Europe after the Peace of Paris

The Organization of the Peace Conference

1. The negotiations for the peace settlement were held in Paris at the Quai d'Orsay, the French Foreign Ministry. They were dominated by the **Council of Four**:
   (a) Clemenceau - France: his main concern was for security for France;
   (b) Wilson - US: his main concern was to create a new world order;
   (c) Lloyd George - Britain: mediated between the other two;
   (d) Orlando - Italy: wielded little influence.
2. The main common aims of the statesmen were:
   (a) to destroy German militarism, which had almost defeated its rivals single-handedly;
   (b) to restore stability in states where established regimes had disappeared;
   (c) to redraw the map of Europe, satisfying the aspirations of various nationalist movements;
   (d) to create a new world order in which such a general war could not happen again.
3. Peace treaties were drawn up separately with each of the defeated powers, and signed in various chateaux in the environs of Paris, from which they took their names:
   (a) The Treaty of Versailles - with Germany (28th June, 1919);
   (b) The Treaty of St-Germain - with Austria (10th September, 1919);
   (c) The Treaty of Trianon - with Hungary (4th June, 1920) ;
   (d) The Treaty of Neuilly - with Bulgaria (27th November, 1919);
   (e) The Treaty of Sèvres - with Turkey (10th August, 1920);

The Treaty of Versailles with Germany (28th June, 1919)

1. German territorial losses:
   Alsace-Lorraine to go to France
   Eupen and Malmedy to Belgium;
   Northern Schleswig to Denmark;
   Poznania, West Prussia (the "Polish Corridor") and part of Silesia to Poland;
   Danzig to be administered by the League of Nations;
   Memel to Lithuania;
   The Saar and its produce to the League for 15 years, then a plebiscite (The produce of the coalfields would go to France for the first five years).
2. Allied armies of occupation were placed west of the Rhine and east of the Rhine at three bridge-heads: Cologne, Coblenz and Mainz.
3. All overseas German territories were to go to the League of Nations, which gave mandates* to Britain, France Australia, New Zealand, South Africa and Japan to administer them.
4. German concessions and trading rights in China, Egypt etc. were forfeit.
5. Germany was forbidden to unite with Austria, which was now entirely German in population.
6. Military restrictions were imposed:
   (a) A demilitarized area was established 30 miles east of the Rhine.
   (b) The General Staff was abolished.
   (c) The Army was limited to 100,000 men.
   (d) The navy to be handed over to the Allies.
   (e) No submarines were to be built or maintained.
   (f) No military air force to be maintained.

(g) The fortifications of Heligoland were to be demolished

7. The **War Guilt Clause** placed sole blame for the war on Germany: "The Allied and Associated Governments affirm and Germany accepts the responsibility of Germany and her Allies for causing all the loss and damage to which the Allied and Associated Governments and their nationals have been subjected as a consequence of the war imposed upon them by the aggression of Germany and her allies." Its main purpose was not so much to apportion blame, as to provide the justification for requiring Germany and its allies to pay compensation. The amount of financial reparations to levied was be set at later date.

8. The Treaty of Brest-Litovsk was to be regarded as void, and Germans were to withdraw from the Baltic provinces.

Aftermath

1. The Americans and French disagreed on the sum Germany should pay.

(a) The Americans, who had suffered hardly at all, and who had ended the war in a wealthier position than when it began, thought that they should pay a smaller sum.

(b) The French, who:

(i) had ended the war in debt;

(ii) had suffered considerable destruction and dislocation by the German invasion;

(iii) and considerable losses of life;

(iv) and who considered hindering and slowing down the German recovery to be in France's interest, considered a high sum appropriate.

In a compromise solution, Germany had to pay only for losses to civilians and their property.

In May 1921 the reparations were fixed at 132,000,000,000 gold marks.

Comment

1. If the main reason for fighting the First World War was to prevent German dominance of the continent, the French idea of breaking up Germany would have been a reasonable one:

(a) There would have been no "Germany" to retaliate;

(b) Germany had only been a single country since 1871, and many Germans, e.g. in Bavaria, regretted the dominance of Prussia and longed for a return to local independence.

2. The US idea of treating Germany leniently would have enabled Germany to return to the community of nations without an inheritance of resentment. The compromise: retaining a united Germany but punishing it harshly, ensured that a resentful Germany would remain to seek revenge.

3. Blaming Germany for the war and imposing reparations was:

(a) unfair, given the complexity of the causes of the war;

(b) unwise, in that it:

(i) Gave the Germans a sense of injustice which could later be exploited by nationalists;

(ii) weakened the Weimar government, making it vulnerable to right-wing charges of collaboration with the Allies.

4. The imposition of reparations on a Germany deprived of 15% of her agricultural land, 16% of her coal, 14% of her iron ore, and 10% of her manufactures precipitated an economic crisis. The economist J. M. Keynes warned of this at the time.

The Treaty of St-Germain with Austria (10th September, 1919)

1. The Austro-Hungarian Empire was to be broken up:

(a) Austria and Hungary became separate states.

(b) The new state of Czechoslovakia was recognized.

(c) The new state of Yugoslavia was created.

(d) Parts of the former Austrian Empire were given to:

   (i) Poland (Galicia),

   (ii) Rumania (Transylvania),

   (iii) Italy (South Tyrol, Trentino and Istria).

2. The Boundaries of Austria were defined with a plebiscite in Southern Carinthia.

3. Austria was forbidden to unite with Germany without League of Nations approval.

4. Limitations were placed on the size and composition of the Austrian armed forces.

5. A war indemnity was imposed on Austria, the amount to be determined later by a commission.

The Treaty of Trianon with Hungary (4th June, 1920)

1. The Austro-Hungarian Empire was broken up (as above).

2. Hungary was reduced in size by the creation of the new nations and the expansion of Rumania, creating a future problem.

3. Limitations were placed on the size and composition of the Hungarian armed forces.

4. Hungary was liable to pay a war indemnity, the amount to be determined later.

Comment

1. The breakup of the Austro-Hungarian Empire was particularly unfortunate:

   (a) Minorities were left in all the new states, and these minorities were much more conscious of their inferior status in the new, supposedly national states, than they had been in the old multi-national Austro-Hungarian Empire, e.g. Hungarians in Rumania, Germans in Czechoslovakia, Slovaks in Czechoslovakia, Slovenes and Croats in Yugoslavia.

   (b) Many states were left with border disputes, e.g. Czechoslovakia with Poland, Hungary with Rumania, Yugoslavia with Italy.

   (c) The new borders cut across the old trading area of the Austro-Hungarian Empire, based upon the River Danube. The new national rivalries ensured that these became obstacles to trade and the development of the region.

   (d) Vienna, a cosmopolitan centre of culture and learning, slipped towards provincial status.

   (e) Many of the Germans in the rump of the old Empire would wish to unite with Germany, ading to its territory and strength.

2. The creation of small nation states out of the multi-national Austro-Hungarian Empire, with the stimulation of nationalism which that would entail, was a deliberate attempt to reduce the appeal of social revolution and Bolshevism in that area.

3. Forbidding the union of Austria with Germany (*Anschluss**) ran counter to the professed respect of the Allies for the principle of self-determination.

The Treaty of Neuilly with Bulgaria (27th November, 1919)

1. Bulgaria lost territory:

   (a) to Yugoslavia: areas in Macedonia;

   (b) to Greece: Western Thrace.

2. Bulgaria gained territory from Turkey in Eastern Thrace.

3. Limitations were placed on the size of the Bulgarian armed forces.

4. Bulgaria was liable to pay a war indemnity, the amount to be determined later.

The Treaty of Sèvres with the Ottoman Empire (10th August, 1920)

1. The Ottoman Empire lost territory:

    (a) to **Greece**: Eastern Thrace including Adrianople and the northern coast of the Sea of Marmora, eastern Aegean islands and Smyrna and a surrounding area on the mainland of Anatolia, which would be occupied for five years when a plebiscite would be held;

    (b) to **Bulgaria**: part of Eastern Thrace;

    (c) to **Italy**: Adalia on the mainland of Anatolia;

    (d) to **Britain**: Cyprus (which Britain had occupied since 1878);

    (e) to the **League of Nations**, which gave mandates to Britain (Iraq, Palestine and Transjordan), France (Syria);

    (f) **independent states** e.g. Hedjaz and Arabia.

2. The **Straits** (Dardanelles and Bosporous) were placed under an international commission

3. The **Dodecanese Islands** would be transferred from Italy to Greece (by a separate convention)

4. Britain, France, Italy and Greece would retain troops in Turkey.

Comment

1. This was the final destruction of the Ottoman Empire, which stimulated a distinctively Turkish nationalism.

2. The division of the Middle East between the victorious powers was a betrayal of the promises made to the Arabs in order to gain their support against the Turks. The result was that Arab nationalism was aroused and then frustrated.

The Revision of the Treaty of Sèvres

1. Although the Sultan accepted the terms of the Treaty, **Mustapha Kemal** led a revolt of Turkish Nationalists against the empire and the treaty.

2. The Turkish Nationalists sought to create an exclusively Turkish nation-state. The Kemalists drove out the surviving remnants of the **Armenian** population. In towns with significant numbers of returned Armenians, massacres were organised. The news of this caused some to resist, and these were annihilated. Most abandoned their homes and became refugees once more. Once again, Allied troops stationed in the Middle East did not attempt to save lives.

3. Lloyd George persuaded the Greek prime minister, Eleftherios Venizelos, to enforce the terms of the Treaty by defeating the Kemalist forces in Anatolia. In the **Greco-Turkish War**, the Greek Army quickly advanced upon Ankara.

4. When Venizelos was defeated in a general election and King Constantine restored to the throne of Greece, experienced officers were replaced by royalists better known for their loyalty to the thron than their military ability. Kemal successfully counter-attacked the already over-stretched Greek lines forcing a retreat whichh soon became a rout. The Greek Army was evacuated from Anatolia.

5. The Allies were no longer united:

    (a) The French were supporting the Kemalists with arms.

    (b) The Italians saw the Greeks as regional rivals.

    (c) All saw the importance of a revived Turkey in the oil-rich Middle East.

    The Allies proposed an armistice.

6. Kemal demanded the evacuation of Anatolia as a precondition of talks, which they refused. In August and September 1922 the Turks then drove the remaining Greek population to Smyrna, and massacred all those there which could not escape, together with other Greeks within their

territories, while Allied warships looked on.

7. When Kemalist forces confronted the British troops occupying the Straits at Chanak. Lloyd George accepted Kemal's demand for a revision of the Treaty.
8. Kemal was able to do this because the Powers were divided.

The Treaty of Lausanne (24 July 1923)

1. The provisions relating to Arab countries remained.
2. Turkey regained Eastern Thrace and the islands of Imbros and Tenedos from Greece. Both sides of the new Greek-Turkish frontier were demilitarized.
3. The Straits to be demilitarized under Turkish control.
4. All foreign troops were to be removed from Turkey.
5. No restrictions were to be imposed on Turkey's armed forces.
6. Reparations were cancelled.
7. The Italians retained the Dodecanese.

Aftermath

1. Turkey was proclaimed a republic. Kemal became its first president.
2. A massive exchange of populations between Greece and Turkey was agreed. Except for the Greeks of Constantinople and the Turks of Thrace, Greek Muslims went to Turkey and Turkish Christians to Greece. This created a huge refugee problem.

Comment

1. The acquiescance of the Allies with the Turkish *fait accompli* is an early example of appease-ment.*
2. The failure of the world to intervene to protect the Armenians or the Asia Minor Greeks, to punish those guilty of **genocide**,* exposed the hollowness of the international system of security set up by the Powers. This act of genocide would provide a lesson in ruthlessness to Hitler, while the lesson of the advantages to be gained by ruthlessly changing demographics* on the ground was later to be copied by Israel.

The League of Nations

1. Several statesmen suggested the foundation of an international organisation to settle international disputes: President Wilson of the USA, Lloyd George, and Jan Smuts of South Africa.
2. The **League of Nations** had two main aims:
    (a) to **maintain peace** through collective security. If one state attacked another, the League would restrain the aggressor by economic or military sanctions;
    (b) to **encourage international co-operation** in the solution of economic and social problems.
3. The aims and constitution of the League were set out in the **Covenant of the League**, which was written into all the peace treaties concluded in Paris.
4. Membership originally consisted of the Allies who signed the peace treaties and neutral states. New applicants would have to be approved by two-thirds of the Assembly.
5. The League was composed of several institutions:
    (a) The **Assembly**: of all member states with one vote each. It met annually.
    (b) The **Council**, composed of the USA, Britain, France, Italy and Japan (permanent members) with four additional elected members met at least three times a year.

(c) The **Secretariat**: led by a Secretary-General, financed by the members of the League, which organised the meetings and carried out the decisions of the League.

(d) a Permanent **International Court of Justice**: which consisted of fifteen judges who judged points of international law when both parties to a dispute brought a case to them. It sat at the Hague in the Netherlands

(e) various **commissions and committees**. The main commissions handled mandates, military affairs and disarmament. There were committees for labour, health, narcotics, refugees, women and children.

6. The League headquarters and most of the institutions were housed at **Geneva**, in neutral Switzerland. The International Court of Justice was located at the **Hague**, in the Netherlands.

7. Member states undertook:

(a) to submit disputes to arbitration, to refer disputes to the Council and not to go to war for three months after a Council;

(b) to work to reduce armaments;

(c) to take economic sanctions against a member which resorted to war. If further action were needed, the Council could request contributions from members for military action. Offending members could be expelled.

Unanimous agreement would be required for decisions, except where otherwise agreed.

8. All treaties should be made public and should be consistent with the Principles of the League

9. The colonies of the defeated countries would become mandated territories where "the well-being and development of (the) peoples form a sacred trust." The Powers undertook to look after them, reporting to the Council, advised by the Mandates Commission.

10. Members undertook to co-operate for the common good (e.g. concerning conditions of labour, colonial subjects, drug trafficking and health matters, to bring existing organizations in these fields under the League and to encourage the Red Cross.

Limitations of the League of Nations

1. The US, having played the major role in setting up the League of Nations, refused to join. The Republican dominated Senate refused to ratify US membership of the League:

(a) The usual reason given is that they were pursuing an **isolationist*** strategy. However, the US was at the time engaged in a naval building programme, designed to allow the projection of US power across the Pacific.

(b) The main Republican objection was that the League infringed upon US sovereignty and the rights of the US Congress. i.e. Constructing a system of international law and order would hamper the actions of the US, now the most powerful nation in the world.

(c) Also, as R. A. Stone points out, some US Republicans were appalled that the vote of "a nigger" from Liberia, Honduras or India would equal that of the "great United States." They were simply not prepared to treat people of non-Caucasian races as equals.

2. The Japanese were offended by the rejection of her attempts to have a statement of racial equality written into the Covenant of the League. The Australian Government had objected.

3. With the Central Powers and the USSR initially excluded, the League lacked legitimacy as a world body, and appeared to be a club of (some of) the victors.

4. The League possessed no armed forces of its own, and so would be dependent upon the cooperation of its members to enforce international good behaviour and punish misbehaviour. But events in Turkey already showed that "changing the facts of the ground" to one's own advantage by force seemed to serve a nation's self-interest better than co-operation.

Assessment of the Peace Treaties

1. The previous redrawing of the map of Europe in 1815 led to a state of general peace for ninety-nine years. This attempt was to last for barely twenty. That speaks for itself.
2. The defeated states regarded the Treaty as unjust:
    (a) The Allies claimed to be redrawing the map on the basis of national self-determination. Yet they were inconsistent. They ignored self-determination when Germans or Magyars (Hungarians) were involved.
    (b) The war guilt clause was considered unjust.
3. Many of the allies of the victors were disappointed with the treaties:
    (a) The Allies were also inconsistent when joining up the West Slavs: Czechs and Slovaks in Czechoslovakia, and the South Slavs: Serbs, Montenegrins, Croats, Slovenes, Bozniaks, etc. in Yugoslavia. The statesmen considered that many small states (Balkanization*) would lead to a power vacuum which would cause regional instability.
    (b) The Italians were dissatisfied with their gains.
    (c) The Japanese were incensed at their failure to have a statement of racial equality written into the Covenant of the League.
    (d) The Chinese were angry that German concessions in China had been given to Japan.
4. The new states of Czechoslovakia and Yugoslavia were almost as multi-national as the Austro-Hungarian Empire they replaced, which was considered out of date precisely for that reason. Both fell apart of their own volition in the 1990s; Czechoslovakia peacefully and Yugoslavia violently.
5. When the settlement was seriously challenged by the Turks, the Allies were shown to be divided, irresolute, and unwilling or unable to enforce their will.

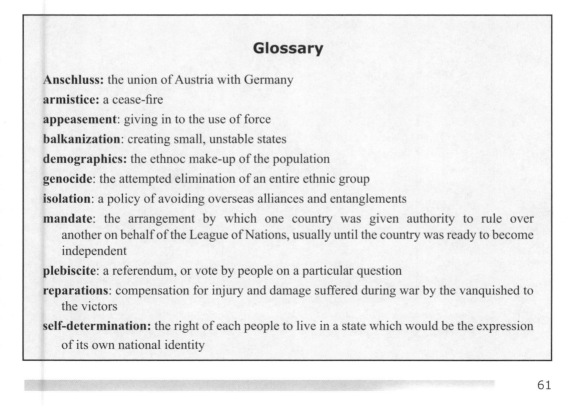

Glossary

Anschluss: the union of Austria with Germany

armistice: a cease-fire

appeasement: giving in to the use of force

balkanization: creating small, unstable states

demographics: the ethnoc make-up of the population

genocide: the attempted elimination of an entire ethnic group

isolation: a policy of avoiding overseas alliances and entanglements

mandate: the arrangement by which one country was given authority to rule over another on behalf of the League of Nations, usually until the country was ready to become independent

plebiscite: a referendum, or vote by people on a particular question

reparations: compensation for injury and damage suffered during war by the vanquished to the victors

self-determination: the right of each people to live in a state which would be the expression of its own national identity

Bibliography

Barker, B., *Versailles: The Peace and After*, History replay, Blackwell (Oxford, 1979)

Goldstein, Erik, *The First World War Peace Settlements, 1919-1925*, Seminar Studies in History, Longman (London, 2002)

Lederer, I. J., *The Versailles Settlement: Was It Foredoomed to Failure?* Heath-Harrap (Boston, 1960)

Sharp, A., *The Versailles Settlement: Peacemaking in Paris*, 1919, Macmillan (London, 1991)

Leon Trotsky

3. The Russian Civil War

[For the background to the Russian Civil War, see the chapter on "Lenin's Russia" in the companion volume "Single-Party States"]

The Causes of the Russian Civil War

1. There were many groups in Russia opposed to the Bolshevik take-over of the country:
    (a) Counter-revolutionaries:*
        (i) Those who supported the Tsarist system in some form;
        (ii) Those who wished for a Western style state: either a constitutional monarchy or republic;
        (iii) ambitious generals who saw the opportunity to gain personal power;
    (b) Non-Russian nationalists, who saw an opportunity to gain national liberation;
    (c) Revolutionaries who resented Bolshevik domination:
        (i) the Social Revolutionaries (SRs);*
        (ii) anarchists.
2. Following the Treaty of Brest-Litovsk, with its massive sacrifice of territory, the opponents of Lenin and the Bolshevists began to find common cause:
    (a) The Whites, including all counter-revolutionaries: supporters of the Tsar, the landlords or democracy.
    (b) The non-Bolshevik left: left SRs and anarchists: who had been alienated by Lenin's dissolution of the Constituent Assembly and by the Treaty of Brest-Litovsk.
3. Resistance to the Communists began at the end of 1917, leading to civil war between the Bolsheviks and their opponents. By summer 1918 different factions of the "Whites"* had set up provisional governments in various places. At the same time, the Left SRs attempted a coup. Attempts were made to assassinate Lenin and leading officials.
4. In addition, Allied governments were opposed to the Bolshevik takeover:
    (a) Fearful of revolution among their own populations, they hoped, in Churchill's words, "to

strangle the revolution in its cradle."

(b) The repudiation of foreign debts and the confiscation of foreign assets had hurt and infuriated the French.

(c) The Treaty of Brest-Litovsk was a disaster for the Allies, who considered intervention in Russia:

(i) If they could link up with nationalist Russians and reopen the Eastern Front, they might save their exhausted armies in France from facing the full force of the Spring onslaught the Germans were launching in an attempt to break through the lines before the arrival of fresh American forces.

(ii) They might also save Allied war *materiel* that had stacked up in Russian ports from seizure by the Germans or Bolsheviks, and distribute it to Russians still willing to fight the Germans.

5. Britain, Japan, the USA, France, Rumania, Poland, Serbia and Greece sent troops to Russia. Czech and Slovak deserters from the Austro-Hungarian army, whom the Tsarist government had allowed to form their own units, took control of the Trans-Siberian Railroad. Direct intervention by Allied military forces involved about 200,000 soldiers.

The Course of the Civil War

1. Resistance to the Bolsheviks had begun by mid-winter 1917.
2. By mid-1918, alternative governments were set up in various parts of Russia:
    (a) Admiral Kolchak set up a "White" government in Siberia.
    (b) General Denikin held the Caucasus region.
    (c) General Wrangel held Crimea.
    (d) Socialist revolutionaries had set up a government at Samara on the River Volga.
    (e) The Czechoslovak Legion, comprising POWs from the Austro-Hungarian Army who had fought against the Germans under the Provisional Government. Following the peace of Brest-Litovsk, they had been permitted to leave the country by way of the Trans-Siberian Railway and Vladivostock, on the Pacific Coast. When attempts were made to disarm them, they seized control of the Trans-Siberian Railway and set up their own administrations.
3. Allied military forces began to land in Russia:
    (a) The French landed in the Ukraine, at Odessa.
    (b) The British landed in the Murmansk region in the north.
    (c) The Americans landed at Archangel, in the north, and in the Far East.
    (d) The Japanese established themselves systematically in the Far Eastern provinces.
4. Among the early victims of the Civil War were the members of the former imperial family. Nicholas II, his wife, and his children had been moved in the spring of 1918 to Yekaterinburg. The local soviet feared that Nicholas might be liberated and become a rallying point for counter-revolutionaries, so on the night of July 16-17th, 1918, all the members of the family were taken to the cellar of their prison house and shot.
5. By August 1918, the Czechs and White allies captured Kazan, 400 miles from Moscow. Leon Trotsky, the Commissar for War, rushed to the area by rail to assemble a local force to block the road to Moscow. Not only did he raise a force, he recaptured Kazan.
6. With the end of the World War in November 1918, and the end of the pretext of reactivating the Eastern Front, it became clear that the real reason for foreign intervention was the desire of the capitalists to suppress the revolution.
7. Early in 1919 General Kolchak approached Moscow, the new capital city, from the Urals with three armies.

8. By this time, Trotsky had built upon the foundation of the Red Guards and created a Bolshevik Red Army to defend the Revolution. He accepted the assistance of many officers from the old Tsarist Army. They were not given their uniforms or right to receive salutes back, but they were called commanders, and under the supervision of political commissars, could exercise full rights to command. The soldiers' revolutionary committees were abolished.
9. Kolchak was driven back in early summer.
10. The French in the Ukraine were:
    (a) bewildered by the confused struggle between Bolsheviks, Russian Whites and Ukrainian nationalists;
    (b) unsure of the loyalty of their own troops, who were absorbing revolutionary sentiments.
    They withdrew their forces during March and April 1919, having hardly fired a shot.
11. The Americans and British in the Arkhangelsk and Murmansk areas did some fighting, using poison gas against the Bolsheviks, before withdrawing their forces in the early fall of 1919.
12. The Czech Legion was defeated.
13. In October 1919, General Denikin took advantage of a cossack rising against the Bolsheviks in the Ukraine to conquer most of Ukraine. He advanced from the south and reached within 250 miles of Moscow before being defeated.
14. At the same time, General Yudenich made a thrust towards Petrograd from the Baltic region, before being driven back.
15. General Pyotr N. Wrangel launched an attack from the Crimea in 1920, but failed.
16. During these campaigns Trotsky moved from one front to another in an armoured railway car, directing efforts.

The Russo-Polish War

1. Taking advantage of the chaos in Russia to increase their own territory and influence in the region, the Polish Army invaded under Marshall Pilsudski in 1920, advancing as far as Kiev.
2. In response, the Red Army drove the Poles back almost to Warsaw. In doing so the Red Army was joined, for what were essentially patriotic reasons, by many officers of the old Tsarist Army who had not previously fought in the Red Army.
3. The Russians expected that Polish workers would rise against the bourgeoisie and participate in the World Revolution. But nationalism proved stronger than socialism.
4. The French sent assistance to Poland under General Weygand, and Polish resistance stiffened.
5. Polish and French troops then invaded the Ukraine.
6. By the **Treaty of Riga (1921)** the Russians were forced to give up parts of White Russia and the Ukraine.
7. The Russo-Polish War demonstrated that relations between Soviet Russia and other states would be of the type normal between state powers, and not fundamentally affected by the Bolshevik character of the Soviet state.

War Communism

1. **War communism** was introduced in mid 1918 to mobilize the state, party and people against the counter-revolutionary forces which threatened the Revolution. Lenin enacted emergency decrees to take control of all the resources of the state. Lenin said: "War communism was thrust upon us by war and ruin... It was a temporary measure."
2. Measures included:
    (a) conscription;
    (b) forced requisitions of grain. Many peasants resisted this, leading to a drop in production

and the development of a black market.*

(c) The foundation of the **Pan-Russian Extraordinary Commission for Struggle against Counter-Revolution (Cheka)**, a committee for fighting counter-revolution, was created, headed by the Polish Bolshevik, Felix Dzerzhinsky. It came to employ a staff of 30,000 to run a political police force and its own army. During early 1918 it rounded up and imprisoned many prominent SRs and anarchists.

Eventually, in September 1918, the government proclaimed a campaign of "Red terror," which authorized the shooting of hostages, and gave increased powers to the Cheka of summary arrest, trial, and the execution of suspects.

3. During this period many of what would later be thought of as the distinguishing characteristics of the Soviet system were set:

(a) Industrial production was paramount, since socialism could only be built after production was able to meet everyone's needs. (This was known as **productionism.***)

(b) **a siege mentality***: the belief that all other powers and classes were dangerous enemies against which the Bolshevik state had to struggle to survive.

The Reasons for Bolshevik Success

1. The quality of Lenin's leadership:

(a) Although the economy had collapsed, Lenin managed to mobilise sufficient resources to sustain the Red Army and workers in industry.

(b) By admitting the right of the non-Russian peoples to secession, he won the forbearance of the non-Russian nationalities, because the Whites did not recognise that right. This prevented the disintegration of the empire, and allowed it to remain a multinational state.

(c) By making the industrial workers the new privileged class, favoured in the distribution of rations, housing, and political power, he retained their loyalty.

(d) Giving into the peasants' demand for the land from the gentry, church, and crown, without compensation, he won over the peasants.

2. Trotsky was a brilliant war leader. He increased the Red Army from half a million to five and a half million men.

3. The Whites:

(a) Lacked unity and could not co-ordinate their efforts. Stephen J. Lee points to the "amazing variety of anti-Bolshevik regimes" which were set up at the beginning of the war;

(b) They frequently worked against each other, in an attempt to place themselves in an advantageous position after victory over the Reds;

(c) Were associated with the foreigners, and so appeared unpatriotic;

(d) Were associated with capitalists, who were suspected of wishing to exploit Russia's resources for their own profit;

(e) Were associated with the landlords. On the territories that they won, they restored landed property to the previous owners and punished peasants who had dared seize the land. Although the peasants' detested the Soviet's grain requisitioning, when forced to choose between Reds and Whites, they chose the Reds;

(f) Treated potential opponents with great severity, imposing a "White Terror" on the areas they occupied;

(g) Were committed to preserving the unity of the empire, and so were unable win the nationalist movements among the non-Russian peoples to their side;

(h) were violently anti-Semitic, killing perhaps 100,000 Jews in the Ukraine, alienating the Jewish population.

4. Foreign intervention was ineffective because:

    (a) J. L. H. Keep points out that , the war on the Western Front took priority, so no full scale invasion took place.

    (b) The various Allied expeditions were uncoordinated.

    (c) The soldiers were war weary.

    (d) Many of the foreign soldiers sympathised with the revolution. French ships in Odessa had to withdrawn after a mutiny. British trades unions urged the withdrawal of British troops.

5. Holding the central core of European Russia throughout the war, the Reds:

    (a) Held the industrial heartland, which contained most of the military stores.

    (b) Lay at the centre of the railway system, and so could communicate and move men and equipment more easily than the Whites, whose bases were on the periphery and so were cut off from one another.

6. The morale* of the Bolsheviks was always high because they confidently expected that the Revolution would quickly spread to the rest of the developed world.

7. Little credit can be given to **war communism**,* which:

    (a) increased the unpopularity of the Bolsheviks, especially among the workers and peasants who were their natural allies;

    (b) reduced the efficiency of their own economy.

The Results of the Civil War

1. The breakdown in normal services and production entailed by:

    (a) The World War,

    (b) The Revolution,

    (c) The Civil War,

    (d) The Polish War,

led to a widespread famine which caused five million deaths.

2. Between 1914 and 1926 some fourteen million people died prematurely. There were millions of refugees and orphans.

3. In 1920, when the Civil War was for all practical purposes over, industrial production was about one-quarter of what it had been in 1913, and the number of employed workers had fallen by roughly one-half.

4. Since the civil war gave Russians only two alternatives, and one was not acceptable, the civil war might be said to have kept the Bolsheviks in power despite their unpopularity in 1918.

5. The political system which emerged victorious from the civil war, was one in which the soviets had been pushed to one side. All power belonged to the Communist Party, members of which occupied all the posts in the Soviet of People's Commissars, and the key posts at all the lower levels of government. The party itself was governed by its Central Committee, dominated by Lenin.

6. The style of Bolshevik government was dictated by the needs of war. Robert C. Tucker notes that this was based upon the **militarization** of the Party:

    (a) ready to resort to coercion;

    (b) rule by administrative *fiat;*

    (c) centralised administration;

    (d) summary justice.

7. The Communist victory was a defeat for the various nationalist movements of the non-Russian peoples. The Communists proclaimed the right of self-determination, but in practice they imposed Russian hegemony on them.

Glossary

black market: illegal market established to avoid rationing

Cheka: Pan-Russian Extraordinary Commission for Struggle against Counter-Revolution

counter-revolutionaries: those working to overthrow a revolution

productionism: the belief that improving production is the key to creating the conditions for the building of socialism, focus upon increasing production

siege mentality: a defensive approach to others

Socialist revolutionaries (SRs): a Non-Marxist revolutionary socialist party

war communism: Lenin's attempt to place Soviet Russia on a war economy to win the Civil War

Bibliography

Davies, Norman, *White Eagle, Red Star, The Polish-Soviet War, 1919-1920*, Macdonald (London, 1972)

Deutscher, Isaac, *The Prophet Armed: Trotsky 1879-1921,* Oxford University Press (Oxford, 1974)

Footman, D., *Civil War in Russia*, Faber & Faber (London, 1961)

Hosking, Geoffrey, *A History of the Soviet Union*, Fontana (London, 1985)

Luckett R., *The White Generals*, Longman (London, 1971)

Radkey, O., *The Sickle Under the Hammer: the Russian Socialist Revolutionaries in tnbe early months of Soviet Rule,* Columbia University Press (Ithaca, NY., 1976)

Rigby, T. H., *Lenin's Government: Sovnarkom, 1917-1922,* Cambridge University Press (Cambridge, 1979)

Schapiro, Leonard, *Origin of the Communist Autocracy: political opposition in the Soviet state*, 2nd ed., Macmillam (London, 1977)

Francisco Franco

4. THE SPANISH CIVIL WAR

"I am responsible only to God and history." (Francisco Franco)

BACKGROUND

The Republic

The Government of Zamora and Azaña (1931-3) *[Moderate Left]*

1. The new republic faced many problems:
    (a) the hostility of the Church, army and landowners.
    (b) Economic difficulties caused by the Depression:
        (i) Agricultural prices fell, wine and olive exports declined, land went out of cultivation, peasant unemployment rose.
        (ii) Iron production fell by one-third, steel production by one-half, unemployment in the cities rose.
    (c) Left-wing parties wanted social revolution, and the overthrow of the democratic republic. Syndicalists encouraged riots, strikes and assassinations.
2. Azaña and Zamora began attacks upon supporters of the dictatorship and enemies of democracy:
    (a) the Catholic Church:
        (i) Church and state were separated.
        (ii) the state was to cease paying priests' wages.
        (iii) Jesuits were expelled from the country.
        (iv) Religious education in schools was to end.
        (v) Religious orders were to be banned from teaching.
        Zamora resigned as prime minister over the attack upon the church, and was replaced by Azaña. Zamora became president.
    (b) The army:
        (i) It had been accustomed to make and unmake governments, and was unlikely to fight

another major war. A large number of the higher officers with which it was top-heavy were compulsorily retired.

(ii) Universal conscription was introduced, although with ways to ameliorate* service for the rich.

(c) The power of the landowners was limited by the **Agrarian Reform Bill** (1932):

(i) Tenants were protected from eviction.

(ii) An eight-hour maximum day was introduced for labourers.

(iii) arbitration boards were set up to supervise collective bargaining.

(iv) A start was made on the nationalization of the largest estates.

3. By the **Statute of Catalonia,** that region was allowed some self-government:

(a) a Catalan parliament with powers of provincial government;

(b) equality to Castilian and Catalan as national languages.

4. Attempts were made to raise wages in industry. Workers were given an eight-hour day.

5. The reforms led to opposition. There were clashes between peasants and the hated civil guard, which behaved in many areas like an army of occupation. Their leader, General Sanjurjo, took revenge, and many peasants were executed in reprisal. Conspirators gathered around Sanjurjo:

(a) monarchists,

(b) right-wing republicans,

(c) *africanistas.*

The coup was planned for 10 August 1932. The **Sanjurjada** was successful in Seville and Jerez, but nowhere else did risings take place. Sanjurjo surrendered, was sentenced to death and reprieved.

6. Some officers also tried to overthrow the government in 1932, but failed.

7. A new right-wing party, the **CEDA**, with its youth movement JAP, was formed to defend the Church and the landlords, led by **Gil Robles**. It leaned towards the Italian-style corporate state.

8. In Jan. 1933 police set fire to houses in a village near Cadiz to smoke out anarchists. Twenty five people were killed. This lost the government the support of the left.

9. During 1933 the **Falange**, a fascist party on the Italian model, was founded by Jose Antonio Prima de Rivera, son of the former dictator. The "Traditionalist Spanish Phalanx of the Juntas of the National Syndicalist Offensive" was influenced by Italian Fascism, the Falange joined forces (in February 1934) with a like-minded group, the Juntas de Ofensiva Nacional Sindicalista, and issued a manifesto of 27 points. It:

(a) repudiated the republican constitution and party politics;

(b) repudiated capitalism;

(c) repudiated clericalism;

(d) sought strong government;

(e) national glory and Spanish imperialist expansion;

(f) a national-syndicalist state organised along corporative lines;

(g) the redistribution of land.

Despite parades and strident proclamations, the Falange made little headway in its first three years. It appealed mostly to students from wealthy families.

10. An election in Nov. 1933 returned a right-wing majority, with the biggest party, the CEDA. The majority in Spain had rejected liberal anti-clericalism.

The Government of Robles (1934-36) *[Right]*

1. The new government, headed by Lerroux and then Samper cancelled most of the reforms of the previous government, including restrictions on the activity of the Church and landlords.

2. It interfered with Catalonian self-government and refused to grant self-government to the Basques. The Basques, who had supported the CEDA, switched to the left.
3. Robles withdrew CEDA from the coalition, threatening its fall, and to avoid this was made prime minister.
4. Resistance grew:
> (a) Anarchists derailed the Barcelona-Seville express.
> (b) Catalonia briefly asserted local autonomy.
> (c) A general strike was held.
> (d) The miners in the Asturias revolted and captured Oviedo. This was suppressed with great bloodshed by General Franco using the Foreign Legion. 30,000 people were imprisoned.
5. The economic situation deteriorated.
6. During 1935 at a meeting of the Comintern it was suggested that the various left wing parties combine in a **Popular Front**. The communists combined with **POUM**, the popular Trotskyite party of the revolutionary workers and peasants.
7. In elections of Feb. 1936, the anarchists decided to participate for the first time, and the Popular Front was victorious.

The Government of the Popular Front

1. The new government, with Azaña as prime minister, lasted until April when Azaña became president, and was replaced as prime minister by Casares Quiroga.
2. It turned out to be ineffective, since many would not join it, hoping for a revolution which would overthrow the existing social order when the bourgeois republic collapsed, while the right opposed it.
3. Disorders grew, with:
(a) a wave of strikes;
(b) the bombing of churches and monasteries.
4. The Falange expanded from 5,000 to 500,000 members in six months.
5. Gil Robles and CEDA became more stridently fascist in appearance and style.
6. Largo Caballero of PSOE, the socialist party, called for revolution, although his party had no paramilitary force.
7. A conspiracy of army officers who sympathised with the Falangists and had connections with the *africanistas* was formed. Azaña saw the danger and moved high-ranking officers to separate them. This did not stop General Mola from continuing to plot. Contacts were made with CEDA and the Falange. General Sanjurjo was to be the figurehead of a coup d'état, which would seize Madrid.
8. A pretext was required. This was provided on 12th July with the assassination of **Calvo Sotelo**, the leading monarchist politician. Mola set 18th July as the day for the rising. The failure of this coup attempt would lead to civil war.

The Causes of the Civil War

1. The country was **divided** between:
> (a) Those who wished to **preserve** traditional Spain;
> (b) Those who wished to **replace** it with something else.
> The latter were divided between:
>> (i) Those who wanted a **social revolution;**
>> (ii) Those who wanted local **self-government or independence**.

2. There was no tradition or understanding of liberal democracy, which was actively supported by only a small minority of educated middle-class people. The majority of people in the country favoured the destruction of the Republic:

   (a) The Church and many Roman Catholics resented its attacks upon the privileges of the Church.

   (b) The army feared loss of influence and a social revolution.

   (c) Monarchists wanted a monarchy restored.

   (d) Capitalists and landlords feared loss of privileges.

   (e) Fascists wanted a dictatorship.

   (f) Revolutionary socialists and anarchists wanted a social revolution.

   (g) Catalans and Basques wanted self-government or independence.

3. The republic had to cope with the consequences of the Great Depression and was associated with economic hardship and failure.

4. In Spain there was no tradition of tolerance or compromise, only of ideological fanaticism.

5. The murder of a leading right-wing politician, **Calvo Sotelo**, by the police was the trigger for an attempted military coup.

The Civil War

The Failed Coup

1. The coup attempt began prematurely at Melilla in Morocco when it was betrayed to the authorities. General Franco assumed leadership of a revolt of the army in Morocco. Its aims were:

   (a) the overthrow of the republic;

   (b) the saving of traditional Spain from:

      (i) social revolution,

      (ii) local separatism.

2. On the mainland it began when General Quiepo de Llano seized Seville. In many cities the army and civil guard collaborated successfully. In Madrid, General Fanjul was besieged in the Montana barracks by workers' militias and defeated.

3. Fighting broke out all over Spain. The Prime Minister, Caseres Quiroga, refused to arm the people, allowing the nationalists to gain control in many places. Several of the Falange's principal leaders, including Primo de Rivera, were arrested and shot by Republican firing squads.

4. By late July it was clear that:

   (a) The rising had been successful in Old Castille, in Navarre, where Carlist support was decisive, and, in Saragossa, Seville, Cordova, Valladolid, and Cadiz, Galicia and most of Andalucia. The Nationalists held the food-producing areas.

   (b) Catalonia and the Basque provinces were loyal to the government because the republic guaranteed their autonomy. In Madrid and Barcelona the security forces, helped by the workers who were armed by the government, defeated the officers. Thus the Republic held the centre, the East coast, Catalonia, and the Basque industrial zones. The Republic also controlled the Navy and Air Force.

5. The role of the workers in defeating the rising made their organisations powerful in the Republican zone. The legal government was bypassed or replaced by local committees and trade unions; while the workers' militia replaced the dissolved army.

6. In many parts of Spain a social revolution took place. Factories and farms were collectivised.

Many who resisted the nationalist coup were divided between:
  (a) bringing about the revolution;
  (b) defeating the rebels.
7. This revolution was unwelcome to:
  (a) the right-wing Republicans;
  (b) the Communist Party, which rapidly grew in number and influence because it controlled the supply of arms from the Soviet Union.
8. In September 1936 Largo Caballero became prime minister, and the CNT was brought into the government. The important trade unions were replaced by the political parties. Fighting the Nationalists was to take precedence over the Revolution.
9. This provoked resentment in Catalonia. The **Workers' Party of Marxist Unification** (Partido Obrero de Unificación Marxista (**POUM**)), set off a rebellion in Barcelona in May 1937. The Communists and Republicans used this as an excuse to oust Largo Caballero. A government was set up led by a Socialist Juan Negrin.
    Some have argued that this restored military discipline to the republican side, others that it undermined the will to resist Franco.
10. General Mola and General Franco both failed to take Madrid in 1936. The successful resistance of the city, which was stiffened by the arrival of the International Brigades and Soviet arms, meant that the Civil War would be prolonged. Victory would go to the side with the best army, with unified political control, and with adequate arms supply.

Foreign Intervention

1. The Republic consistently hoped that France and Britain would allow them to acquire arms. Partly because of fear of a general war, partly because of domestic pressures, both powers backed non-intervention.
2. During autumn 1936 the Non-Intervention Committee was created and met, at the instigation of Britain and France, in London to secure non-intervention in the war by the powers. It was feared that the divisions in Spain would make worse internal divisions in other countries, and even spread into the rest of Europe, leading to a World War. Roosevelt also imposed a "moral embargo" on arms sales to both sides. The effect of this was that the legitimate government of Spain was unable to purchase arms except from Mexico.
3. Mussolini sent 50,000 "volunteers" to help the nationalists. He wished to gain influence in the Western Mediterranean, and gained a naval base at Palma de Majorca.
4. Hitler was persuaded by Admiral Canaris, a friend of Franco, to aid the nationalists. Goering used the war to allow his air force to gain experience and to practice tactics. Hitler also needed Spanish iron for his rearmament programme. 12,000 men, including the Condor Legion, were involved.
5. Dictator Salazar allowed Portugal to be used by the nationalists as a base of operations.
6. The USSR sent advisers, food, tanks and aircraft to the government side. The result was that the Republican Government had to increasingly conform itself to the wishes of the Communists.
7. The Comintern organised international brigades of volunteers to fight for the government, which included George Orwell from the UK, Tito from Yugoslavia, and Togliatti from Italy.
8. Other international brigades were formed to fight for the nationalists, e.g. of Catholic Irishmen.
9. Hitler and Mussolini both supplied aircraft early in the war. The Germans, in return for mineral concessions, supplied the Condor Legion (one hundred combat planes).
10. The Italians sent ground troops; both supplied tanks and artillery.
11. The Western democracies protested at violations of the embargo by members of the Non-

intervention Committee but did nothing. This aided Franco and the Nationalists.

12. The Soviet Union alone responded to the breakdown of non-intervention by supplying arms to the Republican side. Soviet supplies were of great importance (tanks, aircraft, and a military mission) after October 1936. In 1938, Soviet supplies dropped off.

The Course of the Civil War

1. In February and March 1937 further attempts were made by the Nationalists to take Madrid, which failed, including an Italian attack at Guadalajara.
2. Foreseeing a long war, Franco introduced conscription in the areas which the nationalists controlled.
3. The foreign forces aiding the Nationalists were frequently dismayed by **Franco's excessive prudence** in advancing, which was extending the war.
4. Franco was concerned:
   (a) that foreign troops should not gain the credit for important advances;
   (b) that his rivals in the nationalist army should not gain the credit for important advances;
   (c) that the advance should be slow enough to enable the Nationalists to eliminate Republican sympathisers as they advanced.
5. General Franco transferred his effort to the north, where he was able to launch a bombing campaign, of which the destruction of Gernika (**Guernica**), on April 26, 1937, by German planes, was the most famous incident, and outraged public opinion in the democracies. This incident was immortalised in painting by Pablo Picasso. The fall of the Basque Country followed.
6. In Catalonia in particular, anti-clericalism* showed itself in the looting and burning of churches and the shooting of priests and monks.
7. When General Franco concentrated again on capturing Madrid, the Republican army staged its most effective offensive in the **Battle of Teruel** (launched Dec. 15, 1937). General Franco recovered Teruel, drove to the sea, and committed his one strategic error in deciding on the difficult attack on Valencia. To relieve Valencia, the Republicans attacked across the Ebro (July 24, 1938); but once more they failed to exploit the breakthrough. This battle exhausted the Popular Army.
8. The final Nationalist campaign in Catalonia was relatively easy. **Barcelona fell** on 26th January 1939.
9. On the Republican side, the question of the feasibility of continued resistance, which was supported by the Communists and Negrin, caused acute political divisions. On March 7, 1939, a civil war broke out in Madrid between Communists and anti-Communists. On March 28 the Nationalist forces entered a starving capital.
10. By 1st April all resistance was over.

The Consequences of the Civil War

1. 700,000 people had been killed in battle.
2. A policy of *limpieza* or "cleaning up" was followed by Franco. To have supported the Republic merited death, imprisonment or lesser sanctions. About 250,000 were imprisoned in camps.
3. South-West France was flooded with refugees.
4. 200 towns totally destroyed. 250,000 houses left uninhabitable.
5. 60% of the railways destroyed.
6. 5,000 churches burned down or severely damaged.
7. Nearly 500,000 Spaniards went into exile, mostly in France, Latin America and the USSR.
8. Spanish society remained divided until Franco's death in 1975.

Basque and Catalan rights, including the languages, were suppressed.

Trade unions were prohibited and strikes suppressed.

9. Hitler and Mussolini had been brought together through their co-operation in the civil war in Spain and on the non-intervention committee.

10. Their experience on the non-intervention committee taught them to expect appeasement and inaction in the face of determined aggression from the Western democracies.

11. Mussolini's absorption in Spain allowed Hitler to carry out the *Anschluss** without harming German-Italian relations.

12. Hitler was able to use the war to train German pilots for **Blitzkrieg**.

13. It further demonstrated the ineffectiveness of the League of Nations. The failed non-intervention committee was an *ad hoc* body which by-passed the League altogether.

Reasons for the Nationalist Victory

1. Franco was skilful in holding together under his own **control** the various groups opposing the Government: Church, landowners, capitalists, monarchists, Falangists, etc. Their diversity was less than the parties on the other side. Pope Pius XI made it possible for the nationalists to see themselves as crusaders.

2. Franco was skilful at defusing tensions within his own side.

3. The nationalists had a unified military leadership under Franco, and fought a single war. No single unified army command was achieved on the government side, so that the Republic fought a number of local campaigns and its men were unwilling to fight in areas other than their own.

4. The **divisions** on the government side were fatal. Anarchists and communists actually fought each other for some time in Barcelona.

5. The Republican generals were often inept, and worked at cross-purposes.

6. The Republic had a volunteer army, whereas the Nationalists commanded a regular army.

7. Any attempt to impose strong leadership was resisted by the rival groups on the Government side. This was an obstacle to their own programmes.

8. The **foreign intervention** was more effective on the nationalist side, particularly German and Italian intervention. The Germans provided 16,000 military advisors and the Condor Legion. Italy sent 50,000 troops, nearly a hundred vessels and a thousand aircraft. By banning arms sales to both sides, in an agreement which virtually no one else observed, the British actually deprived the Government of weapons.

    By contrast, Stalin was unwilling to fully commit the USSR because of fear of Germany. He insisted on being fully paid in gold.

Significance of the Spanish Civil War

1. E. H. Carr called the Spanish Civil War a "European civil war fought on Spanish territory." The war appeared to be:

    (a) a *practice* for, and

    (b) a *preview* of,

    the Second World War. It involved the same line up: fascism or populist conservatism against liberal democracy and communism.

2. Inside Spain itself, however, the Spanish Civil War was

    (a) on the nationalist side a crusade to preserve the traditional Spain, which had been created during the 1490s;

    (b) on the other side a war to destroy the Spain of the 1490s and enter the twentieth century.

Glossary

africanistas: army officers who had made their careers by serving in the Moroccan campaigns.

ameliorate: make easy

anti-clericalism: opposition to the power of the Church

Blitzkrieg: "lightning war", a style of mobile mechanised warfare practised by the Germans during the Second World War

Carlists: supporters of a dispossessed branch of the Spanish royal line, absolute monarchists, based largely in Navarre

CEDA: Confederación Española de Derechas Autónomas - right-wing monarchist group led by Gil Robles

CNT: Confederación nacional de Trabjo - anarchist syndicalist trades union

Falange: Fascist movement founded by Jose Antonio Prima de Rivera in 1933

JAP: Juventud de Acción Popular - CEDA youth movement

limpieza: "cleansing" of political opposition by Franco

millinarian: a quasi-religious belief in a sudden deliverance which will usher in a paradise on earth

POUM: Partido Obrero de Unificación Marxista - Non-Stalinist Socialist Party founded in 1935

Sanjurjada: Attempted coup led by General Sanjurjo in 1932

Bibliography

Beevor, Antony, *The Spanish Civil War*, Peter Bedrick Books (New York, 1983)

Blinkhorn, Martin, *Democracy and Civil War in Spain 1931-1939*, Lancester Pamphlets, Routledge (London & New York, 1990)

Brenan, Gerald, *The Spanish Labyrinth: An Account of the Social and Political Background of the Spanish Civil War,* 2nd ed., Cambridge University Press (Cambridge, 1950)

Browne, Harry*, Spain's Civil War*, *2nd ed.,* Seminar Studies in History, Longman (London & New York, 1996)

Madagiara, S., *Spain: A Modern History*, Cape (London, 1946)

Payne, Robert, *The Civil War in Spain*, Secker & Warburg (London, 1970)

Preston, Paul, *The Coming of the Spanish Civil War: Reform, Reaction, and Revolution in the Second Republic, 2nd ed.*, Routledge, (London & New York, 1994)

Preston, Paul, *The Spanish Civil War 1936-9*, Weidenfeld & Nicolson (London, 1970)

Thomas, Hugh, *The Spanish Civil War*, 3rd ed. Penguin (London, 1968)

Watters, William E., *An International Affair: Non-Intervention in the Spanish Civil War*, Exposition Press, (New York, 1971)

Jiang Kaishek

5. The Chinese Civil War

"The people of China have stood up." (Mao Zedong)

Background

1. China is a vast country, covering an area larger than the USA and containing a quarter of the world's population. Mountainous and covering many varied types of terrain, communications in the interior were often very difficult.

2. The country had long been subjected to pressure from the US and European powers who wished to take advantage of potential markets there by establishing foreign **enclaves** where Chinese law did not run, and where Chinese (except for the very wealthy) were treated as inferiors. This provoked resentment and **xenophobia**.

3. For centuries China had been ruled by emperors. Traditionally, a good emperor was a strong ruler, who:

    (a) strictly enforced the laws, so that the dykes were maintained and irrigation was not interfered with, agriculture flourished and flood and famine were avoided.

    (b) Kept the powerful in order, so that civil war and internal disorders were avoided and foreigners did not take advantage to invade and devastate the land.

    A strong, successful emperor was known as the "Son of Heaven" and was said to enjoy "the mandate of Heaven".

4. In 1908 the throne of China was inherited by Pu-Yi, a boy of two years of age - the most extreme form of "weak emperor". This weakened the control of the Manchu dynasty over the empire.

5. Near the end of 1911 **Sun Yat-sen**, head of the nationalist party the **Guomindang** or **GMD (Kuomintang - KMT)**, set up a republic and was proclaimed president. In Beijing Yuan Shih-kai took control as Prime Minister, determined upon personal rule.

6. In 1912 Pu Yi was forced to abdicate and a republic was proclaimed with Yuan Shih-kai as president. Yuan outlawed the Guomindang and dismissed parliament. The Guomindang then set up a rival government under Sun in Canton.

7. At the meeting of the first parliament of China in 1913 the Guomindang argued for a democratic

republic on the Western model, while Yuan favoured strong personal rule by himself.

8. In 1915 Yuan died. A number of generals seized control in different provinces, leading to a period of chaos and civil war known as the **War Lord Era**.

9. The **Guomindang or GMD (Kuomintang - KMT)** had been founded by Dr. Sun Yat-sen with three aims, called **The Three Principles**:

   (a) Nationalism: To rid China of foreign interference and rebuild it as a strong united power;

   (b) Democracy: To introduce democracy, following the education of the people;

   (c) Land Reform: rent restraint, and after a period of time, a more equitable redistribution of land.

   The organisation of the GMD was modelled on that of the Soviet Communist Party.

10. The Guomindang had its own army, which fought the War-Lords. Little was achieved, since:

    (a) the army was so weak that it had to rely upon the support of some of the War Lords.

    (b) Sun Yat-sen was not an effective military leader.

11. Some Chinese turned to Marxism-Leninism as a pattern for reform, and in 1921 the **Chinese Communist Party (CCP)** was officially founded. Most meetings of the national party were held on a boat in a lake in Shanghi to avoid the attention of the police. Mao Zedong was present.

12. In 1923, under pressure from the USSR, the members of the CCP also became members of the GMT, forming a united front. The GMD:

    (a) accepted Russian assistance;

    (b) received Russian advisers;

    (c) sent some members to Moscow for training;

(d) and adopted, in part, the Leninist organisation of the Soviet Communist Party, although not its ideology.

13. In 1924, after witnessing demonstrations by peasants in his native village of Shao-shan, who had been angered by the news of the shooting of dozens of Chinese by foreign police in Shanghai, Mao Zedong became aware of the revolutionary potential of the peasantry. He had previously adopted the traditional intellectual's view of the peasants as ignorant. His Marxism had already forced him to change his view of the urban proletariat, and now he turned to the peasants for support. This was a policy for bringing about revolution which differed from those of Marx and Lenin, but was better adapted to Chinese conditions.

14. In 1925 Sun Yat-sen died, and General Jiang Kai-shek (Chiang Kai-shek) succeeded him as leader of the GMD. Although the GMD was receiving help from Soviet Russia, Chiang supported the landowners and businessmen rather than the left-wing and the communists, and he removed left-wingers from positions of influence in the party.

15. In 1926 Jiang set out on the **Northern March** to destroy the power of the War Lords in the centre and north of China. In 1927 the GMD captured Shanghai and Nanjing (Nanking); and in 1928 Beijing.

16. In 1927 in Shanghai, Chiang Kai-shek organised a massacre of left-wing members of the GMD, especially those who were also members of the CCP. The Communists organised resistance. This was the beginning of the Chinese Civil War.

17. It was announced that the provision of "democracy" by the GMD would need to be postponed indefinitely, and that henceforward, Nationalist China would be a single-party state.

The First Phase of the Civil War: 1930-37

1. The CCP split into two parts:
   (a) The Moscow-trained central leadership went underground in Shanghai. They called upon the members of the CCP to launch urban revolutions. Although Moscow sent an agent, Heinz Neumann to assist them, the urban revolts failed.
   (b) Mao led another group into the countryside of Hunan and Jiangxi (Kiangsi), where they established independent soviet areas. There Mao and Zhu De (Chu Teh) founded the Red Army.

2. Between 1930 and 1934 Chiang Kai-shek launched a series of five military encirclement campaigns against the Communists in the Kiangsi Soviet.

3.. From 1931 Mao Zedong (Mao Tse-tung) used the failure of the Moscow-directed leadership to consolidate his power as the real leader of the CCP.

4. During the extermination campaigns Mao and Zhu De (Chu Teh), the commander in chief of the army, successfully developed the tactics of guerrilla warfare from base areas in the countryside.

5. The Communists of Jiangxi (Kiangsi) successfully fought off four Nationalist **Campaigns of Encirclement and Extermination** using tactics of mobile infiltration and guerrilla warfare developed by Mao.

6. In the fifth campaign Jiang gathered about 700,000 troops and established a series of blockhouses around the Communist positions. The Central Committee of the CCP abandoned Mao's guerrilla strategy and used regular warfare tactics against the better-armed and more numerous Nationalist forces. As a result, the Communist forces suffered heavy losses and were nearly crushed.

7. In order to avoid extermination, on Oct. 15, 1934, the remaining 85,000 troops, 15,000 administrative personnel, and 35 women broke through the Nationalist lines and fled westward. This was the beginning of the **Long March.** At that time Mao was not in control of events; Zhu

De commanded the army, and Zhou Enlai (Chou En-lai) was the political commissar.

8. During the first three months of the march the Communists were subjected to constant bombardment from Chiang's air force and attacks from his army, and lost more than half of their men. Morale was low when they arrived in Tsun-i, in the south-western province of Kweichow. At a conference there in January 1935, Mao established his dominance of the party.

9. The remnants then headed toward Northwest China, near the safety of the Soviet border. In June 1935 a force under Jiang Kuo-tao, a long-time Communist leader, joined the main army, and a power struggle took place. Jiang's group, accompanied by Zhu De, headed toward the extreme south-western part of China. The main body, under Mao, went on toward northern Shaanxi (Shensi), where the Communist leaders Gao Gang and Liu Zhidan had built up another Soviet area.

10. Mao arrived in Shaanxi (Shensi) in October 1935 with only about 8,000 survivors. Along the route some Communists had left the march to mobilise the peasantry; but most had been killed or had starved. Only one tenth of the original marchers survived.

11. Mao's troops joined the local Red Army contingent of 7,000 men. Other units, including that of Zhu De, swelled their ranks by late 1936 to about 30,000.

12. The Long March:
    (a) decisively established Mao's leadership of the Chinese Communist Party;
    (b) enabled the embattled Communists to reach a base area beyond the direct control of the Nationalists;
    (c) established Mao as a potential leader of all China with the mandate of Heaven.

13. In December 1936 the Communists settled in Yanan (Yen-an) in Shaanxi (Shensi), where they remained throughout the war with the Japanese. From this base they grew in strength.

The Truce

1. In 1936, seeing the threat from Japan, the CCP began promoting the idea of a United Front against the external threat. This was popular throughout China, but Jiang remained more concerned to defeat the Communists that to protect the country against Japan.

2. On December 12th 1936 Jiang Kaishek was kidnapped by the Manchurian Warlord at Xian (Sian), who mutinied and forced him to agree to a truce with the CCP in order to focus upon fighting the Japanese, after which he was released.

3. Although the anti-Communist fighting was ended, a blockade of Red Yanan continued.

4. When the Japanese began their undeclared war by bombarding Wanping following an incident at the Marco Polo bridge on July 8th 1937, both groups fought them in uneasy alliance. The Japanese enjoyed initial success. When Beijing fell they opened a second front at Shanghai. When Nanjing (Nanking) was threatened, Jiang moved his capital inland to Chungking. The fall of Nanjing (Nanking) was followed by a massacre known as the **Rape of Nanjing (Nanking)** in which 100,000 civilians were killed.

5. Thus the Chinese gave up space to buy time, and the Japanese Army found itself bogged down in a war which it could never decisively win.

6. In fighting the Japanese, the communists seemed the more successful, and communism flourished among the peasants. The Communists broke up a substantial portion of their army into small units and sent them behind the enemy lines to serve as nuclei for guerrilla forces that effectively came to control vast areas of the countryside stretching between the cities and communication lines occupied by the invader. As a result, they:
    (a) expanded their military forces to somewhere between 500,000 and 1,000,000 at the time

of the Japanese surrender

(b) established political control over a population that may have totalled as many as 90,000,000, where socialist agrarian policies secured broad support among the peasantry.

7. Meanwhile, in Yanan, Mao:

(a) developed his own version of Marxism, based upon the **"Sinification" of Marxism,** its adaptation to Chinese culture and conditions;

(b) established his control over the Party

8. **Maoism** was created during this period in Yanan, although not called by that name until the Cultural Revolution.

(a) Mao thought "book-learning" useless if not accompanied by real-life experience: "There can be no knowledge apart from practice." The young cadres* were taught to listen to the old men from the countryside.

(b) He considered the peasants as the vanguard of the revolution.

(c) In place of **democratic centralism** he preferred "the mass line", based upon the practical experience of the peasants.

(d) History was not moved merely by impersonal forces. The revolutionary will of the peasantry could, if harnessed, move mountains.

(e) Mao saw and accepted the need to retain and intensify state power to build socialism. Western writers debate whether Mao's ideology was:

(i) a new form of Marxism adapted to Chinese conditions and ways of thinking, or

(ii) nothing more than Stalinism

9. The differences between Mao and the Soviet-oriented faction in the party came to a head at the time of the **Rectification Campaign** of 1942-43. This program aimed at:

(a) giving a basic grounding in Marxist theory and Leninist principles of party organisation to the many thousands of new members who had been drawn into the party in the course of the expansion since 1937;

(b) the elimination of "foreign dogmatism": blind obedience to Soviet experience and orders.

10. In March 1943 Mao achieved official leadership of the party, becoming chairman of the Secretariat and of the Politburo. Shortly after that, the Rectification Campaign took the form of a purge of those disloyal to Mao.

11. The Yan'an legacy left a tradition of:

(a) Mao's leadership;

(b) Maoism;

(c) popular education;

(d) the practice of organising campaigns in the villages to ensure that policies were properly carried out;

(e) economic self-sufficiency

(f) useful experience of government by the Chinese Communist Party.

12. A US delegation known as the **Dixie Mission** visited Yanan in 1944 in order to see how a resumption of the Civil War could be prevented after the defeat of the Japanese. The delegates were impressed by what they saw at Yanan.

13. General Joseph Stilwell was sent to "keep an eye on" Chiang for the US Government. He came to think that the GMD was hopeless, and Gen. Patrick Hurley was sent in Oct. 1944, to persuade Jiang to give up command of all his forces to Stilwell. He refused. Stilwell was then recalled and replaced by General Wedermeyer.

Post-War China

1. During the war, the USA and USSR both recognised Chiang as head of the legitimate Chinese government.
2. US policy was ostensibly to create a strong central government which would be "the US of Asia." The US hoped:
    (a) To reform the GMD under US supervision. General Wedemeyer recommended this in July 1947. The China Aid Act and the Sino-American agreement by which the GMD would put its house in order (1948) were passed as a consequence.
    (b) to bring the GMD and the CCP together under the moderates of the Democratic League. These attempts failed as both sides were too suspicious of each other. The talks broke down over the failure to merge the two armies.
3. The GMD received US aid, and was assisted by US forces in taking over all those areas occupied by the Japanese.
4. After the war Stalin's policy was to:
    (a) Prevent the rise of a strong central government;
    (b) To nibble away at China's borderlands.
Since Stalin thought that Mao would make a stronger ruler of China than Jiang, his policy was supportive of the Nationalists and hostile to the Communists.
    (a) An anti-Chinese revolt was engineered in Xinjiang (Sinkiang) in 1944, and a secessionist republic was set up.
    (b) By declaring war on Japan in the last days of the war he was able to occupy Manchuria.
        (i) Japanese industrial plant was removed to the USSR;
        (ii) The area was returned to the GMD.
    (c) Outer Mongolia, nominally under Chinese sovereignty but really controlled by the USSR, was abandoned by the Chinese at the Russo-Chinese Treaty of August 1945.
5. Following the Japanese surrender there was a race by GMD and CCP forces to occupy the lands vacated by the Japanese, including valuable arms and military supplies. In this race the Communists were better placed to liberate most occupied areas.
6. The USA and the USSR handed over areas they took over to the GMD.

The Second Phase of the Civil War: 1946-49

1. US objectives were to create a pro-American China as:
    (a) a huge market for US capital and trade;
    (b) a pro-American neighbour of the USSR.
2. Initially the USA sponsored negotiations between the GMD and the CCP under General George C. Marshall, posing as impartial arbitrators, but when they broke down, reverted to supporting the nationalists.
3. Serious fighting broke out again between the armies of the GMD and CCP in Manchuria in April 1946. Initially, the Nationalists were successful. In March 1947 they seized Yanan.
4. By mid-1947 the Nationalist army was overstretched in occupying all the areas gained, and a successful Communist counter-offensive began in Manchuria.
5. The PLA won victories in Manchuria in 1948, took Beijing (Peking) early 1949 and Nanjing (Nanking) in April 1949.

6. Chiang resigned from the presidency Jan. 1949 and the GMD asked the US to mediate with the CCP, hoping to retain the south. The CCP, sensing victory, was no longer interested in an armistice. Their advance continued.
7. On October 1st 1949, the Peoples' Republic of China was proclaimed.
8. On December 8th, Chiang and the remnants of the GMD fled to Formosa (Taiwan), taking the country's gold reserves with them. Lacking marine forces, the Communists could not pursue them, not take the nearby islands of Jinmen (Quempy) and Mazu (Matzu), which remained in the hands of the Nationalists.
9. On Dec. 18th 1949, Mao visited Moscow as head of state.

Reasons for the Success of the Communists

The nationalists had many advantages:
1. They were recognised and supported by the USA *and* the USSR.
2. They had a large, US equipped army.
3. The experience of the PLA was in fighting a guerilla war, rather than with large conventional armies using modern weapons.
4. The nationalists had a monopoly of air power.
However:
5. The CCP were able to present themselves as more patriotic nationalists than the GMD, who would more reliably resist foreign influences.
6. They were seen as more effective fighters than the GMD in the Sino-Japanese War.
7. Mao's policy of cultivating the peasants and using them as a power base was successful.
8. The land reform policy of the CCP was compromised during the war, being limited to restricting rent rises, and giving the land of only the largest landowners to the poorest peasants. This won the support of the smaller landowners.
9. The glamour of the Long March assumed the proportions of a national epic and its spell captivated the peasants, and suggested that Mao would be "an emperor with the mandate of Heaven".
10. Mao had able generals, e.g. Zhu De (Chu Teh) and Lin Biaou (Lin Piao).
11. Mao and Zhou Enlai (Chou En-lai) were shrewd enough to take advantage of the many weaknesses of their opponents *[see below]*.
12. The GMD was a government of industrialists, bankers and landlords. It made no attempt to gain the support of the masses.
13. It was inefficient in everything it did, from fighting the Japanese to coping with the economy, to introducing much needed reforms:
    (a) Little attempt had been made to improve the lot of the masses.
    (b) High taxes and forced labour were resented.
    (c) The administration of the GMD was notoriously corrupt:
        (i) The laws were not applied impartially to rich and poor alike. What had been done, e.g. laws against child labour, was not seriously applied.
        (ii) During a series of droughts and consequent bad harvests and famines the GMD had not prevented the hoarding of rice by profiteers. Many of the profiteers had links with the GMD.
        (iii) US aid went straight into the pockets of officials. Even President Truman referred to the GMT leaders as "grafters and crooks".
14. The GMD had paid for the wars against the Japanese and the Communists by printing money.

This led to inflation, which meant more hardship for the poor, and ruin for the middle classes. After the end of the Sino-Japanese War inflation got out of control.

15. The army of the GMD was allowed to loot the countryside, making it very unpopular. By contrast, the PLA did not.

16. The GMD relied heavily upon a hated secret police system.

17. The GMD army was badly led, with no good generals.

18. In the final stages of the Civil War Chiang would not countenance retreats. This led to disastrous defeats and to mass desertions.

The Character of the Struggle

1. The coming to power of the CCP was, in Marxist terms, unorthodox, being neither by:
    (a) a proletarian revolution, nor
    (b) liberation by the Soviet Army.

2. It was the outcome of a long struggle against:
    (a) Feudal exploitation of the peasants by the landlords;
    (b) Western and Japanese control of China.

3. The movement was fired by:
    (a) nationalism;
    (b) the demand for reforms leading to social justice;
    (c) the desire for a strong and efficient central government.

4. It was part of the cycle of peasant movements for national liberation which swept Asia and Africa after the Second World War. This was seen by the emerging nations of the Third World, which regarded Communist China highly.

5. The success of the communists in China owed nothing to help from the USSR.

6. In 1949, it was the first time that most of China had been united under a strong government since the decline of the Manchu dynasty in the nineteenth century.

Glossary

CCP: Chinese Communist Party

democratic centralism: Lenin's belief in a highly disciplined party

enclave: an area set apart

GMD: Guomindang or Kuomintang (KMT) - party founded by Sun Yat-sen to modernize China

KMT: Kuomintang or Guomindang (GMD) - party founded to modernize China

Sinification: developing in a Chinese way

Sino-: Chinese

xenophobia: fear and hatred of foreigners

Bibliography

Eastman, Lloyd E., *Seeds of Destruction : Nationalist China in War and Revolution, 1937-1949*, Stanford University Press, (Stanford, CA., 1984)

Emperor Hirohito

6. The Sino-Japanese War

"The Western Powers taught the Japanese the game of poker, but after acquiring most of the chips they pronounced the game immoral and took up contract bridge." (Yosuke Matsuoka, Japanese Foreign Minister)

Background

1. In response to intrusion by Europeans, Japan went into complete isolation from the outside world until the mid-nineteenth century.
2. This period of isolation was ended when the US Commodore Perry forced Japan to open up to the outside world.
3. The Tokugawa* shoguns* were forced to concede unequal treaties giving to the Great Powers:
   - (a) economic advantages,
   - (b) territorial concessions.
4. Under the last of the *shoguns* the Japanese began to try to catch up with the West in military organisation and technology.
5. In 1868 the **Meiji Revolution** (named after the Meiji emperor):
   - (a) restored belief in the divinity of the Emperors;
   - (b) brought a group of far-sighted samurai statesmen to power;
   - (c) revived the ancient local Shinto* religion;
   - (d) created a modern centralized state;
   - (e) restored the power of the Samurai warrior caste;
   - (f) began the transformation of Japan into a modern industrialised state;
   - (g) began the development of an army modelled on the Prussian Army and a navy on the British Navy.
6. In 1894-5 Japan won a war against China, forced her to give up territory in Korea and Southern Manchuria, but was forced by the powers to hand it back. The Japanese resented this.
7. In 1889 the outward trappings of modern liberal parliamentary democracy were introduced. Despite the appearance of western democracy, Japan was ruled by an oligarchy.* The *genro* * coordinated civilian and military affairs. The government did not resign if it lost an election, only

if it lost the confidence of the aristocracy, the bureaucrats and the military chiefs.

8. Powerful industrial companies developed: Mitsui, Mitsubishi, Sumitomo and Yasuda. These **zaibatsu*** provided their workers with housing, health care, education, entertainment. etc. in return for their work and loyalty.

9. In 1898 the USA began to establish itself as a dominant power in the Western Pacific with the annexation of Guam, Hawaii and the Philippines.

10. The Anglo-Japanese Alliance was concluded in 1902. It was a result of Britain's fear of Russian expansion in the Far East. It was regularly revived.

11. After the 1904-5 Russo-Japanese War, in which the Japanese defeated the Russians:
    (a) Manchuria was divided into Japanese and Russian spheres of influence;
    (b) The Japanese Army won the right by their victory to direct access to the Emperor, bypassing the ordinary government.

12. The Japanese had gone on to build up a small empire:
    (a) by conquering Korea;
    (b) by taking over the Russian position as hegemonic power in Manchuria.

13. During the First World War Japan:
    (a) seized Kaichow and all German islands in the Pacific;
    (b) presented Twenty-One Demands to China to ensure that it would enjoy a leading role in the post-war exploitation of China.
    (c) benefited from the temporary removal of the Allies as competitors, allowing Japan to build up its commercial and industrial power. The Japanese merchant fleet doubled in size.

14. In 1917, a Japanese expedition was launched to rescue the Czechs who held the Trans-Siberian Railway and to prevent Amur falling into Bolshevik hands. The Japanese remained in Eastern Siberia until 1922, and in North Sakhalin until 1927.

15. Japan was given a permanent seat on the Council of the League of Nations. But due to Australian opposition, a Japanese bid to include a statement of racial equality in the Covenant of the League was dropped.

16. The US became concerned that growing Japanese power would rival its own dominance of the Pacific. At the **Washington Conferences** of 1921-2 it was agreed that:
    (a) Japan could have a navy three-fifths the size of the US and British navies;
    (b) Japan would withdraw from the Kiaochow and Shantung provinces of China;
    (c) Japan would keep all former German islands in the North Pacific as League mandated territories;*
    (d) The Western powers would build no more naval bases in the Western Pacific.

17. The Anglo-Japanese Alliance was allowed to lapse under pressure from the USA, which wished to increase its own influence in the Pacific at the expense of the British.

18. In 1922 the Japanese signed the **Nine-Power Treaty** recognizing the sovereignty of China, and promising not to create special rights in that country. This was the culmination of a long period during which the Americans had sought to limit the penetration of the other imperial powers in China under the cover of an Open Door Policy, which gave equal rights to all countries in China. They were hoping in the long run to create a united China under US influence.
    This left Japan supreme in the Far East with the world's third largest navy, which she could concentrate in that area, unlike the British and Americans, who had commitments in other areas.

19. In 1924 the US Congress singled out the Japanese by banning immigration into the USA.

20. In 1925, universal manhood suffrage* was introduced; although at the same time, the government was given wide powers to suppress Communists and other radicals.

21. During this period, the army had been democratized. A new generation of army officers drawn from the countryside, poorly educated, highly nationalist, and fiercely loyal to their profession, brought a new extremism and instability to the behaviour of the army.

Japanese Foreign Policy Problems at the End of the 1920s

1. In 1928 the US concluded a trade agreement with China. This suggested:
    (a) A revival of US interest in creating in China a pro-western, Christianized country open to US trade, investment, influence and exploitation.
    (b) The end of the existing system of foreign privileges in China, to the detriment of the Japanese. Japanese exports to China dropped by one half between 1929 and 1931.
2. A resurgent nationalism under the Guomindang (GMD or Kuomintang (KMT) led by Jiang Kai-shek (Chiang Kai-shek) also threatened Japanese influence in China. In particular, Manchuria seemed a soft area for expansion, but Jiang Kaishek and the GMD were threatening to establish greater control over the region.
3. The effect of the great depression and the drop in international trade led to fears that Japan would not be able to afford the foreign exchange to buy the oil, coal, iron, rubber and soya beans which were obtained from China and South-East Asia. The western powers had their colonial empires to protect themselves from the effects of the depression. Japan did not have an overseas empire.
4. At the London Naval Conference of 1930 the Japanese delegation was persuaded to accept a limit on Japanese cruisers, destroyers and submarines which many at home considered a "sell-out" to the west.

Internal Power Struggle

1. As the members of the genro died out, effective coordination of civilian and military affairs ceased.
2. There was a banking crisis during 1927. In the end thirty-six banks collapsed.
3. The zaibatsu took advantage of the banking crisis to take over many medium sized industrial companies.
4. The effects of the depression were severe in Japan, since silk, a major export to the USA, was a luxury product, and people do not buy luxury goods when times are bad.
5. As a reaction to the economic crisis, hostility, grew to the *zaibatsu*. Ideas of nationalism and state socialism under military rule, known as the **Showa Restoration**, began to take hold.
6. The countryside, which was worst affected by the depression, became a breeding ground for chauvinistic* nationalism and militarism.*
7. During the early 1930s, civil government began to lose the confidence of the people, and power gradually passed from politicians to the military
    (a) Democracy was not popular with influential groups, such as the army and conservatives.
    (b) Ordinary people revered the divine emperor, rather than political leaders.
    (c) The politicians were perceived as corrupt, in the pockets of the *zaibatsu*.
    (d) The world economic crisis led to increasing unemployment as other countries raised tariff barriers. Politicians were blamed for the rise in poverty.
    (e) A series of good harvests brought down the price of rice and impoverished the farmers.
    (f) Industrial workers and farmers tried to organise, but were suppressed by the police. It seemed that democracy supported the capitalists.
    (g) The London Naval Conference of 1930 was felt to have been a "sell-out" of Japan's interests to the western powers. This led to a reaction among the military and the people in

favour of nationalists, and against those who favoured a pro-western policy.

(h) Many young army officers were attracted by fascism, and wanted to install a strong nationalist government.

(i) Writers like Kita Ikki argued for "national socialism" at home and an aggressive foreign policy abroad.

The Manchurian Crisis (1931)

1. Japan had interests in Manchuria: the South Manchuria Railway and the banking system. It also had troops there to guard them.

    (a) The Japanese generally believed that as a country lacking in natural resources, their economic survival depended upon their exploitation of Manchuria;

    (b) It seemed a "soft area" for expansion, but the successes of Jiang Kaishek (Chiang Kai-shek) in establishing control over China seemed to suggest that if the Japanese did not act soon, they would lose their chance to expand there.

2. In 1928 Japanese Prime Minister Tanaka sent a small force into northern China to check the advance of the Guomindang (GMD).

3. Shortly afterwards, Chang Tso-lin, the war lord of Manchuria, was assassinated near Mukden, when his railway carriage was bombed. Japanese officers were generally regarded as the culprits.

    This was later learned that this was to have been the signal for a Japanese Army plan to seize Mukden, but the plan fell through when senior officers would not go along with it. The Chief of the General Staff and other high ranking officers were unwilling to take any disciplinary action against the plotters, as this would undermine the prestige of the Army. This set a precedent for indiscipline among the officer corps.

4. By 1930, the Army was distressed at:

    (a) The suffering of the peasants of northern Japan, an area from which recruitment was traditional;

    (b) The government forcing the chiefs of the Navy to accept the results of the London Naval Disarmament Conference; The Army felt that it might also be forced to accept unpalatable agreements in the future.

    (c) Subservience to the West in general;

    (d) The government's "soft" policy towards China.

5. This led to considerable violence:

    (a) An attack was made on the life of liberal Prime Minister Hamaguchi on Tokyo Station.

    (b) A new conspiracy of Army officers was formed to plan a coup and impose a military government on Japan, which included some high ranking officers. In March, it came to the notice of General Ugaki, who ordered it ended, in what was known as the **March Incident.**

6. For several months before September 1931 there had been tension between the Japanese Army and the new warlord of Manchuria, who had begun to build new railway lines competing directly with those under Japanese control. A conspiratorial group of extreme nationalists, the **Imperial Way Faction**, was formed among younger army officers in Manchuria. They wished to take over Manchuria because:

    (a) They believed that war would "spiritually regenerate" the nation, and lead it away from corrupting western ideas and ways.

    (b) The army wished to establish a base outside the country, and outside political control, as a counter- weight to the influence of the *zaibatsu*.

    (c) The Chinese were trying to squeeze out the Japanese.

(d) Manchuria was sparsely populated, compared with Japan, and it was thought that it might solve Japan's overpopulation problem.

7. In September 1931, middle-ranking army officers blew up a section of the South Manchurian Railway, blamed it upon the Chinese, and then proceeded to seize Manchuria without Japanese government permission.

8. This action led to an outburst of nationalist sentiment among the population. The Emperor deplored it, but did not order it to cease.

9. In the face of international protests, the Japanese government agreed to withdraw, but the Army continued its advance. The discrepancy between the professions of the Japanese government in Tokyo and the behaviour of the Japanese Army in Manchuria led most foreign observers to believe that Japanese government was being deliberately deceitful. In fact the Japanese government did not know, and could not control, what the Japanese Army was doing.

10. The League of Nations called upon the Japanese to withdraw. The government agreed to do so, but the army ignored them and continued the occupation of Manchuria.

11. In March 1932 a Manchurian Independence Movement, financed by the Japanese army established the puppet state of Manchukuo, supposedly under Henry Pu Yi, the deposed Chinese emperor, but effectively it was ruled by the Japanese army.

12. The Japanese extended complete control over Manchuria by the **Tangku Truce** (1933). They:
    (a) Suppressed opponents, especially Marxists;
    (b) Rigidly controlled education;
    (c) Built up armaments;
    (d) Used the area as a base for further attacks upon China.

13. The response of the Great Powers was one of **appeasement**:*
    (a) US President Hoover was following an isolationist policy and wanted no involvement in the Far East. The **Stimson Doctrine of Non-Recognition** was adopted., whereby the USA "refused to recognise" the *fait accompli*.
    (b) Sir John Simon, British Foreign Secretary, actually defended Japanese actions.
    (c) The League of Nations sent Lord Lytton to report on the situation. He travelled to the area very slowly, and then issued a report condemning Japan, but saying that there was fault on both sides. In response, Japan withdrew, from the League altogether.

14. This was:
    (a) the first failure of collective security;*
    (b) the first example of appeasement.*
    It is sometimes said that this act of aggression was the real beginning of the Second World War.

15. Manchukuo was administered by the army on "national socialist" lines and not exploited by the *zaibatsu*. Control over this area gave the army an independent base outside the country, and strengthened their position against the *zaibatsu*. Effectively, the Japanese armed forces were beyond the control of the civilian government.

The Establishment of a Single-Party State

1. The effect of the acquisition of an area larger than Japan, containing 30 million people and valuable agricultural and mineral resources made the army and the nationalists very popular within Japan itself.

2. At the same time as the Manchurian invasion took place, another coup plot was discovered in Tokyo. This one planned the bombing of the cabinet and the establishment of a military junta. Once again, in this October Incident, only nominal penalties were imposed on the guilty.

3. In 1932, fighting broke out between the Chinese and a Japanese Naval Party at Shanghai.

Extensive bombing of the city by Japanese naval aeroplanes and a rescue mission by the army was necessary to recover them. The Japanese were forced to leave by the British.

4. In 1932 the **League of Blood** a group of peasants led by a Buddhist priest, pledged to assassinate the ruling clique who were held to be responsible for the misery of the farmers. Before being identified and eliminated, they had killed several high officials, including the Finance Minister.

5. After their elimination, bands of army and naval cadets continued their work. In May 1932 they struck at the government, the *zaibatsu* and the political parties, killing the Prime Minister Inukai, and others. The assassins received much public sympathy and short prison sentences.

6. Afterwards, the army refused to supply a Minister of War to a Prime Minister who was the leader of a political party.

7. At this time, the Army itself was rent by internal factions, both nationalist:

(a) *Kodo-ha* (Imperial Way School): contained younger officers and was the more radical, obsessed by the need for war with the USSR.

(b) *Tosei-ha* (Control School): preoccupied with the need to take control of China.

8. Police repression and the establishment of a semi-military dictatorship followed. The power of the political parties in the Diet* decreased during this period, and real authority passed to a small group of cabinet ministers under the leadership of the armed forces.

9. Teachers were forced to give greater attention to:

(a) the Shinto religion;

(b) military training;

(c) nationalist ideas.

10. Internal repression increased with:

(a) the arrest of left wing political leaders and workers' leaders;

(b) the censorship of newspapers;

(c) attacks upon western values.

11. In 1933 the Japanese advanced piecemeal into NE. China taking advantage of the ongoing Chinese Civil War.

12. In summer 1934 a civilian plot to bomb the entire cabinet was foiled.

13. From the end of 1934 the Imperial Way School began to lose ground to the Control School. This led to killings and an attempted coup by supporters of a Showa Restoration. They seized part of central Tokyo. It collapsed only when the emperor ordered their surrender. On this occasion there were executions, including the patron of the "Showa Restoration,"* Kita Ikki. Following this coup attempt radicals were arrested.

14. Between 1934 and 1936 the Japanese threw off the restrictions of the Washington Conference and began a naval building programme.

15. The army assumed greater and greater control of the national life.

(a) By late 1936 the Minister of Finance referred to a "quasi-wartime economy."

(b) When Japan signed the Anti-Comintern Pact in December 1936, the negotiations were conducted by the army, and not the Foreign Ministry. This treaty was directed against the Soviet Union.

16. In January 1937 there were protests in the Diet about the army's usurpation of power, and Prince Konoye became prime minister in 1937.

17. Following Hitler's successes:

(a) Political parties were dissolved (they were already virtually impotent), and replaced by the **Imperial Rule Assistance Association** (modelled upon European fascist parties);

(b) All trade unions were dissolved and were replaced by "associations for service to industry."

18. Although like European fascism in many ways, it was different in that:
    (a) there was no sudden seizure of power;
    (b) there was no outright break with constitutional democracy:
    (c) there was no charismatic* leader. The emperor filled this role.
19. The *zaibatsu* elite who had supported the Westernisers now changed sides and supported the reformers in the armed forces. These began a programme of rearmament in preparation for overseas conquest.

The Background to the Sino-Japanese War

1. Following the establishment of Manchukuo, the Japanese followed a policy of supporting the assertion of independence by local governments in the north of China. This had the effect of:
    (a) weakening the Nationalists and the unity of the country;
    (b) extending Japanese influence over Northern China.
2. In May 1934 the Japanese proposed to the USA that the US should be regarded as the "stabilizing power" in the Eastern Pacific, and Japan in the West. The US rejected this division of the Pacific into two spheres of influence. US Secretary of State Cordell Hull asserted that the USA "had a special interest in preserving peace and order in China;"; that is, the USA regarded itself as the hegemonic power across the entire Pacific and its coastal states in the Far East.
3. In August 1934 the Japanese Navy began to push for the abrogation of the existing naval agreements. At the London Naval Conference, the Japanese requested recognition of its right to build a navy as large as that of the USA. The USA refused to accept this, and in December the Japanese unilaterally renounced the existing arrangements, which were based on the Washington Conference of 1922.
4. Threatened by the Civil War with the Communists, in 1935 Jiang Kai-shek (Chiang Kai-shek) offered the Japanese a compromise:
    (a) The Nationalists would recognise Manchukuo;
    (b) The Japanese would respect and support Guomindang (Kuomintang) rule in China.
    The Japanese military decided instead to continue the policy of detaching the northern provinces from China under the cover of independence.
5. In 1936 the Japanese Navy began to plan to enforce its hegemony over the Western Pacific Ocean in opposition to the USA:
    (a) As the Japanese oil supply was dependent upon the US, it was clear that this would involve manoeuvring into a good position for the exploitation of the resources of the southern seas, particularly oil. Private Japanese businesses began to penetrate S. E. Asia.
    (b) A naval building programme was begun.
6. By 1936, a large part of Inner Mongolia and Northern China as far south as Beijing was effectively under Japanese control.
7. In December of that year, Jiang Kaishek was kidnapped by the Manchurian Warlord at Xian (Sian) in an attempt to divert his attention from harassing the Chinese Communists to focusing upon resisting the Japanese.
8. Fighting broke out between Chinese and Japanese troops at the Marco Polo Bridge near Beijing on 7th July, 1937, when, the Japanese claimed, Chinese soldiers fired upon a Japanese night patrol. The Japanese Minister of War, General Sugiyama, promptly sent reinforcements from Manchukuo and Korea. The prime minister, Prince Konoye (Konoe) Fumimaro, first tried to resist this escalation of the fighting, then gave way. Thus outright war broke out.
9. China appealed to the League of Nations, which condemned Japanese aggression. But the Japanese were not members of the League, and they would not attend an international conference

called to address the situation.

10. The Europeans were preoccupied with Hitler and the Spanish Civil War at the time, while the US was intent upon maintaining its policy of isolation.

The Causes of the Sino-Japanese War

1. Japan had a high population on land, much of which is unfit for agriculture, and poorly provided with natural resources. It needed:
    (a) food and raw materials for industry;
    (b) markets for manufactured goods.
    Control of China would go some way to meeting this.
2. This desire for territory was fed by the desire to achieve autarchy to escape the effects of the international depression and future trade fluctuations.
3. There was a "soft area" for expansion in China:
    (a) If Jiang Kaishek were allowed to be successful in establishing a strong central government, the chance to expand there would be lost;
    (b) More likely, in the opinion of the Japanese, rule by the incompetent and corrupt Jiang Kaishek would lead inevitably to the success of the Communists and the spread of Bolshevism throughout the region, and an increase in the power of the USSR in the area.
    Both possibilities provoked precipitate action.
4. The Japanese resented Europeans' assumption of racial superiority. This led them to desire to achieve equality with the Great Powers by winning local hegemonic status and an empire.
5. The army wished to try out their western-style forces, win victories, and so obtain prestige and greater power within the state, and during the 1930s, the government came to be dominated by the armed forces.
6. The Americans and the League of Nations had failed adequately to respond to the Manchurian adventure. This appeasement suggested that there would be nothing to stop further Japanese actions against China.

The Course of the War

1. In August fighting began in Shanghai.
2. Japanese naval officers bombed and sank the *USS Panay* in the River Yangtze, and an artillery unit shelled the British gunboat *HMS Ladybird*. The US and UK decided to maintain their policy of non-intervention.
3. In December the Japanese captured Nanjing (Nanking). Atrocities were committed with the wholesale massacre of the population in what became known as the "rape of Nanking."
4. In Summer 1938 Japanese and Soviet troops fought at the borders of Korea, Manchukuo and the USSR. For the first time, the emperor exercised some restraint on the army.
5. In the autumn the Japanese captured Hankow and Canton.
6. The nationalists under Jiang Kaishek and the Communists under Mao Zedong (Mao Tse-tung) decided to end their civil war and combine against the Japanese.
7. A new capital was established by the Nationalists inland at Chongqing (Chungking).
8. Japanese control of China outside the cities was limited to the coastal regions except in the north-east, and was always shallow outside the towns.
9. Serious fighting broke out between Soviet and Japanese forces at Nomonhan between May and September on the borders of Manchukuo and Outer Mongolia.
10. Early in 1941, Japanese Foreign Minister Matsuoka Yosuke concluded a **Neutrality Pact** with Stalin, effectively securing this border.

11. This Sino-Japanese War was the beginning of the fighting which escalated into the Second World War.

The Consequences of the Sino-Japanese War

1. The Sino-Japanese War "soaked up" Japanese resources which both:
    (a) made war with the USA and Britain more likely, in order to obtain the resources required to win the war;
    (b) made the defeat of Japan more likely, since its resources were hopelessly overstretched in fighting both China and the Western Allies.
2. It made the victory of the Communists in the Chinese Civil War more likely, since it revealed the incompetence and lack of patriotism of the Guomindang leadership to the Chinese people.
3. The death and destruction set back the development of China, making the task of reconstruction in 1949 that much more difficult.

Glossary

appeasement: offering conciliation in the face of aggression

charismatic: able to attract and command support by the power of personality

chauvinistic: aggressive, bellicose

collective security: the arrangements made by the Great Powers to provide for their own security and for the avoidance of a general war between them, replacing the former alliance system and the balance of power

Diet: the Japanese parliament, made up of a House of Nobles and a House of Representatives

genro: oligarchic council which ruled Japan at the turn of the century

Guomindang (Kuomintang) - GMD (KMT): party founded by Sun Yat-sen to modernize China

mandated territories: territories officially taken over by the League of Nations, and administered on behalf of the League by one of the Great Powers

Meiji Revolution: late nineteenth century economic and social revolution launched from above, designed to modernize Japan

militaristic: glorifying the military and the values of the military

oligarchy: rule by a small elite

Samurai: the members of the traditional warrior aristocracy

Shinto: the traditional Japanese nature religion

shogun: feudal military leader

Showa Restoration: a projected "cleansing" of the nation of western corruption, named after the Showa emperor, Hirohito

Tokugawa system: Japanese feudal system

Zaibatsu: financial conglomerates

Bibliography

Allen, L., *Japan: the Years of Triumph*, MacDonald (London, 1971)

Beasley, W. E. *Japanese Imperialism, 1894-1945*, Oxford University Press (Oxford, 1987)

Boyle, John Hunter, *China and Japan at War, 1937-1945: the Politics of Collaboration,* Stanford University Press, (Stanford, CA., 1972)

China's Bitter Victory: The War with Japan, 1937-1945, eds. James Chieh Hsiung & Steven I. Levine, Armonk, (New York, 1992)

Coble, Parks M., *Facing Japan: Chinese Politics and Japanese Imperialism, 1931-1937*, Council on East Asian Studies Harvard University, (Cambridge, Mass., 1991)

Fewster, S., *Japan*, Longman (London, 1988)

Hung, Chang-tai, *War and Popular Culture: Resistance in Modern China, 1937-1945*, University of California Press (Berkeley, CA., 1994)

Lamb, Margaret & Tarling, Nicholas, *From Versailles to Pearl Harbour: The Origins of the Second World War in Europe and Asia,* Palgrave (London, 2001)

Livingston, J., Moore, J. & Oldfather, F., *The Japan Reader: Imperial Japan, 1800-1945*, Penguin (London, 1976)

Storry, Richard, *A Modern History of Japan, rev. ed.*, Penguin (London,1960)

Williams, B., *Modern Japan*, Longman (London, 1987)

Neville Chamberlain

7. The Second World War

"How horrible, fantastic, incredible it is that we should be digging trenches and trying on gas-masks here because of a quarrel in a far-away country between people of whom we know nothing." (Neville Chamberlain)

The Approach to the Second World War

Overview

1. In 1931 the German and Austrian governments began negotiations to create a customs union. The French protested that this would breach the Treaty of Versailles. The

2. In 1932 Chancellor Brüning announced that Germany could pay no more instalments of its war reparations.

Hitler's Foreign Policy Aims

Hitler personally controlled foreign policy, formulating strategy and tactics. His aims were set out in *Mein Kampf*, the *Secret Book* and the Hossbach Memorandum.* They were:

1. To re-establish Germany's position in world affairs: ending the humiliations attending the Treaty of Versailles. This would involve the defeat of France and the recovery of pre-1918 boundaries of Germany

2. To complete the work of Chancellor Bismarck by uniting all ethnic Germans in a "Greater Germany" - a goal made possible by the break up of the Austro-Hungarian Empire.

3. The conquest for Germany of *Lebensraum*.* Hitler believed that this space needed to be acquired in the east as far as the Ural Mountains, so as to secure for Germany the Ukrainian "bread basket" and open up vast territories for German colonisation. Hitler found justification for such conquests in:

   (a) his notions of German racial superiority over the Slavic peoples who inhabited the lands he coveted.

   (b) He saw the Bolsheviks who now controlled Russia as the vanguard of the world Jewish conspiracy.

4. To establish German military dominance of Europe:

(a) Control of the East would be the foundation for Germany's economic and military domination of Europe.

(d) The "Jewish Problem", which threatened German racial integrity, needed to be solved.

Most of these goals were not possible without war, and Hitler was clearly aware of this.

5. Rearming of Germany, begun in secret in 1933, was made public in March 1935 when he announced
    (a) the creation of an air force;
    (b) the reintroduction of conscription to provide the manpower for thirty-six new divisions in the army.

6. In June 1933 he concluded the **Anglo-German Naval Agreement** with the British that allowed a German naval build-up of up to thirty-five percent of Britain's surface naval strength and up to forty-five percent of its tonnage in submarines.
    This agreement between Britain and Germany to renegotiate the terms of the Treaty of Versailles without reference to France made the French much more cautious and less determined in confronting Germany, since they did not feel that they could rely upon British backing.

7. In June 1933 Germany defaulted on all its foreign debts.

8. In October 1933 Hitler withdrew from the Disarmament Conference and the League of Nations.

9. On March 7, 1936, he moved German forces into the demilitarised Rhineland. Neither the British nor the French defended the Treaty of Versailles.

10. By 1936 Hitler was spending 10.2 billion marks on rearmament, and Göring was placed in charge of a Four-Year Plan to prepare the German economy for war. On Nov. 5, 1937, Hitler gathered his general staff and admonished them to be prepared for war in the east no later than 1942 or 1943. This is recorded in the **Hossbach Memorandum**.

11. As a cover for his true intentions during the first years of power, Hitler frequently expressed his desire for peace. As evidence of his pacific intentions he signed, in January 1934, a ten-year nonaggression pact with Poland.

12. In July 1934 Hitler encouraged the Nazi party in Austria to attempt an overthrow of the government of Chancellor Engelbert Dollfuss. Dollfuss was successfully assassinated, but Mussolini rushed Italian troops to the Austrian border and forced Hitler to abandon the Austrian Nazis.

13. His agreement with the Japanese in 1936, the Anti-Comintern Pact, was directed towards portraying Nazi Germany as the West's last bulwark against Bolshevik expansion.

14. In the same year, Hitler and Mussolini cooperated in aiding General Francisco Franco's rebel Nationalist forces in the Spanish Civil War.

15. In March 1938, Hitler annexed Austria to the Reich, (known as the *Anschluss**). Britain and France did nothing to stop this further violation of the treaties. [*See below*]

16. Hitler then claimed that the Czechs were persecuting the German minority in the Sudetenland. The British Prime Minister, Neville Chamberlain, held a succession of meetings with Hitler and persuaded the Czechs to yield to his demands. [*See below*]

17. On March 15, 1939, Hitler broke up Czechoslovakia, taking over the West, Bohemian and Moravia.

18. A few days later, he took Memel from Lithuania.

19. Britain and France warned Hitler that a similar attack upon Poland would lead to a general war.

20. In late May 1939, Hitler signed his **Pact of Steel** with Mussolini.

21. Hitler then surprised the world with the **German-Soviet Nonaggression Pact** of August 24, 1939. Secret clauses detailed the division of Eastern Europe between Germany and the USSR.

22. On Sept. 1st 1939, Hitler launched his invasion of Poland.
23. On Sept. 3rd, Britain and France declared war on Germany.

The Austrian Crises

1. In May 1932, Engelbert Dollfuss formed a Christian Socialist government with a majority of one seat in the *Nationalrat*, the Austrian Parliament. The Christian Socialist Party was opposed by the Marxists and the Nazis. Dollfuss decided to replace parliamentary government with a more authoritarian system.
2. In March 1933 an argument arose over the voting procedure. The leading officials of the *Nationalrat* resigned. Dollfuss declared that parliament was unworkable, and afterwards ruled by emergency decree, founding the "Fatherland Front" to unite all conservative factions.
3. Dollfuss, who relied upon the Austrian Fascist party, the *Heimwehr*, turned to Mussolini for support when, on February 12th, 1934, civil war broke out. After four days of fighting, Dollfuss was victorious.
4. An authoritarian constitution was imposed. Elected assemblies were replaced by advisory bodies. "Republic" was removed from the official name of the state.
5. On July 25, 1934, Nazis seized the chancellery in an attempted coup. They killed Dollfuss., but the plotters were compelled to surrender, and their leaders executed. When Mussolini rushed four divisions to the Brenner Pass, Hitler disowned his Austrian followers.
6. Kurt von Schuschnigg became chancellor on the death of Dollfuss. He wished to restore the Habsburgs, but dare not.
7. He negotiate an agreement with Hitler on July 11th, 1936, by which Germany promised to respect Austrian sovereignty, and in return Austria acknowledged itself to be "a German state."
8. In January 1938 the Austrian police discovered a Nazi conspiracy. Schuschnigg went to meet Hitler at Berchtesgaden on Feb. 12th. He was confronted with threats of military intervention and was forced to agree to:
   (a) a general amnesty for the accused Nazis;
   (b) the inclusion of leading Nazis in Schuschnigg's cabinet;
   (c) the appointment of Arthur Seyss-Inquart, a leading Nazi as Minister of the Interior
9. Schuschnigg decided to pre-empt any move by Hitler by announcing that a plebiscite would be held on March 13th to decide on Austrian independence.
10. Hitler noted that:
   (a) Neither Mussolini not the British would oppose the union of Austria with Germany.
   (b) The French Government was preoccupied with a political crisis.
11. On March 11th, 1938, Hitler demanded:
   (a) the postponement of the plebiscite;
   (b) the resignation of Schuschnigg.
12. Schuschnigg resigned.
13. A Nazi government was set up headed by Arthur Seyss-Inquart.
14. The Anschluss was proclaimed and Hitler entered Vienna in triumph on March 14th. Austria was effectively absorbed into the *Reich*.
15. France and Great Britain protested, but accepted the *fait accompli*.
16. A plebiscite was held on April 10th throughout "Greater Germany," resulting in a vote of more than 99% in favour of Hitler.
17. Immediately after the invasion, the Nazis arrested the leaders of the Austrian political parties. Many Austrians, especially wealthy Jews, went into exile.

The Sudetenland Crisis

1. About three million people in the Sudeten Mountains of Czechoslovakia were of German origin. Many were Nazis led by Konrad Henlein.
2. Already, before the achievement of the *Anschluss*, Hitler had denounced the Czechs for alleged persecution of this minority, and demanded their incorporation into the *Reich*.
3. The incorporation of the Sudeten Mountains, with their strong defences, into the *Reich*, would leave the rest of Czechoslovakia defenceless against attack from Germany.
4. In April, Hitler ordered Keitel to prepare for the invasion of Czechoslovakia by October, even if the French should intervene. He was prepared for a war with France.
5. Chamberlain warned Germany against military intervention, while at the same time urging Czech president Beneš to compromise with Henlein. Hitler, however, was encouraging Henlein to avoid coming to an agreement.
6. Hitler made inflammatory speeches demanding that the Germans of the Sudetenland be reunited with their homeland. A war scare developed.
7. The Czechoslovaks were relying on their defensive alliances with France and the USSR. The USSR was committed to the defence of Czechoslovakia if France intervened. Stalin indicated his willingness to cooperate with France and Great Britain and called for a conference, but his offer was ignored by Western leaders.
8. In mid-September, Neville Chamberlain, the British prime minister, held a meeting with Hitler at Berchtesgaden. As a result they agreed that:
    (a) Hitler would take no military action without further talks.
    (b) Chamberlain would try to persuade the French to accept the results of a plebiscite* in the Sudetenland.
9. The French premier, Edouard Daladier, and his foreign minister, Georges Bonnet, visited London, and agreed that all of the Sudetenland with more than 50% Germans be handed over to Germany. The Czech government, not consulted, at first rejected the proposal, but was pressured to accept it.
10. On September 22nd, Chamberlain met Hitler at Godesberg. There he discovered that Hitler had increased his demands. He now wanted in addition:
    (a) the Sudetenland occupied by the German army;
    (b) Czechs and Slovaks evacuated from the area by September 28th.
    Chamberlain agreed to present these new demands to the Czechs.
11. The British cabinet, the French and the Czechs rejected these demands.
12. On the 23rd September, the Czechoslovaks ordered a general mobilisation of their army, and on the next day, the French did the same.
13. Chamberlain proposed a four-power conference to avoid war, and Hitler agreed. On September 29th, Chamberlain, Daladier, Hitler and Mussolini met in Munich. Mussolini introduced a written plan which had secretly been drawn up by the German Foreign Office:
    (a) The German army was to occupy the Sudetenland by October 10th.
    (b) An international commission would decide the future of other disputed areas.
    This was accepted by all the parties. The Czech Government was informed by Britain and France that it had the choice of resisting Germany alone or submitting to the agreement. The Czechoslovak government chose to accept the **Munich Agreement**.
14. Chamberlain and Hitler also signed an agreement declaring their desire to resolve all their differences through peaceful consultations. Chamberlain and Daladier returned home to cheering crowds who were relieved that the war scare was over. Chamberlain announced that he had achieved "peace with honour."

15. It was afterwards reported that Hitler was angered by the result, feeling that he had been cheated of his war.

16. When German troops marched into the Sudetenland, Poland seized the disputed Teschen district.

17. In October the Nazis encouraged the Slovak minority in Czechoslovakia to set up autonomous governments.

18. In November, Hitler offered Hungary the area north of the Danube taken from it in 1919.

19. On March 13, 1939, the Gestapo kidnapped the Slovak leader, Monsignor Jozef Tiso, took him to Berlin, and demanded that he declare Slovak independence in order to break up the country. When Tiso returned to Bratislava, he told the Slovak Diet that the only alternative to being taken over by Germany was to do as they were ordered. They submitted to Hitler's will.

20. In Prague, President Emil Hacha now governed only the rump* regions of Bohemia and Moravia. Hacha was summoned to Berlin and made to request that Bohemia and Moravia be incorporated into the Reich. The country he had promised at Munich not to take by force no longer existed. On the next day, March 16, the German Army occupied Bohemia and Moravia.

21. The Skoda armaments works was now at the disposal of the German war machine, and the boundaries of the Reich had been consolidated.

Reasons for the Signing of the Munich Pact

1. Britain needed time to rearm. R. A. B. Butler, a junior minister at the time, testified that the British Chiefs of Staff had warned Chamberlain that Britain was not ready for war:

   (a) which might involve Italy in the Mediterranean and Japan in the Far East;

   (b) that Britain's air defences were not ready, and France's were primitive. (Everyone exaggerated the strength of the *Luftwaffe)*;

   (c) that the 2,500 mile long Czech frontier with Germany, created after the *Anschluss*, could not be defended.

   In the UK, the year following the Munich Agreement was used for intensive preparation for war, e.g. rearmament, the manufacture of fighter aircraft and training of pilots, the building of radar stations along the coast, the development of civil defence preparations, etc. It has been argued by defenders of Chamberlain's policies that this justified the Agreement. However, opponents argue that Germany made better use of the intervening year. (See below)

2. The French Army had no plans for invading Germany.

3. Although the USSR claimed readiness to honour its alliance with Czechoslovakia:

   (a) The ways open to them were few without transit rights across Poland or Rumania, which the Poles and Rumanians refused.

   (b) In view of Stalin's 1937 purge of his entire officer corps, it was unlikely the Red Army would be effective.

   (c) The USSR was engaged against Japanese forces on the Manchurian border.

   (d) The Czechs themselves were nervous of Russian intervention. Czech General Jan Syrovy said, "We don't want the Russians in here, as we shall never get them out."

4. Despite their protestations of principle, Czechoslovakian borders had been drawn by the Allies at Paris without any regard for the self-determination of Germans or Hungarians, many of whom were included in the new state, where they were treated as second-class citizens. Thus even if Hitler would have to be dealt with, the Czechoslovak issue was not a good enough *casus belli* with which to justify a general war.

5. The League of Nations was not capable of dealing with the crisis, as the USA had never joined it, and Germany, Italy and Japan had already left it.

The Significance of the Munich Pact

1. It is not clear whether, for the Allies, the Munich Pact was:

    (a) An attempt to right some of the wrongs of the Treaties of Versailles, Saint Germain and Neuilly, and so create a more stable and peaceful Europe;

    (b) An attempt to buy time to prepare for war against the Axis Powers.

2. The most diverse judgements have been made about the wisdom of the Munich agreement:

    (a) Popular opinion in Britain and France was expressed in the receptions the leaders received upon returning home.

    (b) Winston Churchill regarded Munich as an unmitigated defeat.

3. It gave Britain time to rearm, so that she was able to withstand Hitler alone in the Battle of Britain, until such time as the Axis drove the USSR and USA to action in self-defence.

4. It gave the Germans more than it secured for the British and French:

    (a) The acquisition of Czechoslovakia gave Germany:

    (i) Skoda: the second most important armaments works in Europe;

    (ii) The thirty-five best equipped divisions in Europe (the Czech Army);

    (iii) A strong defensive border, in the Sudeten Mountains, without a shot being fired;

    (iv) A potential Soviet air base situated between Berlin, Vienna and Munich.

    (b) Germany rearmed during 1938-9 more efficiently than Britain and France. At the time of Munich, the Germans lacked the tanks for a *Blitzkrieg* against France.

    (c) With more resolution, Poland might have been involved on the Allied side.

    (d) With more resolution, the leadership of the German Army might have moved against Hitler.

5. The US supported Chamberlain at Munich. Roosevelt's comment to him afterwards was "Good man." Afterwards, when appeasement had to be given up, and its disadvantages had become obvious, they tended to dissociate themselves from it, stressing their own lack of responsibility for what had happened there.

The Polish Crisis

1. After the destruction of Czechoslovakia there was a lot of speculation about the next victim Hitler would choose: Romania with its oil reserves, the Ukraine, Poland, or even the Netherlands, which suffered an invasion scare in January.

2. On March 17th 1939, Chamberlain attacked Hitler's untruthfulness and evident intention of dominating the continent by force.

3. Three days later Hitler demanded a "corridor across the [Polish] Corridor" to East Prussia and restoration of Danzig to Germany.

4. On the 22nd March, he forced Lithuania to hand over Memel to Germany.

5. On March 31st, the British announced their support for Poland.

6. Mussolini occupied Albania on April 7th.

7. Hitler who reacted to the British guarantee with the oath, "I'll cook them a stew they'll choke on!" renounced his 1934 pact with Poland and the Anglo-German Naval Treaty on the 28th. Germany and Italy then turned their Axis into a military alliance known as the Pact of Steel on May 22.

8. Unable to defend Poland without Soviet help, in the late spring of 1939, the British and French approached Stalin with a request for collaboration against Hitler. It was too late.

9. Stalin decided that:

    (a) the Western powers would leave most of the defence of Poland to the USSR;

(b) war might generate rebellion at home;

(c) He was not ready for the inevitable war with Germany;

(d) With Britain's guarantee to Poland, Hitler could only safely take that country at the cost of war with the British and French. Thus Hitler would need the USSR as an ally.

The Molotov-Ribbentrop Pact

1. Since 1938, secret contacts between Berlin and Moscow had been maintained.

2. On May 3rd, Stalin replaced his Jewish Foreign Minister, Litvinov, with Vyacheslav Molotov, sending a signal to Berlin that Stalin was prepared to deal with the Nazis.

3. On August 23rd 1939, Ribbentrop and Molotov signed the **German-Soviet Nonaggression Pact** in Moscow. This ten-year nonaggression pact contained secret clauses:

    (a) Poland was to be partitioned between the USSR and Germany, along the Curzon Line.

    (b) Hitler conceded the USSR a free hand in the countries which had been part of the Tsarist Empire: Finland, the Baltic states, and Moldova.

4. From Hitler's point of view, this treaty would:

    Allow him to invade Poland with out fear of having to fight a war on two fronts. Thus it fulfilled the same function as the Schlieffen Plan in the First World War, enabling Hitler to dispose of France before having to deal with the USSR.

5. From Stalin's point of view, this treaty would:

    (a) Take the pressure off him in Europe, so that he could deal with the Japanese in Manchuria;

    (b) Give him time to prepare for the inevitable war against Hitler's Germany;

    (c) Allow him to recover the Russian lands lost in 1919 by the Treaty of Brest-Litovsk.

The Approach to War

1. On 25th August, Chamberlain concluded a full alliance with Poland.

2. Hitler delayed his planned invasion of Poland for a week in the hope of reaching an agreement on British neutrality, with guarantees of security for the British Empire.

3. Hitler then demanded that a Polish representative go to Berlin on August 30th to settle the issue of Danzig and the Polish Corridor immediately.

4. When the ultimatum expired, the German army staged a border provocation, a mock attack on the German border by Germans in Polish uniforms, and invaded Poland on September 1st 1939.

5. The British and French declared war on Germany.

The Failure of Collective Security

After the First World War the Great Powers had sought to achieve security from aggression, and to avoid another war by means of:

1. The peace settlements drawn up at Paris;

2. The League of Nations;

3. Various Treaties (later dismissively called "pieces of paper").

The Failure of the League of Nations
The Work of the League

1. The League had some successes:

    (a) In a quarrel between Sweden and Finland over the Aaland Islands in 1920, the League ruled in favour of Finland. Sweden accepted the verdict of the court.

(b) When Poland and Lithuania both claimed Vilna, the League was overruled by the Conference of Ambassadors.

(c) When Poland and Germany quarrelled over Upper Silesia in 1921, the League partitioned it.

(d) When Greece invaded Bulgaria in 1925 after shooting incidents on the frontier, the League ordered a withdrawal and fined Greece.

(e) When Turkey claimed Mosul the League decided in favour of Iraq (a British mandated territory).

(f) A quarrel between Peru and Colombia was settled.

(g) A quarrel between Bolivia and Paraguay was settled.

(h) Much good work was done by the commissions and councils, e.g.

    (i) The International Labour Office persuaded many states to enforce a maximum working day and week and minimum wages for workers, and to introduce sickness and unemployment benefit and old age pensions.

    (ii) The Refugee Organisation helped half a million Central European prisoners marooned in Russia to return home.

    (iii) The Health Organisation successfully combated a typhus epidemic in Russia, which might have spread to the rest of Europe.

    (iv) The Mandates Commission successfully supervised the administration of the Saar and, after a plebiscite, its return to Germany.

2. But its failures were more obvious and important:

(a) When Mussolini bombarded and then invaded Corfu in response to a shooting on the Albanian-Greek border, he threatened to leave the League if it ruled against him, and the Conference of Ambassadors intervened and ordered Greece to pay a fine.

(b) When the League condemned the Japanese invasion of Manchuria in 1931, the Japanese simply withdrew from the League, and nothing was done to force her to comply. The Japanese subsequently ignored the League in their attacks upon China.

(c) The World Disarmament Conference (1932-33) failed when Hitler walked out.

(d) The League condemned the Italian invasion of Abyssinia and applied economic sanctions. But these excluded the products crucially important to waging a war: coal, oil, iron and steel, and were ignored by non-member states. The League was seen to be ineffective.

(e) After 1935 the League was not taken seriously as a means of settling international disputes or deterring aggression. It had become irrelevant.

Thus when the British wished to monitor and prevent intervention in the Spanish Civil War, they set up an *ad hoc** body, the Non-Intervention Committee, which itself proved a vehicle for appeasement.

Reasons for the Failure of the League

1. It was linked closely with the treaties of the Peace of Paris. This gave it the air of an organisation of the victorious powers. The defeated powers were not allowed to become members for some time.

2. In March 1920 the isolationist Republican-dominated US Congress refused to ratify membership of the League. Having worked so hard to set it up, Wilson was unable to join the League, so the League lost the financial and psychological benefit which would have accrued from US membership. This made the League look like an Anglo-French enterprise.

3. The Conference of Ambassadors twice overruled the League:

(a) over the Polish and Lithuanian claims to Vilna;

(b) over Mussolini's invasion of Corfu.

4. There were problems with the Covenant:

(a) It was difficult to achieve the unanimous decisions required;

(b) There was no military force of the League, which had to rely upon individual nations to supply troops in the event of military sanctions being decided upon.

5. States tended to seek security independently of the League by signing mutual non-aggression pacts. This undermined confidence in the effectiveness of the League.

6. Economic problems after 1929 encouraged the growth of bellicose* nationalist regimes which sought to achieve autarchy and divert attention from internal problems by foreign adventures.

7. There was a tendency for the main members of the League to appease powerful aggressor states. This began early, in 1923 with the appeasement of Mussolini over Corfu. It became apparent with the appeasement of Japan over the invasion of Manchuria in 1931, and impossible to ignore over the Italian invasion of Abyssinia in 1935. Aggressor states were able to ignore the League because its leading states were not prepared to enforce its decisions by serious economic sanctions* or by the use of force.

The "Pieces of Paper"

The most important of these included:

1. The Franco-Polish Pact (1921)

2. The Washington Conference (1921-2):

(a) limited the Japanese navy to three-fifths those of Britain and the USA;

(b) allowed Japan to keep all German islands in the North Pacific;

(c) The Allies agreed to build no new naval bases near Japan.

3. The Genoa Conference (1922) Lloyd George sought to:

(a) improve Franco-German relations;

(b) re-establish relations with Russia.

(c) The French refused compromise, so the Germans and Russians withdrew and signed:

4. The Treaty of Rapallo (1922) between Germany and Russia, by which Russia agreed to allow the Germans secretly to evade some of the terms of the Treaty of Versailles, e.g. to maintain an air force on Russian soil.

5. The Franco-Czechoslovak Pact (1924).

6. The Locarno Treaties (1925) The most important was that by which France, Belgium, and Germany would respect their common frontiers. Britain and Italy would assist any state attacked. No guarantee was given to the states on Germany's eastern frontiers.

7. The Franco-Rumanian Pact (1926)

8. The Franco-Rumanian Pact (1927)

9. The Kellog-Briand Pact (1928) Originally a Franco-American pact renouncing war, it was signed by 65 states renouncing war as an instrument of policy (including Japan, Italy, Germany and the USSR).

10. The German-Polish Pact (1934): a ten-year non-aggression pact.

11. The Rome-Berlin Axis (1936) between Germany and Italy.

12. The Anti-Comintern Pact (1936) between Germany, Italy and Japan.

13. The Molotov-Ribbentrop Pact (1939) between the USSR and Germany, outwardly a ten-year non-aggression pact, but with a secret protocol on the division of eastern Europe.

They failed to keep the peace because no one was prepared to back them up or keep their word if it meant war. This was a consequence of the horrors of the First World War.

Appeasement

1. "Appeasement" is the policy of meeting threats of force with compromise or concessions, rather than meeting force with force.
2. It is an important topic, because the revisionist historian A. J. P. Taylor argued that the passive response of world leaders to Hitler's policies and actions encouraged his expansionism, led him to miscalculate, and so precipitated the war.
3. In dealing with this topic we should always bear in mind the distorting effects of hindsight,* that is, of looking at events in the past in the light of what happened afterwards. *We* know that the policies of the Western Allies led to the worst war in history, but at the time when such policies were formulated and carried out, those concerned *did not* know what was still at that time in the future, and the future was unknown to them. To understand their motives, we must:
    (a) consider what lay in their recent past, upon which their judgements would be made;
    (b) discount what lay in their future (which we know, but which they did not).
4. The tendency of the Great Powers to appease aggression from any quarter had been apparent since the end of the First World War. The main examples of appeasement include:
    (a) Kemal's rejection of the Treaty of Sevres and its renegotiation (1920-2);
    (b) Mussolini's bombardment and occupation of Corfu (1923);
    (c) the Japanese invasion of Manchuria (1931);
    (d) the reintroduction of conscription and rearmament in Germany (1933);
    (e) the Italian invasion of Abyssinia (1935);
    (f) the German remilitarization of the Rhineland (1936);
    (g) the ignoring of German/Italian intervention in the Spanish Civil War (1936-9);
    (h) the *Anschluss* (1938);
    (i) the demand for the Sudetenland (1938);
    (j) the invasion of Bohemia and Moravia (1939).

An Analysis of Motives
General factors

1. The First World War had been the largest man-made catastrophe in human history. In some countries virtually an entire generation of men had been killed. The repeat of such a disaster must be avoided at all costs.
2. It was believed that the next world war would be even worse than the first, because of the development of bombers, and of incendiary, gas and explosive bombs. "The bomber will always get through" Stanley Baldwin. Immediately upon the declaration of war death would rain down upon capital cities, annihilating them within hours. Civilisation would probably be destroyed. These fears are evident in the fiction of the day, with titles like *The Gas War of 1940*, *The Poison War*, *The Black Death*, *The Shape of Things to Come*, *War on Women* and *Air Reprisal*.
   This belief was based upon the application of imagination to the memory of the strategic bombing of the First World War. In fact no air force was capable of sustained offensive long-range bombing until 1939.
3. A basic moral principle is that it is always right, if forced to choose between evils, to choose the lesser. In view of the points made above, war would almost never actually be the lesser evil.
4. This was assisted by Hitler's always proceeding one step at a time, while disclaiming in advance future aggressive moves, and so disarming his opponents.
5. As a reaction to the First World War, pacifism, the belief that violence is always morally wrong, was prev-

alent e.g. among "Christian Socialists". This was illustrated by the "King and Country" debate in the Oxford Union (the debating society of Oxford University, oldest debating society in the world).

6. Among western politicians there was considerable sympathy for the view that the treaties at the end of the First World War had been unfair to the defeated powers, and in particular that the Treaty of Versailles had been unjust to Germany. In particular some of its provisions were intolerable violations of national sovereignty (a basic concept of modern political life), e.g. the demilitarisation of the Rhineland. By removing such limitations of national sovereignty, Hitler was removing reasonable causes of German discontent, and so making Europe a safer place and war less likely.

7. There was a lack of unity among the other powers, e.g. French distrust of the British following the Anglo-German naval agreement, which effectively broke up the Stresa Front.

8. Fear of Communism, and therefore of the USSR, led to the belief that a strong Germany under an anti-Communist Hitler was desirable, since it would form a strong buffer against the spread of communism from the east. e.g. This probably led to failure to cooperage with Stalin during the Munich Crisis.

9. Economic co-operation was much desired as being in the interests of all. This would not happen if hostile relations developed between the main trading nations.

10. Due to the Depression, western governments were under pressure to improve the standard of living of the people rather than rearm. As a consequence, they were not prepared for war and needed to rearm first.

11. In view of the unpopularity of war at this time it would have been electorally difficult for democratic leaders to act in an apparently reckless or aggressive way in standing up to the dictators if war might result.

Reasons Peculiar to Great Britain and France

1. There was a tendency to overestimate the effect of German rearmament, particularly the power of the *Luftwaffe*, during the key years 1933-37.

2. A European war would expose the Empires of both countries in the Far East to possible attack from a newly aggressive Japan. Neither Britain nor France could really afford to fight a war in both areas.

Reasons Peculiar to Britain

1. During the crucial years Chamberlain felt that he could trust Hitler.

2. The British did not feel confident in the ability of France to withstand another war, and were reluctant to give the French the impression that they would back them up, to prevent the French from taking precipitate action and involving them in an unnecessary war.

3. The British lacked confidence in US support in the event of a war. Chamberlain said that: "The Power that had the greatest strength was the United States of America, but he would be a rash man who based his calculations on hope from that quarter."

4. Paul Kennedy argues that appeasement had been a traditional policy of British governments since the 1860s, due to
   (a) the application of morality to foreign policy, leading to a preference to settling disputes by negotiation, and the disapproval of resort to force;
   (b) disruption of trade threatened Britain more than her protectionist* rivals;
   (c) Britain's overseas commitments were perceived as out of phase with its resources. Britain was overstretched;
   (d) The British electorate disliked wars, particularly expensive ones.

Thus peace was usually seen as in the national interest.

Reasons Peculiar to France

1. The social fabric of France was in a state of disintegration following the effects of the depression. This led to:
    (a) Political polarisation to the left (Communism) and the right (fascism);
    (b) Strikes and industrial unrest;
    (c) Weak and frequently changing governments;
    (d) reluctance to spend money on rearmament, resulting in unprepared military forces.
2. Due to her geographical position it could be expected that another war would be particularly costly for France in every way, as had the First World War.
3. The High Command overwhelmingly favoured a low-risk defensive strategy unsuitable for anything other than the defence of the homeland.
4. Following the betrayal of the Anglo-German Naval Agreement, the French did not trust the British to support any pre-emptive action they might take.

Reasons Peculiar to the USA

1. Traditional isolationism had reasserted itself as a reaction to American involvement in the First World War.
2. After the depression there was a perceived need for America to concentrate on rebuilding its economy.
3. The US army was small, e.g. smaller than the Czech army, due to traditional US beliefs that standing armies are agencies of royal oppression, and that the USA should be defended by an armed citizenry.
4. The USA was preoccupied with the business of intervening in Carribean, Central and South American states, and in the Western pacific, building up its hegemony over those regions. Europe could wait, its powers exhausting themselves in war in the meantime.

Historiography of the Causes of the Second World War

1. The conventional view is that the war was due entirely to Hitler's plans to dominate Europe and expand Germany, and his aggressive policies. Some, e.g. William Shirer (in *The Rise and Fall of the Third Reich*) suggested that Hitler had a detailed timetable for war.
2. In 1961 the British historian A. J. P. Taylor challenged this with a **"revisionist"*** view by suggesting that:
    (a) Hitler's "ideology" was nothing more than the sort of nationalist sentiments "which echo the conversation of any Austrian cafe or German beer-house";
    (b) that Hitler's ends and means resembled those of any "traditional German statesman";
    (c) that the war came about because Britain and France dithered between appeasement and resistance, leading Hitler to miscalculate and bring war about by accident in September 1939.
    Taylor's thesis makes Hitler's responsibility for the war an error of judgement rather than a wilful crime.
3. Fischer's theses on the causes of World War I are important in assessing Taylor's view, for, if Germany at that earlier time was bent on European and world hegemony, then a case could be made for a continuity in German foreign policy from at least the 1890s to 1945. Supporters of this approach compare Hitler's use of foreign policy to crush domestic dissent with similar

practices by the Kaiser and Bismarck.

But others object that there could be no continuity between the traditional imperialism of the Kaiser's *Reich* and the fanatical racism of the Nazi *Reich*. Hitler was not trying to preserve traditional elites but to destroy them.

4. Alan Bullock proposed a synthesis of the conventional and revisionist views: Hitler had clear long-term aims, but was a flexible opportunist concerning how to achieve them.

5. Soviet writers attempted to draw a causal chain between the development of capitalism and Fascism.

6. T. W. Mason exposed a German economic crisis in 1937. The recovery of the economy in the mid 1930s, together with rearmament, had created an increased demand for the import of fuel, food and raw materials. Germany did not have the exports or foreign exchange to pay for them. (This problem was mentioned at the **Hossbach Meeting**). Conquest of new territories enabled the Germans to:

    (a) seize new resources;

    (b) utilize foreign labour;

    (c) compel countries to trade at a favourable rate of exchange against the mark.

This suggests that the timing of the Second World War was partly a function of economic pressures. However, Hitler regarded himself as the master of economic forces, not their servant.

7. E. M. Robertson considers that **revenge** played a large role, making Hitler's actions sometimes difficult to explain rationally.

8. In the 1970s and 1980s:

    (a) Conscious of US over-extension in the world American historians came to appreciate the plight of Britain in the 1930s.

    (b) The publication of British and French documents of the 1930s enabled historians to understand the reasons for appeasement better.

Glossary

ad hoc: **especially** set up or chosen for a particular purpose at a particular time under particular circumstances

Anschluss: the union of Germany and Austria

appeasement: offering conciliation in the face of aggression

fait accompli: a situation already brought about

hindsight: the fallacy of seeking to understand and explain the motives of politicians in the light of events which happened subsequently, of which they were not aware at the time that they made their decisions

Lebensraum: living space

memorandum: a note of a meeting kept for the record within an organization, and therefore not for public knowledge

revisionist: a radically fresh view of a historical problem which had hitherto had a generally accepted explanation

Bibliography

Adamthwaite, A. P., *The Making of the Second World War*, Allen & Unwin (London, 1977)

Baumant, M., *The Origins of the Second World War,* Yale University Press (New Haven, 1978)

Bell, Philip, Hitler's War? The Origins of the Second World War, in Themes in Modern European History, ed. Paul Hayes, Routledge (London & New York, 1992)

Bloncourt, P., *The Embattled Peace 1919-1939*, Faber (London, 1968)

Bullock, Alan, "Hitler and the Origins of the Second Wold War," in *The Origins of the Second World War,* Esmonde M. Robertson (ed.), Macmillan Student Editions, Macmillan (London, 1971)

Carr, W., Arms, *Autarky and Aggression*, Arnold (London, 1972)

Gehl, J., *Austria, Germany and the Anschluss, new ed.,* Greenwood (Westport Conn., 1970)

Henig, R., *The Origins of the Second World War*, Methuen, (London, 1985)

Kennedy, Paul, *Strategy and Diplomacy 1870-1945*, Fontana (London, 1984)

Marks, S., *The Illusion of Peace, 1918-1933*, Macmillan (London, 1977)

Overy, Richard, *The Origins of the Second World War,* Seminar Studies in History, Longman (London & New York,)

Robbins, K., *Munich, 1938*, Cassell (London, 1968)

Stone, R., *The Drift to War*, Heinemann (London, 1975)

Taylor, A. J. P., *The Origins of the Second World War*, Penguin (London, 1964)

The Origins of the Second World War, ed. Esmonde M. Robertson, Macmillan Student Editions, Macmillan (London, 1971)

The Origins of the Second World War Reconsidered: The A. J. P. Taylor Debate After Twenty-Five Years, ed. G. Martel, (London, 1986)

Thorne, C., *The Approach to War 1938-1939*, Macmillan (London, 1967)

Wolfson, R., *From Peace to War: European Relations 1919-39*, Arnold (London, 1985)

Adolf Hitler

The Course of the Second World War

"Our strength consists in our speed and in our brutality. Genghis Khan led millions of women and children to slaughter — with premeditation and a happy heart. History sees in him solely the founder of a state. It's a matter of indifference to me what a weak western European civilization will say about me.

"I have issued the command — and I'll have anybody who utters but one word of criticism executed by a firing squad - that our war aim does not consist in reaching certain lines, but in the physical destruction of the enemy. Accordingly, I have placed my death-head formations in readiness - for the present only in the East - with orders to them to send to death mercilessly and without compassion, men, women, and children of Polish derivation and language. Only thus shall we gain the living space which we need. Who, after all, speaks today of the annihilation of the Armenians?" (Adolf Hitler)

"Once the Russian war had not been decided within three months, as Hitler had expected, Germany was lost, since was neither equipped for nor could sustain a long war." (Eric Hobsbawm)

The War in Europe

The Invasion of Poland

1. The Germany Army invaded Poland from East Prussia in the north, Pomerania and Silesia in the west and Slovakia in the south. Preceded by aerial bombardment tank units followed by mechanised infantry thrust deep into Polish territory using the tactics which became known as *Blitzkrieg.**

2. The large Polish Army was badly equipped, particularly lacking in aircraft and heavy artillery.

3. On 10th September a general retreat by the Poles began, in order to take up defensive positions.

4. On 17th September, the Red Army invaded from the east.

5. The last resistance was extinguished on 6th October.

6. The invaders had divided Poland among themselves. Border adjustments to conform to the secret treaty were made between the German and Soviet armies on a friendly basis.

7. The Poles had received no assistance from their "Allies", not even a diversionary attack upon Germany from France.

Timetable of the Second World War

1939

Sept 1	German Army invades Poland
Sept 3	Britain and France declare war on Germany
Sept 17	Red Army invades Poland.
Sept 27	Polish Army surrenders
Nov 30	Red Army invades Finland

1940

Mar 12	Finland signs a peace treaty with USSR
Apr 8	British Army lands in Norway
Apr 9	German Army invades Denmark and Norway
May 10	Germany invades the Low Countries and France
May 14	Netherlands surrenders to Germany
May 27	Evacuation of Dunkirk begins
May 28	Belgium surrenders to Germany
Jun 10	Italy declares war on the Allies
Jun 14	German Army enters Paris
Jun 22	France signs armistice with Germany, Vichy regime created
Jul 1940	Battle of Britain begins
Aug 23	Blitz begins
Sept 13	Italian Army invades Egypt
Sept 27	Tripartite Pact signed by Germany, Italy and Japan
Oct 28	Italian Army invades Greece

1941

Mar 1	Bulgaria joins Axis
Mar 11	Lend-Lease Act signed
Apr 10	Axis invade Yugoslavia
Apr 17	Yugoslavia surrenders to Germany
Apr 21	Greece surrenders to Germany
Apr 25	General Rommel invades Egypt
Jun 8	Syria invaded by British Army and Free French forces
Jun 22	Germany invades USSR
Oct 6	German Army approaches Moscow
Dec 7	Japanese attack the US Fleet at Pearl Harbor; US declares war
Dec 8	Japanese invade Malaya, Thailand and the Philippines
Dec 11	Japanese invade Burma

1942

Jan 20	Wannsee Conference
Feb 15	Singapore surrenders to Japanese
May 1	Japanese take Mandalay in Burma
May 6	Battle of the Coral Sea begins
Jun 3	Battle of Midway begins
Jun 21	Rommel captures Tobruk
Jul 7	Japanese land on Guadalcanal
Aug 7	US land on Guadalcanal
Aug 24	Battle of Stalingrad begins
Nov 4	German Army defeated at El Alamein

Nov 8	Allied invasion of Tunisia.
Nov 12	British recapture Tobruk

1943

Feb 25	Anglo-American aircraft begin round-the-clock bombing of Germany
Apr 13	Germany announces discovery of bodies of Polish officers at Katyn
Jul 10	Allies invade Sicily
Jul 25	Mussolini dismissed
Sept 3	Allies invade Italy
Sept 12	Mussolini rescued by Germans
Sept 15	Mussolini establishes a new fascist state at Salo on Lake Garda
Sept 23	Italy signs armistice with Allies
Oct 13	Italy declares war on Germany
Nov 6	Red Army recaptures Kiev
Nov 18	Intensive bombing of Berlin begins

1944

May 18	Allied troops take Monte Cassino
Jun 4	Rome falls to Allies
Jun 6	D-Day landings in Normandy
July 20	Failed plot against Adolf Hitler
Aug 1	Rising of Polish resistance in Warsaw
Aug 24	Liberation of Paris
Aug 25	Romania declares war on Germany
Sept 4	Liberation of Brussels
Oct 2	Warsaw Uprising crushed
Oct 4	British Army land in Greece
Oct 6	Red Army enters Czechoslovakia
Oct 20	US forces return to Philippines
Oct 28	Bulgaria signs armistice with the Allies

1945

Jan 17	Red Army liberates Warsaw
Jan 18	Red Army captures Budapest
Feb 13	Anglo-American carpet bombing of Dresden
Feb 19	Battle of Iwo Jima begins
Feb 28	US Army linerates Manila
Mar 9	American carpet bombing of Tokyo
Mar 22	Western Allies cross the Rhine
Apr 1	Battle for Okinawa begins
April 6	700 plane kamikaze attack sinks or damages 13 US destroyers
Apr 28	Mussolini executed by Italian partisans
Apr 31	Hitler commits suicide
May 2	Commander of German troops in Berlin surrenders. 2nd May, 1945
May 3	Anglo-Indian troops liberate Ragoon
May 7	Germany surrenders
Jul 16	Atom bomb test at Alamogordo, New Mexico
Aug 6	US Air Force drops atom bomb on Hiroshima
Aug 8	Japanese ask Soviets to arrange truce; USSR declares war on Japan
Aug 9	US Air Force drops atom bomb on Nagasaki
Sept 2	Japan surrenders

The Winter War

1. Stalin ordered the Baltic States to invite in Soviet troops, which they did.
2. In December, when the Finns resisted demands for the cessation of significant amounts of territory to the USSR, Stalin declared war.
3. Finland appealed to the League of Nations, and the USSR was formally expelled.
4. Unexpectedly, the Red Army suffered initial defeats due to:
    (a) stiff Finnish resistance;
    (b) Soviet underestimation of the enemy;
    (c) the inexperience of Soviet officers, many of whom had recently replaced those killed or sent to the camps during the purges.
5. Only when reinforcements were sent in February, did they meet with success.
6. On 12th March the Finns concluded a peace agreement, ceding* the territory demanded.
7. The fall of Finland led to the downfall of Daladier in France.

The Battle of the Atlantic

1. In the West the first months of the war were known as the **Phoney War**. Preparations were made once again for the waging of total war, but nothing happened. Many children evacuated from London returned to their homes.
2. The only fighting was at sea, with the beginning of the battle of the Atlantic.
    (a) U-boats began unrestricted warfare against shipping.
    (b) In December the scuttling of the German pocket battleship *Admiral Graf von Spee* was forced in the River Plate, South America.
    (c) In February 1940 the British destroyer *Cossack* freed nearly three hundred British prisoners from the cruiser *Altmark* in a Norwegian fjord.*
3. In this struggle, control of Norway became important:
    (a) the fjords could be used as havens for submarines attacking shipping;
    (b) it had potential as a base for attacking both Germany and the UK;
    (c) Swedish iron ore had to be transported via the Norwegian port of Narvik for seven months each year because the Swedish ports were icebound.
4. On 9th April 1940 Germany invaded Denmark as a step to the occupation of Norway.
5. The invasion of Norway followed almost immediately. There was some resistance. A German cruisers was sunk, and another damaged.
6. Allied forces, sent to help captured Narvik in the north. When the Norwegian king refused to accept the puppet government of Vidkun Quisling imposed upon them by the Germans, and decided to continue fighting, Allied forces tried to take Trondheim, but failed. They were soon withdrawn.
7. On 10th May Neville Chamberlain resigned, and was replaced as prime minister by Winston Churchill.
8. Roosevelt was "sympathetic" to the British and French but he was restricted by:
    (a) extensive pro-German sympathies in the USA:
        (i) by people of Germanic descent;
        (ii) southern racists who were very sympathetic to Nazism.
    (b) an isolationist Congress;
    (c) the Neutrality Laws;
    (d) coming elections (late 1940).
    Great Britain and France were supplied with war materials on the "**cash and carry**" plan. They could buy goods in the US on condition that they

(i) paid in full in advance;

(ii) transported them across the Atlantic in their own ships at their own risk.

Britain was also supplied with fifty old First World War destroyers in return for bases on British islands in the West Indies.

The **Lease- Lend Act** passed in March 1941 to lend war supplies which would be returned at some future date if they still existed.

The Invasion of Western Europe

1. On the same day German troops invaded Holland, Belgium and Luxembourg. Rotterdam was systematically bombed. Holland surrendered on 14th May, and Belgium on 27th May.

2. German forces pressed into Belgium to encircle British and French armies, which fell back on Dunkirk. At the beginning of June, Allied forces were trapped at Dunkirk. Hermann Göring's *Luftwaffe* was allowed to destroy the trapped army, enabling much of it to escape by sea evacuation to Britain.

3. On 5th June, German forces moved south, crossed the Seine and threatened Paris. Mussolini declared war on France. The French government moved to Tours and then to Bordeaux.

4. On 16th June, Reynaud resigned and Marshall Pétain took over, opening cease-fire negotiations with Hitler.

5. Fighting ended on 24th June. The armistice was signed, at Hitler's insistence, in the same railway carriage, drawn up to the same place it had stood in November 1918, when the Germans had signed the armistice at the end of the First World War. By the terms of the armistice:

    (a) the northern and western parts of France were to be occupied by the Germans;

    (b) the south and east were to be under Pétain's government, based at Vichy;

    (c) French troops to be demobilised and the navy disarmed;

    (d) all German POWs were to be returned, while French POWs to remain under German control until a peace treaty had been concluded.

6. General Charles de Gaulle refused to surrender and headed Free French Forces in the UK.

7. On 3rd July, the British sank the French fleet at Oran, in Algeria, rather than see it fall into the hands of the Germans.

The Battle of Britain

1. In June an agreement was made between the USA and Britain whereby Britain would be supplied with arms, provided that:

    (a) the British paid for them in advance;

    (b) the British then took all the risks of transporting them across the Atlantic themselves.

    This was known as **cash and carry**.

2. A German invasion of Britain from the sea, *Operation Sea Lion*, was planned for the autumn. It is still not clear how serious this was, since Hitler was never very keen on war with Britain. It may have been a diversion, to lull Stalin into a false sense of security before attacking the USSR.

3. German command of the air was essential for an invasion. The **Battle of Britain** was a struggle for command of the airspace over the UK. It was almost lost, but then:

    (a) the British developed radar and the technically superior *Spitfire* fighter plane.

    (b) when the battle was almost lost, Churchill ordered the bombing of Berlin by the RAF. The *Luftwaffe* was diverted by Hitler to bomb British cities in retribution.

4. The *Luftwaffe* then concentrated upon trying to undermine civilian morale by bombing cities such as Coventry, Bristol, Southampton and Birmingham in the ***Blitz***.

5. This allowed the RAF to rebuild their resources, and inflict heavy losses on the attackers.

Blitzkrieg

1. After 1918 military strategists devised new tactics for tank warfare:
    (a) J. F. C. Fuller in "Plan 1919" argued for a mass tank attack with air support on a narrow front. The tank units would race to the rear of the enemy lines to overcome their command centres.
    (b) B. Liddel Hart argued that it would be necessary for infantry to accompany the armoured forces.
    (c) In France, De Gaulle argued for a strategy of attack using totally mechanised forces, but the General Staff was in favour of a primarily defensive strategy.
2. The German plans for mechanised attack were developed by General Heinz Guderian, Chief of Mobile Forces, who was heavily influenced by:
    (a) Fuller and Liddel Hart.
    (b) The tradition of *Kesselschlacht*, the infiltration tactics of the German Army during 1918. Armoured forces would assault on a narrow front in overwhelming numbers in order to ensure penetration. Aircraft would be used in support as flying artillery. Mechanised infantry would accompany the tanks and infantry divisions would follow through the gap in order to mop up opposition. It depended upon bluff and surprise, attacking weak points in the enemy defences and causing such disruption and paralysis to the enemy that it was incapable of adequate response.
    (c) Observation of the effect of bombing of cities in panicking the populations and bringing them out onto the roads as refugees, e.g. at Guernica during the Spanish Civil War.
    Guderian's *Achtung! Panzer!* (1937) incorporated many of the theories of the British General J.F.C. Fuller and General Charles de Gaulle.
3. It consisted of:
    (a) surprise attack;
    (b) spearheaded by the Panzer Divisions of tanks, accompanied by motorised infantry brigades, attacking at several points in depth;
    (c) accompanied by bombing of cities to panic civilians into clogging the roads as refugees and hindering the movement of reinforcements to the front, and the use of fighter planes, *Stukas*, as flying artillery;
    (d) followed up by mechanized infantry brigades.
4. Omer Bartov points out that the swiftness and decisiveness of the *Blitzkrieg* campaigns created an impression of invincibility which had the effect of:
    (a) overawing the enemy, an effect which increased with each success;
    (b) fatally convincing the Germans themselves of their invincibility;
    (c) providing the defeated with an excuse for their swift collapse.
5. Unlike most of his reform-minded contemporaries in other armies, Guderian found a sympathetic supporter in his commander in chief, Hitler. He had been designated chief of Germany's mobile troops in November 1938.
6. The central problem posed for all defence establishments was how to respond to the lessons of the stalemate of the First World War. *Blitzkrieg* ("lightning war") was especially attractive to Germany because:
    (a) It was suited to a country liable to have to face a war on two fronts, since it offered speedy victories.
    (b) It would allow Hitler to maintain a "guns and butter" economy, since each new conquest would provide the resources for the next.
    (c) It would allow Hitler to successfully defy other Great Powers whose combined resources

dwarfed those of Germany, since he could deal with them one at a time.

7. Thus *Blitzkrieg* was used effectively in the attacks upon Poland (one month), Denmark (one day), Norway, Belgium (three weeks), Holland (four days), France (six weeks), Yugoslavia and Greece.

8. It is not clear whether *Blitzkrieg* was the result of long term planning, or whether it was all that Germany could manage at the time. The key to understanding this is the German economy.

     (a) The traditional view is that Hitler deliberately organised his economy and army for fighting war in short, sharp bursts. Hitler would have wished to avoid the " repetition of a war of attrition" like WWI. Therefore victory had to be achieved swiftly.

     (b) R. J. Overy has argued that Hitler's planning was geared for long-term war to begin during the mid-1940s. He was caught unprepared for the outbreak of war with Britain and France. Caught at a half-way stage of preparedness the German economy was capable of supporting only short, limited wars. There was no deliberately planned *Blitzkrieg* economy; it was a result of poor planning and the limitations of the economy.

     (c) Omer Bartov argues that there is no evidence that the Nazi leadership were aware of any economic crisis. *Blitzkrieg* was simply an opportunistic military tactic when total mobilization was not considered necessary. It was not adopted as an alternative to total war, but was an adaptation of it to current conditions.

9. Thus according to Alan Bond, it was due to the need to compromise between:

     (i) Hitler's demands, and

     (ii) the ability of the domestic armaments economy to produce war materials.

10. Germany's success in *Blitzkrieg* was due to:

     (a) good leadership;

     (b) good tactical skills;

     (c) the disorganisation of the enemy;

     (d) its psychological effect on the enemy

11. Michael Howard points out that they need not have worked as well as they did. Only Hitler's authority ensured that the High Command accepted these tactics.

     (a) If tanks can attack, tanks could have counter-attacked.

     (b) Tank traps and mines might have created conditions in which tanks could not have operated.

     (c) Air support was necessary and could have been attacked.

     (d) Swift deep penetration leaves the supply lines vulnerable to attack and to cutting.

The North Africa Campaign
The Reasons for the North African Campaign

1. Mussolini wished to create a North African Empire.

2. Hitler wished to:

     (a) Gain control of Egypt and the Middle East, with its oil;

     (b) Cut British access to India and the Far East through the Suez Canal.

The Course of the North Africa Campaign

1. In September 1940 Mussolini ordered the invasion of Egypt from the Italian colony of Libya. The Italians drove some 60 miles into Egypt before being halted.

2. They were then driven out, and the British, in their turn, invaded Libya. At Bedafomm they captured 130,000 prisoners and 400 tanks.

3. In February 1941 Hitler sent Erwin Rommel and the Afrika Korps to strengthen the Italians in

Libya. They drove the British back to Tobruck, taking 2,000 prisoners, and on to Bardia, driving them out of Libya.

4. The Allied forces dug in at El Alamein, 70 miles west of Alexandria. Bounded on the north by the sea and on the south by a salt-pan, the Quattara depression, through which tanks could not pass, it was an excellent defensive position.
5. During summer 1942, two attempts to break through by Rommel failed.
6. On 23rd October, the British successfully counter-attacked through German minefields, driving the Germans back across Libya.
7. In November an Anglo-American force landed in Morocco and Algiers to the west of the German forces (*Operation Torch*). The Germans then found themselves attacked from both sides.
8. In May 1943, Axis forces in North Africa surrendered.

The Consequences of the North African Campaign

1. The campaign was a drain on Axis resources, which could have been employed in the USSR.
2. The ambitions of Hitler and Mussolini for the region were destroyed.
3. The Southern Mediterranean could be used by British shipping;
4. Southern Europe was rendered vulnerable to Allied attack.

The Balkans Campaign

1. Hungary was sympathetic to the Axis Powers. Rumania and Bulgaria soon made their peace with Hitler.
2. On October 28th 1940, Mussolini invaded Greece from Albania.
3. The Greeks repelled the invaders, and themselves pushed into Albania.
4. 60,000 British, Australian and New Zealand troops landed in Greece.
5. One day later, the Germans invaded Greece.
6. The intervention of the British Imperial forces may have been counterproductive:
    (a) It gave Hitler a pretext to invade Greece;
    (b) and disorganised Greek strategy;
    (c) while not being strong enough to protect Greece from the Germans.
7. The Allied soldiers immediately retreated to Crete. Mainland Greece was soon occupied.
8. No plans were made to defend Crete, which was taken by the world's first airborne invasion. The Allied soldiers were evacuated to Egypt.

Consequences of the Balkan Campaign

1. The Balkan Campaign necessitated that Hitler delay the invasion of the USSR, planned for 15th May, for five crucial weeks, in order to avoid leaving his southern flank exposed to Allied forces. This delay ensured that the German invasion would get bogged down in the autumn rains, and then caught in the harsh winter before victory had been achieved. In doing so, it may have ensured the defeat of Hitler in the East, and hence in the War.
    Hitler's Chief of Staff, Field Marshall Wilhelm Keitel, stated during the Nuremberg War Trial: "The unbelievable strong resistance of the Greeks delayed by two or more vital months the German attack against Russia; if we did not have this long delay, the outcome of the war would have been different in the eastern front and in the war in general, and others would have been accused and would be occupying this seat as defendants today".
2. Although the airborne invasion of Crete was successful in that Crete was occupied, it was so costly to the Germans that an airborne invasion was never repeated.

The Great Patriotic War

Background

1. Hitler had always intended to attack the USSR:

    (a) to destroy a rival to German power;

    (b) to destroy Bolshevism, which he considered a Jewish phenomenon;

    (c) to expand Germany's *Lebensraum** and create a slave state to serve Germany's interests;

    (d) to acquire its productive arable land for *Lebensraum*, and its other natural resources.

2. Because he also planned to take revenge on France for the defeat of 1918, he needed some way of avoiding having to fight a war on two fronts - a substitute for the Schlieffen Plan.* By June 1939 he was negotiating with the Nazis. On 23rd Aug. 1939 **the Molotov-Ribbentrop Pact** was signed. Openly, this was a ten-year non-aggression pact, but a secret protocol was appended. It said that if eastern European frontiers were to be "disturbed," the USSR would take Eastern Poland, the Baltic states and Moldova. This was a tremendous achievement for Stalin:

    (a) It secured the recovery of most of the land lost to Russia by the Treaty of Brest-Litovsk without a blow.

    (b) It gave the USSR temporary security in Europe in case of a Soviet-Japanese war.

    (c) It gave the USSR time to prepare for a war with Germany.

    (d) It left Stalin free to prepare to launch a surprise attack on Germany when he was ready.

3. Stalin intended to double-cross Hitler, but thought that he would be given adequate time to prepare for war because it would take Hitler several years to defeat France and Britain. He had prepared an offensive strategy, and had constructed no defences. He was taken by surprise when France fell in a few weeks, but thought that the invasion of England would occupy Hitler during 1941 at least. When signs of an impending invasion were reported to him, he disbelieved them, thinking that:

    (a) The British were trying to deceive him;

    (b) Hitler was not stupid enough to invade without:

    (i) adequate preparation for a major war of attrition;

    (ii) without having defeated the British, so avoiding having to fight a war on two fronts.

    When informants finally gave him the date of the invasion, he considered it too late in the year to be successful, and so not likely to be true.

4. Hitler intended to double-cross Stalin, and by the winter 1940 he had determined to invade the USSR during the following year on 15th May.

5. A complication arose in that Mussolini had invaded Greece from Albania at the end of October 1940, and had been ignominiously ejected. Allied troops had landed in Greece. Therefore, in order to avoid exposing his southern flank, he delayed the invasion for five weeks in order to secure the Balkans.

The *Blitzkriegs*

1. On the 22nd June, the day when Napoleon had invaded Russia in 1812 was chosen for the delayed invasion. That had been too late in the year, and Napoleon's troops had been defeated by the Russian winter, but Hitler thought that it would only take eight weeks for the German Army to reach Moscow because:

    (a) Stalin had executed or imprisoned much of his officer corps, including the most experienced men.

    (b) The Red Army had performed poorly in Finland.

(c) The Soviets would be unprepared, thinking it too late to launch an attack for that year.

(d) His own indomitable will would carry the day.

2. A three-pronged assault was launched:

    (a) in the north through the Baltic States to take Leningrad;

    (b) in the centre to Minsk, Smolensk and Moscow;

    (c) in the south from Rumania through Southern Poland to Kiev, and then south to the Don Region and the Caucasian Oilfields.

3. Since Stalin had forbidden anything which might provoke the Germans, including e.g. the laying of mines along the border or shooting at overflying aircraft, the Germans met no initial resistance. They destroyed aircraft on the ground and took thousands of prisoners, who simply surrendered.

6. The German advance seemed unstoppable:

    (a) By September German forces had besieged Leningrad.

    (b) In the south, most of the Ukraine and Crimea were taken.

    (c) In October a push to Moscow reached the suburbs of the city.

7. The Autumn rains slowed the advance, and the winter cold stopped it, together with stubborn resistance at Leningrad and Moscow. The *blitzkrieg* had run out of steam.

The War of Attrition

1. The war was to be one of attrition, and the Soviet economy was placed on a more efficient war footing than that of Germany. Russian enterprises were moved east out of the path of the advancing Germans into the Urals region.

2. Although initially welcomed by non-Russian Slav populations, the Germans treated the Slavs so badly that they turned most of them into enemies.

3. During the winter of 1941-2 the German Army dug in, and in May 1942 resumed the attack in the south to threaten the Caucusus oilfields.

4. In September the Germans reached Stalingrad. There the Soviets fought valiantly to save the city. As the Germans fought their way in, their armies were surrounded by three armies under Marshall Zhukov, and the besiegers became the besieged. On 31st January 1943, Field Marshall von Paulus and his surviving men surrendered.

5. In the north, the siege of Leningrad was lifted, and in the south the Germans were driven back on a wide front. The tide of war had turned.

6. In early July 1943 the Germans tried to attack at Kursk, but in the largest tank battle in history they were held. That was the last major German offensive. The Russian offensive began later in the month.

7. In a series of offensives, the Red Army drove the Germans out of Soviet territory.

8. In summer 1944:

    (a) The Red Army approached Warsaw. There they stopped to allow the Germans to suppress a rising of the Polish resistance;

    (b) Soviet troops reached East Prussia;

    (c) Rumania surrendered.

9. In autumn:

    (a) Bulgaria surrendered;

    (b) Belgrade was liberated.

10. During the winter of 1944-45:

    (a) Hungary was invaded;

    (b) The advance resumed in Western Poland.

(c) Soviet forces entered Germany.
11. Berlin was occupied, after fierce fighting during April 1945.
12. This was the main theatre of war. Hitler was defeated precisely when the Red Army reached the heart of Berlin.

Reasons for German Failure and Soviet Success

1. The invasion of the Soviet Union only had initial success because:
    (a) Stalin refused to believe the attack was coming;
    (b) He had denuded his army of experienced officers in the purges of the late 1930s.
   When winter fell in 1941, the war in the USSR had not been won.
2. Hitler had been deluded by his successes into thinking that he could deal with the USSR in the same way as the other countries he had invaded, and before his economic base was ready to support a major war. The same method of fighting the war which had been used in Western Europe, *Blitzkrieg,* was totally unsuited to such a country. The area to be crossed before the command centres could be overrun was so vast that:
    (a) the element of surprise, confusion and paralysis was lost. The Soviets had time to recover their morale, to regroup and counter-attack, and to move vulnerable economic targets and command centres when necessary.
    (b) the German supply lines became stretched and vulnerable to attack.
3. Unlike the Germans, the Soviet soldiers were able to function during the harsh Russian winter.
4. The USSR was able to field a mass army better equipped than the Germans because:
    (a) their resources were greater;
    (b) their economy, unlike that of the Germans, was efficiently geared to total war.
5. Soviet artillery was more effective than that of the Germans.
6. The USSR received supplies from the USA and Britain.
7. Stalin learned, after some false steps early in the war, to leave military planning to his generals. Hitler never learned this, and his orders increasingly lost touch with reality.

Occupied Europe

1. The map of Europe was redrawn:
    (a) Neutral states like Spain, Vichy France, Switzerland and Sweden were either sympathetic to the Nazis or had to be accommodating to them.
    (b) Hungary, Rumania and Bulgaria were allies of the Nazis. They retained their rulers, but were dominated by fascist parties. In reality they were client states of Germany.
    (c) In areas under German occupation, such as Norway, Holland, Belgium and Denmark, the Germans used puppet governments.
    (d) Other countries were broken up, e.g.:
       (i) Poland was partly assimilated into the Reich and partly governed as an occupied territory;
       (ii) In Yugoslavia, Croatia was governed by an Italian fascist prince, while the rest of the country was occupied by the Germans.
       (iii) Greece was partly occupied by the Germans, partly by the Italians and partly by the Bulgarians.
2. Economic exploitation of the occupied territories was ruthless:
    (a) Resources were commandeered by the Germans for use in Germany;
    (b) Lower food rations were enjoyed in the occupied lands;
    (c) They were exploited for slave labour for factories in Germany.

3. In the West, local fascist parties were encouraged, and volunteer military units raised "to fight Bolshevism."
4. The local populations were ruthlessly repressed in the East.
    (a) *SS Einsatzgruppen** moved into Poland and the USSR attempting to eliminate the entire Polish intelligentsia, Soviet Communist Party officials and Jews of military age.
    (b) Brutal reprisals were taken against resistance, including the killing of every adult male in a village or town, e.g. Kalavryta, in Greece; Lidice, in Czechoslovakia; Oradour-sur-Glane, in France.
5. Certain groups were targeted by the Nazis for elimination throughout Europe, especially Jews, Roma* and homosexuals. At first they were killed by shooting, but this proved inefficient. They were later rounded up and sent to death camps in Poland, where they would be worked to death or gassed. Six million people were probably killed in these camps, four million being Jews.
6. Resistance movements were founded in many occupied countries. They:
    (a) undertook acts of sabotage;
    (b) informed the Allies of Axis activities;
    (c) in some countries, e.g. USSR, Yugoslavia and Greece, guerilla units fought the invaders.
Almost everywhere, the core of these movements were formed of Communists.

The Italian Campaign
The Reasons for the Italian Campaign
Stalin had been asking for the Western Allies to open a second Front in Europe to take pressure off the Eastern Front. Churchill opted for the invasion of Italy because:
    (a) He claimed that a failed attempted invasion of France would be very costly in lives, and would prevent the liberation of Europe for a generation, because public opinion in America and Britain would not support another attempt for a long time. An invasion of Italy would be less risky.
    (b) It would also be less helpful to Stalin, and Churchill wanted Germany and the USSR to destroy each other before the Anglo-Saxons stepped in to pick up the pieces.

The Invasion of Sicily
1. On 10th July 1943, British and American forces landed in Sicily.
2. In order to pacify the island, the Americans brought with them leaders of the Italian Mafia in the US, reinstalling organised crime in Sicily, where it had been eradicated by Mussolini.
3. On 24th July, Mussolini was summoned to appear before the Fascist Grand Council and criticised. Immediately afterwards, he was dismissed by the King and then arrested.
4. Marshal Badoglio became Prime Minister.

The Invasion of Italy
1. Anglo-American forces crossed into Italy at Reggio on September 3rd.
2. Secret negotiations for the surrender of Italy to the Allies were held in Algiers, and on September 8th the Italian surrender was made public.
3. German forces occupied Italy.
4. Mussolini was rescued from captivity and installed as head of the "**Fascist Republic of Salo**" in the north. He was virtually a prisoner of the Germans.
5. Throughout winter 1943-4 the Allies were held up south of Rome at Monte Cassino. Polish and French forces broke through in May.
6. Rome was liberated in June.

7. Only in April 1945 did the Allies drive north across the River Po.
8. Mussolini sought escape to Switzerland, but was captured by partisans and shot. His body was taken to Milan and hung from a street lamp.

The Consequences of the Italian Campaign
1. It eliminated Italian forces from all theatres of war.
2. It provided the Allies with bases from which to bomb Southern Europe.
3. It tied down German troops which might have been used elsewhere.

The Western European Campaign
1. Preparations for *Operation Overlord*, the invasion of France, were made during 1943-4.
    (a) Men and supplies for the largest seaborne invasion in history were amassed (Americans, British, Canadians and Free French forces);
    (b) Artificial harbours, known as Mulberry Harbours were prefabricated, to be transported across the sea and assembled off the coast of France;
    (c) Pipelines under the Channel (PLUTO) were laid to supply fuel on the French coast.
2. D-Day was 6th June, 1944. The landing on the coast of Normandy met with varied response in different parts of the beach, but was ultimately successful.
3. Several weeks were spent establishing a beachhead, before Allied forces broke out towards the River Seine.
4. On 26th August, Paris was liberated by Free French Forces under General de Gaulle, and Brussels on 2nd September.
5. Later that month, Allied paratroops landed at Arnhem to capture bridgeheads across the Rhine were annihilated. The Rhine was reached in early December.
6. despite initial successes, a German counter-attack, the **Battle of the Bulge**, failed during the winter, with the loss of 250,000 men and 600 tanks.
7. By March 1945, German territory was being invaded from west and east.

The End of the War in Europe
1. By mid-April, with Berlin surrounded by the Red Army, Soviet and American troops met at Torgau.
2. On 31st April, Hitler committed suicide.
3. Admiral Dönitz took over as head of the Third Reich, and formally surrendered on May 7th.

The Reasons for the Allied Victory in Europe
1. The Soviet victory was due to:
    (a) Hitler's many errors:
        (i) in not foreseeing that the war would go on into winter 1941;
        (ii) He refused to mobilize the population against Stalin's regime.
    (b) Stalin's leadership of the USSR:
        (i) His appeal to national patriotism;
        (ii) His retirement from dictating military policy, following initial blunders;
    (c) the movement of the industrial base out of the path of war;
    (iv) the productive capacity of the USSR exceeded that of Germany.
2. Because of the size of the US economy, Churchill stated in his memoirs that once the USA had entered the war, everything that followed was "merely the application of overwhelming force."

The outcome of a war of attrition was inevitable. By the end of 1942 US production had been added to that of the UK and USSR.

Relationships between the Allies

The US took systematic advantage of their uniquely fortunate position as against the Bitish and French:

(a) They used lend lease to obtain British islands as bases in the Caribbean;

(b) Took over civil airline routes from the British;

(c) US oil companies pushed into the Middle East.

The War in the Far East

The Greater East Asia Co-Prosperity Sphere

1. New sources of supplies were required by Japan to continue the war against China. Due to the war in Europe, the European powers were in no condition to defend their Far Eastern imperial possessions:

    (a) Britain's in Malaya and Burma, which had rubber and tin;

    (b) France's in Indo-China;

    (c) Holland's in the Dutch East Indies (now Indonesia) which had oil.

2. The Nazi-Soviet Pact of August 1939 was experienced as a slap in the face by the Japanese. At this time Japanese forces were badly beaten in a clash with Soviet forces under General Zhukov at Nomonhan, on the borders of Manchukuo and Outer Mongolia.

3. In May 1940, following the fall of France, the US fleet was moved to Pearl Harbour to intimidate the Japanese.

4. In July the US imposed a partial trade embargo on Japan, banning the sale of scrap iron, steel and aviation fuel.

5. Vichy France allowed the Japanese to occupy Indo-China, supposedly in order to close the access routes to Chungking. The Japanese set up military bases in September 1940.

6. As a result of Hitler's conquests in Europe, which made it seem overwhelmingly likely that Germany would win the war, Japan concluded the Tripartite Axis pact with Germany and Italy.

7. In September 1940 Britain agreed to close the Burma Road for six months, due to Japanese pressure.

8. In October 1940 Roosevelt agreed to Anglo-American joint staff talks.

9. In April 1941 the Japanese signed a neutrality treaty with the USSR, in order to remove the possibility of a war on two fronts.

10. On July 2nd 1941, the Japanese Imperial Council accepted a grand plan to remove western influence out of the Far East and to replace it with Japanese hegemony an a "Greater East Asia Co-Prosperity Sphere."

11. In July 1941 the Japanese occupied southern Indo-China. This was a threat to the security of Malaya and Indonesia.

12. In response, the USA, Britain and Holland imposed a more severe economic embargo on Japan. The US:

    (a) froze Japanese assets in the US;

    (b) imposed an embargo on oil supplies;

    (c) allowed US mercenaries to assist the Chinese.

13. Inconclusive talks were held between the Americans and Japanese in Washington to solve

the *impasse*.* The US demanded Japanese withdrawal from Indo-China and China, including Manchuria. This was unacceptable to the Japanese Government since:

(a) It would have meant great loss of face, (very important to the Japanese);

(b) It would have reduced the power and prestige of the army within Japan;

(c) It would have been incredibly unpopular with the Japanese people.

14. In Oct. 1941 Prince Konoye resigned as Prime Minister and was succeeded by Admiral Tojo. He saw that:

(a) the need for oil would require either that the Japanese withdraw from China or take the Dutch East Indies with its oil.

This would mean war with the US, but by this time Japan had parity with the combined fleets of the USA and GB in the North Pacific. At the same time, the USA had just embarked on a massive naval construction programme which would overtake Japan's in the future. Short-term advantage and long-term disadvantage dictated war sooner rather than later.

15. Tojo decided that it would be better to launch a pre-emptive war. He gave the US an ultimatum to withdraw its trade embargo, and when that was not lifted on Dec. 7th 1941, the US Pacific fleet in Pearl Harbour was attacked and destroyed. Eight battleships were put out of action. Attacks were also launched upon Hong Kong, Malaya, Singapore and the Philippines.

16. Hitler almost immediately followed this up with his own declaration of war on the USA.

The Causes of the Japanese-American War

1. There was a reaction against western values and a resurgence of traditional Japanese values following the depression.

2. The Japanese required their own sphere of influence in the Western pacific:

(a) Japan had a high population on land, much of which is unfit for agriculture, and poorly provided with natural resources. It needed:

(i) food and raw materials for industry;

(ii) markets for manufactured goods.

(b) Resentment of Europeans' assumption of racial superiority, led to the desire to achieve equality with the Great Powers by winning an empire.

(c) The Japanese desire for territory was fed by the desire to achieve autarchy* to escape the effects of the depression and future trade fluctuations.

3. The Americans were not prepared to concede such a sphere of influence to the Japanese, since it would deny them:

(a) untrammelled American dominance of the entire Pacific;

(b) the free access to China they had demanded in the so-called "open-door" policy.

4. The US oil embargo, an attempt to reduce Japanese activity in the region, had presented them with a choice between retreat from China, which was unacceptable, or war. Thus it had impelled the Japanese into war.

5. The vulnerability of the European colonies during the war presented the Japanese with another attractive "soft area" in Southeast Asia.

The Pacific War

1. In the first few days the Japanese eliminated:

(a) the US Air Force in the Philippines;

(b) *HMS Prince of Wales* and *Repulse* off Malaya.

2. 120,000 US citizens of Japanese origin in California, Oregon and Washington State were

rounded up and interned in concentration camps.

3. By May 1942 Japan had overrun Malaya, Singapore, Hong Kong, the Dutch East Indies, Guam and Wake Island. These provided supplies of oil, rubber, and other important raw materials.

4. Aircraft carrier attacks were launched against Ceylon (now Sri Lanka) and South India.

5. From this position the Japanese threatened:

    (a) Burma and India;

    (b) New Guinea and the northern coast of Australia.

    (c) They had also isolated China.

6. The reasons for these successes were:

    (a) The Americans and British had grossly underestimated them due mainly to their racist beliefs;

    (b) The Japanese quickly established air and sea superiority;

    (c) The Japanese troops were highly-motivated and well-trained.

7. The Japanese were initially welcomed in the newly-acquired territories as liberators from European domination. Local populations of Westerners were interned in POW camps. The Geneva Conventions were not applied, and the Japanese regarded their prisoners as unworthy of consideration simply because they had surrendered. Cruelty was common. In time, their disdain for the local people generated enmity towards them, and led to the rise of resistance movements. A similar cruelty was displayed towards POWs.*

8. In summer 1942 three attacks led to battles in which the Japanese were defeated, and lost the initiative:

    (a) An advance to the Solomons and Port Moresby in Papua New Guinea led to the Battle of the Coral Sea, in which both sides suffered heavy losses and the Japanese withdrew;

    (b) In June 1942, the USA repelled a Japanese attack at Midway Island, sinking two aircraft carriers. This was the turning point in the Pacific War;

    (c) An attack on New Hebrides and Samoa led to the Battle of Guadalcanal.

The main reason for these Japanese defeats was that due to overconfidence, the Japanese committed too few forces to the campaigns. Instead, they were stationed on the Asian mainland.

9. From August 1942, by **island hopping** the Americans and Australians under General MacArthur began to reconquer the Pacific Islands, beginning with the Solomon Islands and going on to the Marianas and then the Philippines.

10. With the American attack upon Iwo Jima, the Japanese began to rely upon suicide planes flown by *kamikazes*.*

11. Meanwhile:

    (a) The British had recovered Burma, and were preparing to recover Singapore.

    (b) The Australians had seized Borneo.

    (c) The Japanese army in China was in retreat.

12. The Japanese, dependant upon foreign supplies, neglected to organise the defence of merchant convoys, anti-submarine measures, etc., and so lost tremendous amounts of shipping.

13. Air defences had also been neglected, and US carpet bombing campaigns against Japanese cities became increasingly destructive. In March 1945 40% of more than sixty cities had been destroyed by incendiary bombs.

14. In April 1945 the USSR announced that it would not be renewing the Neutrality Pact of 1941. In May the Japanese offered Northern Manchuria, the Southern Sakhalin and the Northern Kuriles in return for a renewal. In return for cruisers and minerals, they asked for oil, which was now in short supply, but received no firm reply.

The Nuclear War

1. With Japan's forces in retreat, the economy in a desperate situation, and her cities under merciless attack, there was little option but to consider surrender. The Emperor, the Prime Minister, Admiral Suzuki, and the Foreign and Navy ministers favoured peace. The Army Minister and Chiefs of Staff were for holding out for terms:
   (a) preservation of the Emperor system;
   (b) preservation of the status of the military;
   (c) no army of occupation.
2. In July the Japanese approached the USSR asking if they would receive a delegation headed by Prince Konoye to negotiate peace terms. The Russians replied that a response would have to wait until after the Potsdam Conference. The US Government was aware of this, because they intercepted communications between Tokyo and Moscow.
3. Nevertheless, on 26th July Truman issued a demand that Japan surrender unconditionally or face" prompt and utter destruction."
4. On August 6th, the US dropped an atomic bomb on Hiroshima, killing 84,000 immediately.
5. On August 8th, when the Japanese ambassador finally got to see Molotov to discuss peace negotiations, the USSR declared war on Japan.
6. On August 9th, the US dropped another bomb on Nagasaki, killing another 40,000 instantly.
7. The Americans had demanded unconditional surrender, but the Japanese offered to surrender with the proviso that this did not include "any demand which prejudices the prerogatives of His Majesty as a sovereign ruler."
8. On 13th August, the Americans bombed Tokyo and the Soviet invasion continued.
9. On 15th August, the Emperor broadcast his decision to surrender on condition that the emperor system was maintained. This was accepted. In the decision to surrender, the Soviet declaration of war was as important as the dropping of the atomic bombs.
10. In accordance with Truman's desire to keep the other Allies out of Japan, and to treat it as an exclusively American territory, the formal surrender took place to General MacArthur on the *USS Missouri* on 2nd September.

The Reasons for the Dropping of the Atomic Bombs

1. The much-professed reason was to save American lives which would have been lost in the invasion of Japan. Churchill put the number at one million, even though the total numbers of the projected invasion force numbered much less than that.
2. Sometimes this is expanded to include Japanese lives, since many Japanese would have been killed in any invasion as well.
3. The same effect could have been achieved in open countryside, or at sea off Tokyo, but the US Strategic Bombing Survey said in its official report: "Hiroshima and Nagasaki were chosen as targets because of their concentration of activities and population." Several cities had been spared bombing raids so that the effect of the atomic bomb on cities could be accurately assessed. They were therefore, scientific experiments.
4. Liddel-Hart suggests that the real motive was to end the war as quickly as possible, so as to deny the Soviets any chance to fight, and subsequently to claim a share of Japanese territory as a reward. The Americans had determined not to share Japan with its Allies.
5. Most evidence from primary sources points to the bomb being used as a political tool to intimidate* the world, and especially Stalin and the USSR, with US power.
   [For a fuller treatment of this issue see the companion volume "The Cold War"]

Reasons for the failure of the Japanese

1. In a war of attrition, the Japanese economy could not possibly compete with the US economy.
2. The Japanese became over confident, and committed too few resources to the war at sea; preferring to focus upon the mainland of Asia.
3. The Japanese failed to realise that the aircraft carrier had rendered the battleship obsolete.
4. The Japanese forces, initially so successful, became overstretched.
5. The Japanese, dependant upon foreign supplies, neglected to organise the defence of merchant convoys, anti-submarine measures, etc., and so lost tremendous amounts of shipping.
6. Air defences had also been neglected, and US carpet bombing campaigns against Japanese cities became increasingly destructive.

The Second World War as Total War

Total War
The Concept of Total War

Arthur Marwick popularised this concept as that of a form of war which might be contrasted with the limited wars of the eighteenth century. *[See "Total War" in Chapter 3 "The First World War," above.]*

He used the concept of "total war" to refer to:

(i) Its all-encompassing character;

(ii) Its severity.

(iii) Total mobilization of the nations' resources for victory;

(iv) The undermining of existing social and political structures and institutions;

(v) colossal psychological trauma.

All-Encompassing Character

1. By early September 1941 all the world powers were, or had been, at war. Other states were subsequently drawn in.
2. The war was fought across the world. There were campaigns in Europe, North Africa and in the Far East.
3. The war was fought on land, on the sea, under the sea and in the air. Aircraft were employed for bombing as never before.
4. All the European powers conscripted men into the armed forces.
5. The Second World War was a war for survival between nations. Almost from the beginning civilians were considered legitimate targets by both sides.

   (a) *SS Einsatzgruppen* and others systematically attempted to eliminate entire groups of civilians in the territories occupied by the Nazis.

   (b) Bombing raids were carried out by the Germans as an integral part of *Blitzkrieg*, and by both sides to destroy the morale of civilians and their productive capacity.

   (i) In the greatest single massacre of the Second World War, which surpassed the atomic bomb attacks on Hiroshima and Nagasaki combined, half-a-million ordinary German men, women and children were killed on the night of February 13-14th, 1945 by two massive firebombing attacks, carried out by the US and the British Royal Air Force. Most died of the heat, rather than by burning or choking. On the next morning a third attack was carried out, during which American fighter pilots strafed helpless crowds of injured and terrorized people as they tried to flee along the banks of the River Elbe.

   (ii) One single night time fire-bombing raid on Tokyo took 100,000 lives.

Carpet bombing was by its very nature indiscriminate, and not aimed primarily at military targets.

(iii) The use of the atomic bomb on two Japanese cities, especially spared previous bombing raids in order that US scientists could study its effects, involved the use of a weapon which by its nature could by no means be regarded as limited to military targets.

(c) Civilians in occupied countries were routinely ill-treated by the occupying power, particularly the Germans, who treated conquered populations as a resource for slave labour, and frequently executed hostages in reprisal for partisan activity. Among towns and villages where all adult males, or the entire population, was killed in this way are Kalavryta in Greece, Lidice in Czechoslovakia and Oradour-sur-Glane in France.

(d) The systematic attempts at genocide,* the eradication of entire populations within German-occupied Europe (the Polish intelligentsia, Jews, Roma, homosexuals, etc.) were not new. During and following the First World War the Turkish nationalists engaged in systematic genocide against the Armenians and Greeks within the boundaries of their state. This was a continuation of the same policy.

The construction of the death camps marked an industrialization of genocide. Six million people were probably killed in these camps, some four million of them being Jews.

Severity

1. The casualties of war were even greater than in the First World War:
   (a) About ten million men were killed and about 20 million wounded. There were five million widows left and nine million orphans.
   (b) Large numbers of the wounded were permanently blind or disabled.
   (c) New forms of killing had been used.
2. Ill-treatment of prisoners-of-war by the Germans was routine in Eastern Europe, and by the Japanese.
3. There was a new bitterness between the populations of the powers. Unlike the bitterness artificially generated by propaganda during the First World War, in this case there were usually good reasons for it. National and racial hatred was stirred up by the propaganda and psychological warfare agencies, and justified by Social Darwinism. This led to the extension of the war to civilian populations, and hence to the increased severity of the war.

Government Intrusion into Everyday Life

1. In this second world war governments knew how to interfere in the details of everyday life. The various interferences which had been implemented during the First World War were reimposed during the Second - with additions.
2. In the USSR the government mobilized all men between 16 and 55, and all women between 16 and 45 years of age.
3. The advent of bombing meant that new duties were assumed by governments and new restrictions imposed upon the people, e.g. in the provision of air-raid shelters and gas masks and in the restriction upon showing even a chink of light from a window after dark during the blackout.
4. Because the Germans relied upon *Blitzkrieg* to win short wars, and the defeated countries to provide the resources for the next campaign, Germany was not affected as much as most other belligerents until the failure of *Blitzkrieg* in the east, when Albert Speer was placed in charge of a central Minstry of Armaments and Production. Even then, for ideological reasons, women were not mobilized for industrial or agricultural work. Instead, the Germans relied upon slave labour.

The Undermining of Institutions

1. By the end of the war, the power of Germany and Japan was destroyed. But also, the power of Britain and France was fatally undermined, and these imperial powers would never recover.
2. There were peaceful social revolutions throughout western Europe, as returning soldiers and liberated populations determined that they would not be cheated out of the promised fruits of victory this time, as they had been after the last war, and as the once-more discredited ruling classes hastened to compromise with their people rather than be swept away.
3. The Communist take-over in Eastern Europe swept away the discredited ruling classes of the new states created by the Peace of Paris.

Psychological Trauma

1. A state of profound shock was evident in the literature of the time: e.g. among the existential philosophers, such as Jean-Paul Sartre.
2. Mark Mazower, in *Dark Continent: Europe's Twentieth Century*, notes in the reports of those in occupied countries a certain anti-idealism, cynicism, and preoccupation with domestic concerns and their material welfare.
3. The psychological shock may have been ameliorated, however, because:
    (a) People already knew what to expect, and feared the worst, so there was not much surprise or disillusionment.
    (b) Among the victors, the need for this war was more evident, and the price of failure unacceptable, so people were more reconciled to it.

Diplomacy during the Second World War

The Main Wartime Conferences

1. **Newfoundland** -Aug. 1941 -Churchill and Roosevelt
    Purpose:
        (a) Churchill wanted to cement his friendship with Roosevelt
        (b) begin the process of drawing the USA into the war.
    There was a ceremonial meeting on board in international waters off Canada: Churchill on *HMS Prince of Wales* and Roosevelt on the *Augusta*. On the Sunday there was a joint religious service on the *Prince of Wales*.
    Decisions:
        (a) The Atlantic Charter was issued. This bound the USA to Great Britain, but did not commit the USA to war.
        (b) There were conferences between the joint Naval Chiefs which had the Japanese as well as the Germans in mind.
2. **Washington** - Dec. 1941- Churchill and Roosevelt
    Purpose: Now that the USA was in the war, Churchill wanted complete understanding between the Allies. Decisions:
        (a) Joint action would be taken in North Africa in place of a US plan to invade Europe.
        (b) Churchill persuaded Roosevelt to put the defeat of Germany before the defeat of Japan.
        (c) A joint declaration was issued by the "United Nations."
3. **Washington** - January 1942 - Delegates from the twenty-six Allied nations
    Purpose: To sign a common declaration of all the "United Nations" accepting the principles of the Atlantic Charter
4. **Moscow** - Aug. 1942 - Churchill and Stalin

Purpose: to establish relations with Stalin. Stalin urgently wanted a second front opened in Europe to take the pressure off the USSR. In May 1942 Roosevelt had promised Molotov to open a second front in Europe within a year. Churchill objected:

(a) Ostensibly,* he thought that a second front would fail, as seaborne invasions were difficult to pull off successfully, and that the cost of that failure would make opening another second front impossible for a generation, as the public would not support it.

(b) Churchill wanted the USSR and Germany to destroy each other, allowing the Anglo-Saxon nations to step in and pick up the pieces afterwards.

Decisions confirmed:

(a) The British would occupy N. Norway to secure a route for Arctic convoys to USSR.

(b) *Operation Torch,* an Anglo-American invasion of French North Africa, would go ahead.

5. **Casablanca** - Jan. 1943 - Churchill, Roosevelt, De Gaulle

There was a fear in Washington and London that the Soviets, in disgust at being left to fight alone (except for the small diversion in North Africa), might choose to make a separate peace with Hitler. There was also trouble between De Gaulle and Giraud over which one of them was to represent France.

Decisions:

(a) to concentrate on taking Tunisia, Sicily and then Italy, rather than Sardinia and Italy.

(b) To try to create a situation in which Turkey would join the Allies.

(c) It was reiterated that the defeat of Germany was to take precedence over the defeat of Japan.

(d) Roosevelt decided to accept only the unconditional surrender of Germany and Japan. Italy was deliberately excluded from this, to split the Axis powers. (Roosevelt made a mistake in his speech announcing this, referring to the unconditional surrender of "all" the enemy powers, and so ruining the desired effect).

The demand for unconditional surrender was greeted with glee in Berlin. It took away from the German people any choice about fighting on or surrendering, and ensured the survival of the Nazi regime to the bitter end.

6. **Moscow** - October 1943 - Foreign Ministers of USA, USSR, Great Britain and China

Purpose: To issue a declaration of intent regarding the foundation of the United Nations Organisation.

7. **Cairo** - November 1943 - Roosevelt, Churchill and Chiang Kai-shek

The meeting with the Chinese Nationalist leader was held separately from the later meeting at Teheran because the USSR was not yet at war with Japan.

Purpose: To coordinate the efforts of the Western Allies and nationalist China

Decisions:

(a) To accept only unconditional surrender from Japan;

(b) To take all Japanese conquests in the Pacific from her;

(c) To restore all Japanese conquests from China back to China after the war;

(d) To create an independent Korea after the war.

8. **Teheran** - November 1943 - Churchill, Stalin and Roosevelt.

Churchill met Roosevelt in Cairo first. Churchill wanted East Mediterranean operations, such as the invasion of Rhodes, to persuade the Turks to enter the war on the Allied side. Roosevelt wanted all resources saved for *Operation Overlord*, the invasion of France.

Decisions:

(a) The Western Allies would open a major second front in Europe during May 1944.

(b) The borders of Finland would be extended.

(c) The frontier of Poland would be the Oder in the west and the Curzon Line in the east.

(d) At a suitable time Stalin would declare war on Japan.

(e) An international peacekeeping organisation, the United Nations Organisation, would be set up after the war.

9. **Quebec** - September 1944 - Roosevelt and Churchill

Purpose: To consider the **Morgenthau Plan** for post-war Germany, under which:

(a) The USSR and other occupied countries could remove machinery from Germany;

(b) The heavy industry of the Ruhr and the Saar would be closed down, and these two provinces placed under international control;

(c) Germany would be turned into a largely agricultural and pastoral country.

The proposals were later rejected. When the *Reich* Propaganda Department heard of it, they were able to use it to strengthen German resolve to fight on.

10. **Moscow** - October 1944 - Stalin and Churchill

Purpose: To prevent disagreement among the Allies leading to splits before the end of the war.

Decisions:

(a) The Balkans were divided into spheres of influence. The USSR was accorded an 80%-20% and 75%-25% preponderance of influence in Bulgaria and Rumania, a 50%-50% influence with the USA in Hungary and Yugoslavia, and Britain an 90%-10% influence in Greece. This is the **Percentages Agreement**.

Subsequently, when the Red Army occupied Hungary, a preponderance of Soviet influence there was recognised.

(b) It was reiterated that the Curzon Line would be the boundary of Poland in the east, and Poland would receive compensation for territory lost in the east by receiving German territory in the west, up to the Oder.

11. **Yalta** (Crimea) - February 1945 - Stalin, Roosevelt and Churchill

Purpose: To make immediate arrangements for the post-war situation:

(a) To adopt a general policy towards the liberated states of central and Eastern Europe;

(b) In particular, to settle the future of Poland;

(c) To determine the immediate post-war administration of the conquered territories: Germany and Austria;

(d) To determine voting arrangements in the United Nations Organization.

Decisions:

(a) To administer Germany immediately after surrender in three military occupation zones: Soviet, American and British; while Berlin would be similarly administered in sectors

It was later decided to divide Germany and Berlin into four occupation areas, the extra ones administered by the French.

(b) Austria (and Vienna separately) would also be administered in military occupation zones.

(c) Germany would pay reparations, and a reparations committee was set up. A basis for consideration was initially set at twenty billion dollars, of which fifty per cent should go to the USSR But the British insisted upon not naming a figure, and specifying the purpose of war reparations, so as to destroy German war potential.

(d) Free elections would be held throughout eastern Europe.

(e) The USSR would retain the area of Poland she acquired in 1939. Stalin also demanded all of Germany east of the Oder and Neisse. The others would not agree.

(f) Some members of the non-communist Polish Government-in-Exile in London would be allowed to join the Communist Polish Government set up by Stalin in Lublin.

(g) Stalin agreed to join the war against Japan "within two or three months" of the end of the war in Europe, in return for Sakhalin Island and territory in Manchuria.

(h) The San Francisco Conference to found the UNO was planned, and the Great Powers decided that they would retain a veto on any measures the UN passed.

12. **San Francisco** - April 1945

Purpose: To launch the United Nations Organisation.

13. **Potsdam** - July 1945 - Stalin, Truman and Churchill, later Stalin, Truman and Attlee

Purpose: The war in Europe was over, but they still needed to settle outstanding matters concerning the post-war situation.

The mood was negative:

(a) Truman and Churchill were personally hostile towards the Soviet Union, and Truman was strengthened in his feeling of invincible superiority by the possession of the atomic bomb;

(b) Truman and Churchill were annoyed that Stalin had occupied all of Germany east of the Oder Neisse line, and placed it under the control of the largely communist government of Poland, which had expelled five million Germans living there.

(c) Stalin was annoyed that Truman was using the atomic bomb to exclude the USSR from the invasion of Japan.

No significant decisions were agreed. The Cold War was already evident.

The **Potsdam Declaration,** issued by Truman and Churchill, simply called upon Japan to surrender unconditionally immediately, "The alternative for Japan is prompt and utter destruction."

The Grand Alliance was dead; the USA was talking tough from its position as the world's sole nuclear superpower.

The Reasons why the Axis Powers Lost the Second World War

1. The war became a war of attrition, and the resources of the Allies (USA, USSR and British Empire) far outweighed those of Germany and Japan.

   (a) Germany and Japan suffered from chronic shortages of certain materials, such as nickel, rubber and even, after mid-1944, oil.

   (b) Liddel-Hart says that they, "became stretched out, far beyond their capacity for holding their gains."

   (c) The Allies were able to build up air and naval superiority, which won the battles of the Atlantic and Pacific, and slowly starved the Axis of supplies.

2. The Axis made very serious tactical mistakes:

   (a) Hitler never took his war against Britain seriously. He was always prepared to do a deal. So he did not commit Germany militarily to the invasion of Britain.

   (b) The *Blitzkrieg* invasion of Russia was his chief mistake.

   (i) The Germans did not prepare adequately for a winter campaign in Russia.

   (ii) Hitler failed to win the support of the non-Russian peoples of the USSR and anti-Stalinists, alienating possible support with his racist policies.

   (iii) The invasion of the USSR turned the war into a war of attrition, which the Germans could not win.

   (c) Hitler's contempt for the USA was misplaced, since the USA could be important in a war of attrition.

   (d) The Japanese concentrated on the production of battleships, when it had become evident that they were rendered out of date by aircraft carriers.

(e) Hitler insisted on a policy of no retreat, which lost valuable resources of men and equipment, e.g. at Stalingrad; and increasingly ignored reality.

(f) Hitler decided to focus on producing V-rockets instead of jet aircraft, which may have prevented the aerial attacks of 1944-5.

The Results of the Second World War

1. At least 30 million people were killed. Over half of these were Russians. Six million people, four million Jews, along with gypsies, homosexuals and others, had been exterminated in the death camps.
2. There was immense destruction of infrastructure, homes, etc. One third of all homes in uninvaded Britain were destroyed. European coal production was at 40% of prewar levels. About 23% of Europe's farmland was out of production by the end of the war. In Western Europe, this was to lead to a severe crisis during the harsh winter of 1946-7.
3. In Europe, over 20 million people had been uprooted from their homes and were displaced persons in 1945:
    (a) Refugees fleeing before invading armies;
    (b) Slave-workers from occupied Europe taken to Germany and Austria;
    (c) Prisoners in concentration camps.
    The attempt to solve the problem of displaced Jews was to lead to the disinheritance and displacement, in turn, of the Palestinians by the establihment of the state of Israel, now such an intractable source of suffeing in the the Middle East.
4. There were great internal stresses within formerly occupied countries, between those who had collaborated and those who had resisted. In many countries there were spontaneous reprisals: lynchings and public humiliation of collaborators. In Greece this was to lead to civil war.
5. Fascism was seen to have failed.
    (a) Its militarism had led to defeat;
    (b) Its anti-Bolshevism had led to the extension of Bolshevism over much of eastern and central Europe.
6. European domination of the world was ended. The USA emerged clearly as the world superpower.
    (a) Germany was destroyed as a great power, while Britain and France were effectively destroyed as great imperial powers, although this was not to be apparent for some time, and they were to cling to great power status.
    (b) The USSR had:
      (i) recovered and extended its empire;
      (ii) acquired a *glacis* in the west;
      (iii) become the dominant military power on the continent of Europe;
      (iv) acquired enormous prestige as the chief opponent and victor over Nazism, cancelling out the shame of the Molotov-Ribbentrop Pact (1939);
      (v) as the leading Communist power, acquired great prestige and following outside of its own borders, e.g. in Greece, Italy and France;
      (vi) found itself the only one of the former Great Powers able to resist US domination;
      although mucch weaker than the USA economically, without nuclear weapons, and unlike the USA, very badly damaged by the war.
7. The USA dominated the world by default, being left as the world's only real superpower, checked only by Stalin. Relations between the two predictably cooled quickly, creating the Cold War. *[See companion volume in this series: "The Cold War"]* For this reason, there was no general

peace conference following the Second World War. When a conference would have been to the advantage of one, it would equally, and for that reason, be to the disadvantage of the other.

8. The defeat of Western powers by Japan and the temporary occupation of their Far Eastern colonies, ended the myth of white superiority, made the peoples of the region unhappy with the return of the imperial powers, and eager to win their own independence, by force if necessary. Thus it was a catalyst* for the break-up of the nineteenth-century empires.

9. Racism and anti-Semitism became unacceptble to Western public opinion, except, e.g. in some of the southern states of the USA.

10. All over Europe, the people were radicalized and ready for reform:
    (a) In many Western European countries, the conditions were ripe for social revolution. Governments compromised by instituting socialist measures:
        (i) social security systems;
        (ii) nationalisation of the means of production and distribution ("the commanding heights of the economy");
        (iii) progressive income tax;
        (iv) measures to create full employment.
        e.g. the Attlee Government in Britain, de Gaulle's government in France.
    (b) In Eastern Europe the ruling classes in the new states created by the Peace of Paris were also discredited. The population was ready for the reforms brought by Communism

11. The minorities in Central and Eastern Europe created by the Peace of Paris which had caused such problems before the war tended to disappear. They frequently fled at the end of the war, leaving more nationally homogeneous states in Central and Eastern Europe.

12. The war had stimulated scientific and technological development, e.g. nuclear weapons.

The Significance of the Second World War

1. It could be regarded as the second part of the War of German hegemony, fought to decide whether or not Germany would dominate Europe.

2. It was also a war between the USA and Japan, fought over which of them would dominate the Western Pacific and the Far East.

3. It was the second part of an act of European civil war which was also an act of suicide, bringing to an end the centuries of European dominance of the world, and providing the opportunity for the USA to emerge almost unchallenged as the world superpower.

4. David Mazower, in *Dark Continent*, points out that much of the horror of Europeans at the character of the German Occupation is that the Nazis treated Europeans in exactly the way that Europeans had been accustomed to treat non-Europeans.

The Nuremberg War Crimes Trials

1. US Justice Jackson argued for a formal trial of Nazi leaders by representatives of the major powers, its purpose being to establish a precedent for the future.

2. A four-man tribunal consisting of representatives of the Allied Powers, its procedures determined by an agreed charter, would try the accused with responsibility for:
    (a) crimes against peace: The deliberate planning, initiation and waging of aggressive war, or of war in violation of international agreements;
    (b) war crimes: violations of the laws or customs of war;
    (c) crimes against humanity: inhumane acts against civil populations, prisoners, etc.

3. Twenty-four top Nazis were indicted, breaking with the custom that only lower ranking people

were tried for war crimes. Hearings began at Nuremberg on November 20th. Twelve were sentenced to be hanged, seven to imprisonment and three acquitted. Göring escaped the judgement of the court by committing suicide.

4. War crimes trials were also held in the Far East in 1946. Seven Japanese leaders, including Admiral Tojo, were sentenced to death.

Problems in Evaluating the Nuremberg War Crimes Trials

Milton R. Konvitz pointed out that there are many irregularities with the Nuremberg War Crimes Trials. Others argue that these do not nullify the court's validity, merely the limitations of its concerns to the crimes committed by one side.

1. The states represented on the tribunal were all on the side of the victors, a breach of generally recognised principles of judicial procedure.
2. The states represented on the tribunal had themselves committed crimes of the type for which the defendants were being tried, e.g.:
   (a) The Soviet declaration of war against Finland in 1939;
   (b) The Anglo-American carpet bombing of German cities during 1943-5;
   (c) The dropping of atomic bombs on Japanese cities in 1945 by the USA.

Glossary

Allies (the): USSR, USA, British Empire, and their allies

attrition: wearing down

Axis: Germany, Italy, Japan, and their allies

blitzkrieg: "lightning war" - attack in depth using planes, tanks and motorized infantry

catalyst: an agent in bringing about change in something else

Einsatzgruppen: SS execution squads

genocide: the attempted elimination of an entire ethnic group

impasse: a situation which cannot be readily resolved

intimidate: threaten

kamikazes: "Divine wind" - Japanese suicide pilots

Luftwaffe: German Air Force

ostensibly: on the surface, openly, overtly (as opposed to "covertly")

POWs: prisoners of war

RAF: Royal Air Force - the British Air Force

UNO: United Nations Organisation, successor to the League of Nations

---

Bibliography

Arnold-Forster, M, *The World at War*, Collins (London, 1973)

Bell, Philip, Europe in the Second World War, in Themes in Modern European History, ed. Paul Hayes, Routledge (London & New York, 1992)

Borg, Dorothy, *The United States and the Far Eastern Crisis of 1933-1938, Harvard University*

Theodore Herzl

8. The Arab-Israeli Wars

"On that day the Lord made a covenant with Abraham saying: 'To your descendants I give this land, from the river of Egypt to the great river, the river Euphrates...'" (Genesis 15:18)
"[I]n Palestine we do not propose even to go through the form of consulting the wishes of the present inhabitants of the country." (Arthur Balfour)

The Background

Zionism*

1. Following persecution of the Jews in the Russian Empire, in 1897 the World Zionist Organisation, led by Theodor Herzl, was founded at Basle, Switzerland, with the aim of establishing a Jewish national home in Palestine.
2. From the beginning, the Zionists spoke of Palestine as though it were properly their own. Herzl said: "the most fertile parts of our land [*sic*] are occupied by Arabs."
3. Zionism was an extreme form of nationalist romanticism, to be compared with the grandiose plans of Hitler for German expansion in his "thousand-year *Reich*" or the US belief in "Manifest Destiny." Like all such ideas, it was always advanced with "special pleading,"* as embodying uniquely worthy claims.
4. Between 1882 and 1903, colonies of Zionists, mostly Russians, settled in Palestine. They formed communal agricultural settlements, called *kibbutzim.**
5. The Zionists, in seeking their goal:
    (a) were careful to disguise their ultimate intentions, of taking the land of Palestine and surrounding areas, displacing the Palestinians to create a homeland exclusively for settler Jews, sometimes practising systematic subtefuge* to do so;
    (b) ignored the Palestinians, often denying their very existence;
    (c) "went over their heads" by seeking the assistance of the Great Powers, especially the Turks. Herzl arranged a trip to Palestine to coincide with the visit of the Kaiser;
    (d) When they purchased land for settlement, they drove the Arab tenants off the land.
6. A second wave of Jewish immigration began in 1904 after the death of Herzl, and the collapse of an alternative scheme to take part of Uganda, and lasted until the First World War.
7. In 1909 an exclusively Jewish town was founded north of Jaffa, called Tel Aviv.

8. By 1914 there were 90,000 Jews living in Palestine; 75,000 were settlers, mostly living in exclusively Jewish communities.
9. Resentment of the immigrants by the Arab population was natural, but it was exacerbated by several factors:

(a) The ability of the immigrants to buy up the best land from absentee Turkish landowners;

(b) The tendency of the immigrants to settle in exclusive communities;

(c) Their racist attitudes towards the indigenous inhabitants of the land, including their tendency to seek advantage there by associating themselves with, and working through, the Great Powers;

(d) The difference between their professed intentions in settling in Palestine and their evident long-term aims to take the entire country and set up an exclusive Jewish state.

The Origins of the Palestinian Problem

1. During the First World War, the British made three incompatible promises about the Near East:

(a) In the **Hussein-McMahon Correspondence** (1915-1916) between Hussein ibn Ali, Sharif of Mecca, and Sir Henry McMahon, British High Commissioner in Egypt, the Arabs were promised that they would have an independent state across the Middle East following the break-up of the Ottoman Empire.

This was to encourage the Arab revolt against the Turks.

(b) By a secret agreement (the **Sykes-Picot Agreement** 1916), the British would divide the area with the French. Britain would take control of areas roughly comprising Jordan, Iraq and Jaffa. France would take South-eastern Turkey, Northern Iraq, Syria and Lebanon. Palestine would be under international administration until there had been consultations with Russia and other powers. The Great Powers would decide on state boundaries of those areas.

This was the usual imperialist *realpolitik*.

(c) In the **Balfour Declaration**, made in a letter by British Foreign Secretary Arthur James Balfour, to Lord Rothschild, a wealthy leader of the British Jewish community, for transmission to the Zionist Federation, it was stated that the Jews could have a national home in Palestine, under the condition that nothing should be done which might prejudice the rights of the existing inhabitants. (It is impossible to see how that could be compatible with creating a national homeland for the Jews in the area.).

The British believed that the promise or reality of a Jewish settler colony in Palestine would:

(i) gain the support of the Jews of the Central Powers and Russia for the Allies;

(ii) gain the support of the powerful Jews of the USA, and assist in bringing the USA into the war on the side of the Allies;

(iii) provide a pro-British settler colony which would assist in preserving British domination of the area, to "secure the territorial continuity of Egypt and India," especially by helping to guard the Suez Canal.

Promising everything to everyone was a standard British practice, to gain support in the war at whatever cost.

2. A British army from Egypt invaded Palestine, and General Allenby took Jerusalem from the Turks. British military rule was established.
3. The British were followed by another influx of Jews: 35,000 in four years.
4. Arab nationalism was sparked by the establishment of Feisal's kingdom in Damascus in 1918.
5. At the Peace Conference in Paris, by the of Sèvres (1920), it was the Sykes-Picot Agreement which determined the settlement.

Palestine under the British Mandate

1. In 1919 the population of Palestine was 90% Arab. It contained 68,000 Jews, mostly living in Jerusalem. The majority of these were Orthodox Jews* whose ancestors had lived there for centuries. They generally resented the 16,000 Zionists settlers.
2. The British officially took control of Palestine under a League of Nations mandate* in 1920.
3. The Zionists turned their attention from the Turks to the British to secure the change of the ethnicity of the population they would need to achieve their aims.
4. **Immigration** was adopted as a political strategy to change the demographics* and to establish the political and economic supremacy of the Jews. Using money provided by wealthy Jews in the USA and Europe, they began to buy up the best land in the country for Jewish immigrants, and refused to employ any of the local Arab population on it.
5. Arab reaction to the slow take-over of their country by Jewish immigrants, coupled with unease generated by the Balfour Declaration, led to anti-Jewish riots in Jerusalem in 1920.
6. Foreseeing further trouble, the British introduced quotas on Jewish immigration, but they were so high that they did not alleviate the problem.
7. The Jews founded **Hagganah**, a secret military force to fight the Palestinians.
8. In May 1921 further Palestinian protests took place over:
    (a) The failure of the British to honour the Sykes-Picot Agreement;
    (b) The continuing influx of Jews.
   This led to a very brief halt on Jewish immigration.
9. In 1922, the British promised that:
    (a) There was no intention to hand over *the whole* of Palestine to the Jews;
    (b) There would be no infringements of the rights of the native Palestinians.
    (c) The Palestinians could not expect to gain their eventual independence, like the other Arab states, because of the promises made to the Jews.
10. The British tried to set up a legislative council containing both Arabs and Jews.
    (a) The Jews created the Jewish Agency;
    (b) The Arabs would not cooperate by giving the Jews a guaranteed and disproportionate voice in the government of their country.
11. The Jewish Agency became an unofficial government of the Jews.
12. Jewish immigration continued at the rate of 10,000 a year. By 1928 there were 150,000.
    (a) Some of the earlier settlers became alarmed that this would destabilize the situation;
    (b) Most wished to swamp the indigenous inhabitants, so as to be able to take over exclusive control of the land for themselves.
13. After Arab protests and inter-communal violence in 1929, the British briefly curtailed immigration once more, and set up a commission to examine the causes of Arab unrest.
14. The commission concluded that the Arabs:
    (a) did not accept the British mandate, but desired independence;
    (b) feared the loss of their own land to the Jews;
    (c) desired the withdrawal of the Balfour Declaration;
    (d) demanded the establishment of democratic institutions;
    (e) wished to prohibit the sale of any more land to the Jews.
15. The Jewish settlers and their backers, especially the Jewish lobby* in London, put pressure upon the British government to allow immigration to continue. Jewish rioting broke out in 1933.
16. After Hitler came to power in Germany:
    (a) many Jews wished to leave Germany, and later Austria and Czechoslovakia;
    (b) More Jews became Zionists;

(c) Most Western states, e.g. the USA, closed their doors to the Jewish immigration.

Thus German Jews flocked to Palestine. In 1934, 42,000 arrived. By 1935, 25% of the population of Palestine was Jewish. Inter-communal violence flared up again.

17. In 1936 this led to a six month general strike, which turned into an **Arab Revolt,** as guerilla resistance against the British began. The rebels wanted:

    (a) a constitution;

    (b) an end to Jewish immigration;

    (c) an end to land sales to the Jews.

18. A Jewish group called **Irgun Zvai Leumi** (The National Military Organization) was formed to carry out terrorist attacks against Arabs.

19. When the Peel Commission was expected to decide on the partition of the country, the Jews tried to change the situation on the ground by erecting wooden "tower and stockade" settlements overnight, so that if partition was decided upon, they would be awarded the greatest amount of Palestinian land they could. This was done particularly in areas which would control the precious water supply. The Jews expected that these set-tlements would be protected by the British, and when they were not, they were "de-fended" by *Hagganah*. This was tolerated by the British.

20. The British:

    (a) repressed the Arabs violently, executing the leaders of the resistance and deporting others;

    (b) armed the Jews, the weapons being passed on to *Hagannah* and the Jewish terrorists.

21. During 1936-7 60,000 Jews entered Palestine legally, and many more illegally. By 1937, there were 400,000 Jews in Palestine, and *Hagganah* was also organising systematic illegal immigration.

22. The **Peel Commission proposed** dividing the land into two separate states, one Arab and one Jewish, with Jerusalem remaining under British control.

    (a) Some Jews accepted, as it gave them a large foothold in Palestine from which to expand later, although most were dissatisfied with the amount of land awarded to them at that time, since they wanted the whole of Palestine;

    (b) The Arabs rejected the plan. They saw no reason to surrender any part of their own homeland.

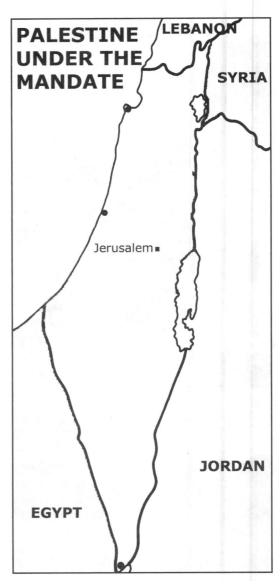

PALESTINE UNDER THE MANDATE

LEBANON

SYRIA

Jerusalem

JORDAN

EGYPT

The Arab Revolt

1. Arab unrest re-erupted. The British soon lost control of Jerusalem, Nablus and Hebron
2. The British tried to restore order. They:
   (a) took civilians as hostages to provide themselves with cover under fire;
   (b) demolished Arab homes as a collective punishment;
   (c) committed atrocities, such as keeping men and boys in the sun all day and then selling water to those who had money, many died.
   The British officer Charles Orde Wingate organized Special Night Squads composed of British soldiers and Hagganah volunteers, which conducted raids on Arab villages.
3. In total, 5,000 Palestinians were killed, and 10,000 injured. 10% of the adult male population were killed, wounded, imprisoned or exiled. The Jewish population suffered 400 killed; the British 200.

The Second World War

1. In 1939, the British began to seek Arab support (and to take measures to secure their oil supplies) for the coming world war. They:
   (a) limited Jewish immigration to 10,000 a year;
   (b) limited land purchase by Jews;
   (c) promised to set up an Arab state of Palestine within ten years.
2. The anti-Semitism of the Nazis naturally appealed to many Palestinians, including Haj Amin, the Grand Mufti* of Jerusalem. More bizarrely, some Jews in Palestine tried to contact Hitler through the Vichy French in Damascus to appeal to Hitler to expel the British so that they could seize the country. One of these, Yitzhak Shamir, later became prime minister of Israel.
3. Lebanon and Syria were granted their independence in 1943 and 1945.
4. At the Biltmore Conference the Zionists decided that British power was waning and that the postwar world would be dominated by the USA. Therefore in the future they would seek US patronage in preference to British. In May 1942 American Zionists declared that they would work for:
   (a) unlimited Jewish immigration to Palestine;
   (b) the creation of a Jewish Army;
   (c) the takeover of the whole of Palestine for an exclusively Jewish state.
   This became official Zionist policy.
5. The Arabs were assured, in letters from Roosevelt and Truman that no post-war settlement of Palestine would be made:
   (a) without full consultation with the Arabs;
   (b) against the interests of the Arabs.

Percentage of the Population of Palestine which was Jewish

Year	Percentage
1922	11.1%
1932	17.7%
1935	25%
1936	28%
1943	31.5%

The Jewish Revolt

1. In January 1944, Irgun called upon the Jews of Palestine to revolt, drive out the British and install a Jewish government. British police stations were attacked. In November 1944, Jewish terrorists murdered the British Minister in Cairo, Lord Moyne.

2. The Zionists moved their pressure onto the US Government, using their electoral power to secure the endorsement of a "free and democratic Jewish Commonwealth" in Palestine by Roosevelt.

3. With the end of the war, there were large numbers of dispossessed European Jews seeking a new homeland. Except for the very wealthy, famous or very well qualified, the USA and Europe did not want to allow them to settle in their own countries.

4. The newly formed **Arab League**, in turn, pledged in March 1945, to prevent the formation of an exclusively Jewish state in Palestine.
   In April 1946 David Ben-Gurion demanded the right for 1,200,000 Jews to settle in Palestine.

5. By this time, *Hagganah* had grown into a semi-professional army. They, together with Irgun, a Zionist terrorist group led by Menachem Begin, a future prime minister of Israel, and the Abraham Stern Gang, an even more extreme faction, began working together in a terrorist campaign against both the British administration and army and the indigenous Arab population. Their most infamous atrocity was the blowing up of the British Military HQ in the King David Hotel, on July 22nd 1946, killing nearly one hundred people.

6. On July 30th, the **Morrison Plan** was published. Palestine would be divided into three regions:
   (a) 43%, including Jerusalem, under direct British rule;
   (b) 40% under Arab local autonomy;
   (c) 17% under Jewish local autonomy.
   The Jews rejected the plan as offering them too little of Palestine.

United Nations Intervention

1. The British mandate was due to expire in 1948, so on 15th February 1947, the British invited the UN to solve the problem they had created by allowing mass Jewish settlement in Palestine.
   (a) Conditions in Britain had deteriorated during the harsh winter 1946-7, and the British Government, which had social reform as a priority, withdrew from several intractable foreign problems: India, Greece and Palestine.
   (b) Truman's interventions to facilitate large-scale Jewish settlement had made solving the Palestinian Problem impossible.

2. The UN appointed a Special Committee on Palestine, which was not recognised by the Palestinians.

3. In August 1947 the UN produced a plan proposing:
   (a) The partition of Palestine, giving half of the country to the Jewish settlers as a national state. (In 1947 Jews were only one third of the population of Palestine and owned 6% of the land. Yet they were granted 55% of the total land area).
   (b) The whole of Palestine was to be treated as a unity economically;
   (c) The British were to administer the country for two more years for the UN;
   (d) During this period, 150,000 more Jews were to be admitted.

4. The reasons for this remarkable development were:
   (a) a feeling of guilt towards the Jews after their suffering during the Nazi era;
   (b) the large numbers of dispossessed European Jewish refugees seeking a new homeland, which the Western countries did not want to take in, as they had problems with their own Jewish minorities, and did not want to stimulate further anti-Semitism;
   (c) the successful Zionist portrayal of Palestine as the only refuge for Hitler's victims;

(d) the desire of Truman wished to gain as many Jewish votes as possible in New York State in the election of 1948. Thus the USA pressured the British into allowing 100,000 Jewish immigrants to go to Palestine, but the British resisted.

(e) Many small states were subject to improper pressure by the US. e.g. US Congressmen warned the Philippines that it would not get US economic aid unless it voted for partition.

It hardly seemed to occur to anyone that it was not ethical to solve one injustice by creating another.

5. The Jews outwardly accepted the settlement, but the Zionist leader David Ben-Gurion instructed *Hagganah* to prepare "to safeguard the entire community and the settlements - *wherever they may be*, to conquer the whole country or most of it, and to maintain its occupation until the attainment of an authoritative political settlement."

6. The Arabs refused to accept the settlement and tried to take the case to the International Court, but were blocked.

7. The UN voted in November 1947. The USA and USSR put pressure (including bribery and threats) on smaller countries to accept the plan, which effectively:

(a) provided legal cover for the Jewish land grab;

(b) compromised the United Nations Organisation in its earliest days. It was seen as a tool of the Superpowers.

8. The British refused to cooperate with the UN and their forces confined themselves to barracks and police stations.

Glossary

demographics: the composition of the population

Grand Mufti: the leading Muslim cleric in Jerusalem

Hagganah: the Jewish secret army

kibbutzim: Jewish colonial settlements in Palestine run on Socialist lines

lobby: groups organized to put pressure on politician to secure their common interest,

subtefuge: lying, deceit

Zionism: the belief in the appropriation of Palestine as an exclusively Jewish settler state

---

Bibliography

Segev, Tom, *One Palestine Complete*, Abacus (London, 2001)

David Ben-Gurion

The First Arab-Israeli War

"When the Lord your God brings you into the land which you are entering to take possession of it, and clears away many nations before you ... and when the Lord your God gives them over to you, and you defeat them; then you must utterly destroy them; you shall make no covenant with them, and show no mercy to them." (Deuteronomy 7:1-2)

"We must use terror, assassination, intimidation, land confiscation, and the cutting of all social services to rid the Galilee of its Arab population." (David Ben Gurion)

"We will expel the Arabs and take their places ... with the force at our disposal." (David Ben Gurion)

The Origins of the First Arab-Israeli War

1. Following the UN intervention, the Jews immediately, prepared for armed conflict, by training men, hiding arms caches, etc.
2. Resenting the impending loss of half of their homeland to Jewish settlers, in December 1947 the Palestinians began to fight for their land against well-armed gangs of Jewish terrorists. Small-scale fighting soon increased in scale, provoked by Irgun hurling bombs into a crowd of Arabs.
3. Riots broke out across Arab lands against the local Jews.
4. The states of the Arab League proclaimed a *jihad** against the Jews.
5. Lebanese, Syrian and Transjordanian troops, with a small contingent of Saudis, also contributed to the war.
6. Fighter aircraft were imported by the Israelis from Czechoslovakia at the rate of two per day. Others came from America. About 5,000 Jewish volunteers arrived from abroad.

"Ethnic Cleasing"

1. In February the Jews drove out Arabs from parts of Jerusalem, then moved settlers in to take their place. This was the beginning of an attempt by the Jews to use the fighting to change the demographics on the ground in their favour.
2. In spring the British began to withdraw their troops. Hagganah put into operation **Plan D**, a plan

not merely to occupy areas allocated to the Jews, but also Jewish settlements outside that area; and occupy Arab towns and villages near Jewish settlements and drive out their inhabitants.

3. On April 15th Irgun and the Stern Gang deliberately massacred most of the population of the Arab village of **Deir Yassin**, over two hundred and fifty people, mostly women and children. The survivors were paraded through the streets of Jerusalem by Irgun soldiers. The Jews then broadcast their actions, deliberately to create an exodus of the Arab inhabitants from and near the areas allotted them by the UN. Thus 67,000 out of 70,000 Palestinians left Jaffa. The Jews then seized their lands, houses and possessions.

4. Deir Yassin was only one of many such massacres of Palestinians, in what was a systematic policy of ethnic cleansing*, designed to reduce the Arab population of the lands taken by the Jews to manageable proportions.

The Creation of the State of Israel

1. On May 15th, David Ben Gurion declared the independence of the state of Israel. It promised equality of political rights to all, regardless of religion, race or sex, and would guarantee freedom of religion, language and culture. *Hagannah* was transformed into the Israeli Army. Unlimited Jewish immigration was announced. Ben Gurion was its Prime Minister and Minister of War.

2. The US recognised the new state within the first eleven minutes of its existence. Arms shipments were received from Czechoslovakia.

3. On the same day, the Egyptian air force bombed Tel Aviv, but no one was killed; while Iraqi troops crossed the Jordan River.

4. Most of the fighting that ensued took place on territory that was to be part of the Palestinian state or in the internationalized zone of Jerusalem. Thus, Israel was not fighting for its survival, but to expand its borders into the areas "awarded" to the Arabs by the UN.

The Truces

1. After nearly four weeks continuous fighting a four-week truce was arranged by the Swedish Count Folke Bernadotte of the UN.

2. The Israelis used this period to acquire more arms.

3. Count Bernadotte produced his own peace plan:
   (a) The Negev would go to the Arabs;
   (b) Galilee would go to the Jews;
   (c) Jerusalem would go to Transjordan, with its Jews enjoying autonomy.
   Neither side agreed to this.

4. Ben Gurion had to beat off Jewish challenges to his authority:
   (a) Fighting broke out between the new Israeli Army and Irgun at Tel Aviv;
   (b) Senior army officers challenged his appointments within the army.

5. Nazareth was captured and looted by the Israelis, before a second truce on 19th July.

6. Again the Israelis used the time to acquire weapons, this time from the USA and Europe.

7. From July onwards, ethnic of Arabs cleansing continued.

8. On 17th Sept. Count Folke Bernadotte was murdered by the Stern Gang.

9. On October 1st the Grand Mufti of Jerusalem was elected by a National Palestinian Council, meeting in Gaza, as head of the government of all of Palestine. This was recognized by all Arab governments except King Abdullah of Jordan, his enemy. He convened a rival conference in Jericho and announced that:
   (a) Palestine and Trans-Jordan constituted a single entity, the "Arab Hashemite Kingdom";

(b) Palestinians would be elected to the parliament in Amman.

10. When the Israelis were ready to resume fighting, they provoked the Egyptians until (they claimed) they were fired upon, and then attacked.

11. On October 21st, the Government of Israel, forgetting its promises about personal freedoms:
    (a) prohibited non-Jewish Palestinians from visiting or living in certain areas of Israel without a permit;
    (b) allowed the Israeli military to expel Palestinian residents from these zones at a whim.

12. Both sides ignored a third truce when it suited them. The Israelis tried to invade Sinai, but were ordered back by the Americans and British.

13. In January 1949 Jewish Rabbis secured passage of a law to the effect that all meat imported into Israel must conform to Jewish religious laws. The state of Israel was beginning to take on a **religious**, as well as a racist, character.

14. The UN arranged a cease-fire. Armistice talks were held on Rhodes, 1949, with the American Ralph Bunche mediating, and a truce followed in April. A **United Nations Truce Supervisory Commission** policed the frontiers.

15. Israeli officials refused to allow any of the Arabs who had fled their homes to return. Arab villages were bulldozed over, citrus groves, lands, and property were all seized.

Reasons for the Israeli Victory

1. The Arab armies were poorly equipped, and the British, who supplied spare parts for Arab weapons, withheld them. The Jews were well supplied by the Czechs, and by Zionists in the USA and Western Europe.

2. Only 40,000 Arab soldiers took part, compared with 60,000 Jews.

3. The Arab forces were inexperienced and badly (if at all) coordinated.

4. There were rivalries between the Arab leaders.

5. The Jews had their government and army in existence, and had prepared for war, beforehand. The Palestinians only had a government at a late stage, and this was never recognised by all the Arab leaders.

6. The Palestinians were suffering from the British repression of 1936-39, which had decapitated their leadership.

7. The Israelis benefitted from a more compact position and shorter lines of communication.

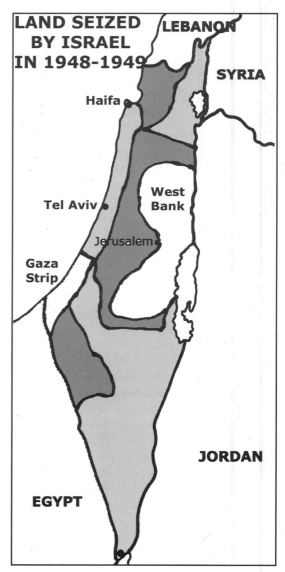

LAND SEIZED BY ISRAEL IN 1948-1949

The Consequences of the First Arab-Israeli War

1. Israel took the opportunity to seize more land than had been awarded them by the UN, including the port of Eilat, taken from Egypt. Jerusalem was divided between Israel and Jordan. Israel held 78% of Palestine.
2. Nearly one million Arabs fled into Egypt, Jordan, Syria and Lebanon, where they lived in miserable refugee camps.
3. In December 1948, the UN passed Resolution 194, which declared that "refugees wishing to return to their homes and live in peace with their neighbours should be permitted to do so" and that "compensation should be paid for the property of those choosing not to return." This resolution was overwhelmingly adopted year after year, but Israel ignored it.
4. In December 1949, The **United Nations Refugee and Works Administration for Palestinians (UNRWA)** was founded. It looked after:
    (a) Some 30,000 Arab refugees who had fled to areas subsequently incorporated into Israel. They could not return to their homes because these were seized by Jews.
    (b) Palestinian refugees who had fled to areas under Arab control:
        (a) On the West Bank administered by Jordan;
        (b) In the Gaza Strip, administered by Egypt;
        (c) In Syria;
        (d) In Lebanon.
UNRWA provided:
        (i) relief;
        (ii) health care;
        (iii) social services;
        (iv) education.
5. The Arab states refused to accept this act of *force majeure,** and none recognised the legitimacy of the state of Israel.
6. In 1950 the Americans, the British and French:
    (a) guaranteed the new borders of Israel; thus recognising the extra land seized by Israel;
    (b) promising to sell only limited arms in the region to avoid an arms race.

The Consequences of the First Arab-Israeli War

1. This was a settler war, of a type common a century earlier, except that the settlers were not representatives of a single Imperial Power, but of a distinctive people scattered across Europe, North America and elsewhere, under the protection of the USA and others.
2. The integrity of the United Nations Organization was compromised from its earliest days by its association with:
    (a) such an extreme example of romantic nineteenth century nationalism;
    (b) imperialist behaviour by the world superpower;
    (c) the unjust disinheritance of much of the Palestinian population;
    (d) as a result of intensive lobbying in Washington.

The Racist State

1. During the late 1940s and early 1950s the Israelis:
    (a) Passed several laws designed to make it impossible for the dispossessed Palestinian Arabs ever to take back their homes and land. Great areas of Arab land were handed over to Jewish ownership;
    (b) Deliberately and systematically bulldozed many Arab villages, so that no claim could

easily be made on them;

(c) Invited Jewish settlers from all over the world, in order to establish a considerable Jewish population, seeking permanently to change the demographics of the area. This culminated in the **Law of Return** (1950), which gave Jews everywhere the right to live in Israel.

2. During the years which followed, there was some infiltration of Palestinians into Israel:

(a) for social reasons: refugees seeking contact with family members who remained in Israel;

(b) for economic reasons:

(c) to avenge wrongs done during the war.

The Israeli response was to treat the border areas as free-fire zones.* Between 1949 and 1956 some 5,000 Palestinians were killed by Israelis.

3. Most Arabs lived in the border areas of Israel and, until 1966, these areas were all declared "military security zones," i.e. under **martial law**.

4. Most of the land was placed under the ownership of the **Jewish National Fund** which prohibits its sale or lease to non-Jews for ever;

5. Government spending was funnelled to Jewish settlements, keeping Arab villages in a state of underdevelopment. Thousands of Israeli Arabs still live in villages declared "unrecognized" and so with no right to any government services, such as electricity.

6. Between 1948 and 1957 some 567,000 Jews were expelled from Arab states in reprisal for the expulsion of the Palestinians. Most settled in Israel.

Glossary

force majeure: using force to compel others

free-fire zones:

jihad: a Muslim holy war

UNRWA: United Nations Refugee and Works Administration for Palestinians

Gamal Abdul Nasser

The Suez War

"The genius of you Americans is that you never make clear-cut stupid moves, only complicated stupid moves which make the rest of us wonder at the possibility that we might be missing something."
(Gamel Abdul Nsser)

Background

1. Although Egypt was minimally independent during the early twentieth century, it was under British hegemony. The British regarded Egypt as a vital part of the British Empire because control of the **Suez Canal** governed the sea passage from the Mediterranean Sea to British possessions in the East, and particularly the Indian Empire.
2. Control of the Suez Canal was vested in the **Suez Canal Company**, largely owned by the British and French. By the Anglo-Egyptian Treaty of 1936, imposed upon the Khedive of Egypt, British troops permanently garrisoned the Canal.
3. During the Second World War the British had summarily taken over the entire country and turned it into a British base.
4. The Egyptians came to resent British hegemony, and felt humiliated by British control of their country.
5. The vast majority of Egyptians were very poor landless peasants, while most of the land was owned by a tiny number of very rich Egyptians. Most prominent of these during the Second World War was King Farouk, who was totally uninterested in the plight of his countrymen.
6. The USA wished to create in the Middle East an alliance similar to NATO as part of their scheme to "contain" the USSR. Thus US, British, French and Turkish governments produced a plan for a **Middle East Defence Organisation (Medo)** which would take over the Suez Canal.
7. The Egyptians:
    (a) rejected Medo
    (b) denounced the Anglo-Egyptian Treaty of 1936, which still had 5 years to run

(c) initiated guerilla attacks on the Canal Zone. In January 1952 there were severe anti-British riots in Cairo.

Nasser's Rise to Power

1. Gamal Abdul Nasser was a poor boy, the son of a postman in the Nile Delta. He was injured in 1935 by the police and expelled from secondary school in Cairo for leading a student demonstration.
2. Although in 1937 he attended law school, he decided to follow a career in the army.
3. While serving in the Egyptian army in the Sudan in 1942, Nasser and three other officers created a secret revolutionary organization, **Society of Free Officers**, whose composition would be known only to Nasser. Their aims were to:
    (a) fight against political corruption in Egypt;
    (b) depose the Egyptian royal family;
    (c) end British domination over Egypt;
    (d) modernise the economy;
    (e) raise the standard of living of the people by a more equitable distribution of land;
    (f) extend the cultivatable area of Egypt;
    (g) lead non-Egyptian Arabs against reactionary regimes
    (h) achieve Arab unity.
4. A major in the first **Arab-Israeli War** (1948), Nasser was besieged for three weeks in the Faluja Pocket and wounded in action.
5. In July, 1952, Nasser led an **army coup** that deposed King Farouk. It was a military collective. Gen. Muhammad Naguib became the nominal head of the government, but Nasser was the real leader of the plotters, and afterwards held power through his control of the **Revolutionary Command Committee.**

The Revolutionary Government

1. The country was initially governed by a Revolutionary Command Council of eleven officers controlled by Nasser, with Major General Muhammad Naguib as the official head of state. For more than a year Nasser kept his own leading role in the new regime hidden.
2. The new government inherited formidable problems with:
    (a) the economy:
        (i) 95% of the land was desert, and the population had to maintain itself on the small area of cultivable land.
        (ii) The economy largely depended upon a single cash crop*: cotton.
        (iii) There was little industry, and what there was was under foreign ownership.
    (b) the British over:
        (i) control of the Suez canal;
        (ii) pressured to join Medo;
        (iii) the future of the Anglo-Egyptian Sudan (technically a condominium*).
3. Moving swiftly against Egypt's hereditary landowners who had formed the main prop of the old regime, landownership was curtailed or nationalized.
4. Opposition parties were banned. The Communist Party and Muslim Brotherhood were suppressed.
5. In 1953 the monarchy was abolished and a one-party republic proclaimed. King Farouk left the country and went into exile.
6. A power struggle ensued between Naguib and Nasser.
    (a) Supporting Naguib were:

(i) the middle class;

(ii) the former political parties;

(iii) the Muslim Brotherhood.

(b) Supporting Nasser were:

(i) the lower ranks in the army;

(ii) the police;

(iii) the working-class, who had been mobilized in the National Union.

Naguib was placed under house arrest, and Nasser named himself prime minister.

7. The Muslim Brotherhood attempted to assassinate him. As a result he cracked down on their activities. He also arrested Naguib for having allegedly known of the plot.

8. Nasser became premier of Egypt.

9. He was in favour of:

(a) ending British colonial influence in Egypt;

(b) ending the existence of the state of Israel;

(c) following a policy of leaned towards non-alignment in the Cold War (Nasser had fallen under the influence of Indian premier Pandit Nehru;

(d) Pan-Arab unity.

10. In February 1953 the Egyptians agreed that the Sudanese should decide their own future. In 1954 an agreement introduced a transitional period of self-government for the Sudan, which became an independent republic in 1956.

11. In July 1954 Nasser negotiated **the Anglo-Egyptian Treaty**, by which the British would leave in 20 months, but retained the right to return if any member of the Arab League or Turkey was attacked by any state other than Israel.

12. In January 1956 Nasser announced a new constitution under which Egypt became a socialist Arab state with a one-party political system and with Islam as the official religion. In June, over 99% percent of the Egyptians who voted did so for Nasser, the only candidate. The constitution was approved by 99.8 percent.

13. He had consolidated his hold on power using radio and television to talk directly to the people, something never before seen in the Middle East.

Arab Socialism

1. The political ideology Nasser developed was called **Arab socialism.**

2. Great Britain and the United States agreed to finance the first stage of the Aswan High Dam project. This was designed to:

(a) irrigate vast areas of land and bring them into cultivation;

(b) make the Nile navigable almost up to the Sudanese frontier;

(c) provide hydro-electric power;

(d) remove the inconvenience of annual inundations in cities;

(e) provide a new fishing industry.

3. He confiscated 2,430 km² farm land from a small group of very wealthy landowners.

4. Guerrilla bands of *fedayeen* ("self-sacrifices") infiltrated across the border from Egyptian controlled Gaza into Israel to recover their homes from the Jewish settlers. In October 1953 the Israeli government began the practice of large-scale "retaliation" using air strikes against the refugees. An attack on Gaza in February 1955 left 38 Egyptians dead.

5. In 1954, a group of Third World countries met in Bandung to decide what action should be taken in the face of the pressure to ally themselves with either the West or the East. They decided to do neither, and instead to remain **non-aligned**.* Nasser, a master of publicity and an expert

manipulator of public opinion, rapidly became one of the leading spokesmen of the non-aligned movement.

6. He sought to **eradicate the remnants of colonialism** in the Middle East:
    (a) pressured King Hussein of Jordan to dismiss his British chief of staff, Glubb Pasha;
    (b) sent aid to Algerians fighting the French for independence;
    (c) pressured Arab states to oppose the British Baghdad Pact.
7. The US and Britain created the Baghdad Pact, (later the **Central Treaty Organisation (CENTO)** an alliance of the US and Middle Eastern states:
    (a) officially to prevent Soviet influence expanding into the Middle East (containment);
    (b) to establish US influence over the Middle East.
    Nasser opposed it, and only Pakistan and Iran joined. This annoyed the US.
8. An Israeli attack and the circumvention by Israel and France of the Tripartite Declaration (1950) limiting arms sales in the Middle East, convinced Nasser that he needed weapons. The West was unwilling to supply them to Egypt, so Nasser concluded an **arms deal with Czechoslovakia** (acting for the USSR).
9. On July 20, 1956, US secretary of state, John Foster Dulles cancelled the US offer to finance the Aswan High Dam. The next day the British also cancelled. This was because:
    (a) The US did not like Nasser and wished to "teach him lesson."
    (b) US cotton interests saw the development of the Egyptian economy as aiding a rival.
10. Nasser recognised the government of Communist China.
11. In order to finance the Aswan High Dam from tolls on the traffic on the Suez Canal, Nasser decided to nationalize the Suez Canal Company, compensating the British and French share-holders.

The Causes of the Suez War

1. Israeli intelligence conducted a bombing campaign of western targets in Egypt to discourage British withdrawal. The plot was foiled, and Egypt executed some of the plotters
2. From 1954 sought to provoke Egypt to war by aggressive strikes across the border, trusting that a retaliation would give them the pretext to launch an attack. This culminated, in February 1955, with an attack upon Gaza, killing 40 Egyptian soldiers. They were intent upon:
    (a) destroying the Egyptian Army
    (b) taking Sinai
    (c) taking the West Bank.
2. British Prime Minister, Sir Anthony Eden, decided that Nasser:
    (a) was out to build a united Arab nation under communist influence,
    (b) threatening the West's oil supply.
3. In secret negotiations, the British, French and Israelis conspired to attack Egypt. The Americans hinted that they would support their action.

The Course of the Suez War

1. By prior arrangement, on 29th Oct. the Israelis suddenly invaded Egypt. Within a week they had captured the Sinai Peninsula.
2. The British and French issued an "ultimatum" to both sides to withdraw from the Suez Canal.
3. When the Egyptians ignored it, the British and French bombed Egyptian airfields and landed troops at Port Said, at the northern end of the Canal.
4. The attacks caused an outcry in the rest of the world. The Americans became afraid that the Arabs would move towards the Communists, and refused to support Britain, France and Israel:

    (a) At the UN they joined with the Russians in demanding withdrawal.

    (b) They also generated a run on the British and French currencies.

5. The British, French and Israelis agreed upon withdrawal, while the UN moved in to police the Israeli-Egyptian border.

6. The Soviets were preoccupied with the suppression of the Hungarian revolt, but Khrushchev threatened Britain and France with inter-continental ballistic missiles (ICBMs).

The Consequences of the Suez War

1. Since the British and French had been seen to fail to topple Nasser, his prestige was increased among the Arabs. He became a focus of Arab nationalism throughout the Middle East.

2. The Egyptians blocked the Canal with sunken ships, causing a disruption of international trade.

3. The Arabs reduced oil exports to the West, causing petrol rationing for a while.

4. British and French prestige and influence in the Middle East waned.

5. Nasser took Soviet money and experts to build the Aswan high dam, and became an opponent of the West in the Middle East.

6. On 5th January, 1957 Eisenhower announced his determination to "contain Communism" in the Middle East. This was known as the **Eisenhower Doctrine**. He offered 200 million dollars in aid to any state in aid against Communist aggression. Only Lebanon accepted.

7. In July the US intervened in Lebanon and the U.K. in Jordan to prop up threatened pro-Western regimes.

8. The UN forces removed the obstructions in the Canal and reopened the waterway to shipping.

The Significance of the Suez War

1. The Suez Crisis had many dimensions:

    (a) It was part of the struggle between Israel and the Arab states.

    (b) It was part of the struggle of the Arab nationalists against British and French colonialism.

    (c) It was part of the Cold War.

2. It showed Israel to have established itself as a state with the intention and ability to engage in territorial expansion, launching wars of aggression while at all times claiming merely to be defending itself.

3. It marked the entry of the Israeli-Arab conflict into the Cold War.

Pan-Arabism

1. The USA decided to step in to fill the vacuum left by the decline of British and French influence in the Middle East with the **Eisenhower Doctrine**. A US representative toured the Middle East offering economic and military aid to any power threatened by a Communist power. The only (unenthusiastic) taker was Lebanon. The offer provoked anti-American riots in Jordan.

2. In 1958 the Syrians approached Nasser with a plan for a union between Egypt and Syria to form the **United Arab Republic,** with Nasser as president. When Nasser visited Syria he received an ecstatic welcome.

3. When the Iraqi regime was overthrown the US sent marines to Lebanon and Britain sent paratroops to Jordan. Khrushchev advised Nasser to defuse the situation, and US and British forces withdrew. Iraq did not join the UAR, but it left the Baghdad Pact.

4. In 1959 Nasser published *Egypt's Liberation: The Philosophy of the Revolution*. Socialist ideas were implemented throughout the UAR:

(a) A free educational system to university level was created.

(b) Labour was to participate in the management of industry, and in sharing its profits.

(c) Nationalisation of most enterprises (except the retail sector) was announced.

(d) A 5-year plan from 1960-65 partially succeeded in increasing GNP.

5. In 1961 there was a military coup d'état in Syria supported by the Syrian bourgeois who were annoyed at the socialist reforms. Syria withdrew from the United Arab Republic. Nasser decided not to impose his rule over Syria by force. He kept the name United Arab Republic for Egypt as a symbol for his aspirations of Arab unity.

6. In spring 1962 a **National Charter** announced that Egypt would be governed in accordance with the principles of "**scientific socialism**". A new mass organization, the **Arab Socialist Union (ASU),** replaced the National Union

7. Nasser sent troops to assist Yemenite republican revolutionaries in their civil war with Saudi Arabian-backed royalists during 1962–67. This was called "Nasser's Vietnam".

8. Strict police control was enforced over the population:

(a) The media were strictly censored, the chief newspapers were nationalized.

(b) There was close surveillance: telephones were tapped, and visitors' rooms searched.

(c) Candidates for office were hand picked by Nasser and his close associates.

(d) Political enemies were imprisoned in concentration camps in the desert.

Glossary

ASU: The Arab Socialist Union

Copts: Egyptian Christians

GNP: gross national product

Medo: Middle East Defence Organisation

Muslim Brotherhood

UAR: United Arab Republic, a temporary union of Egypt, Syria and Yemen

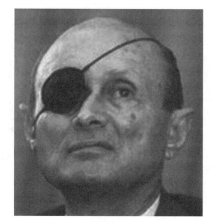

Moshe Dayan

The Six Day War

"Israel must be like a mad dog: too dangerous to bother." (Moshe Dayan)

"What was taken by force, can only be restored by force." (Gamal Abdul Nasser)

The Causes of the Six Day War

1. By 1966 the Israeli government again desired a war. The pretext was to pre-empt an Arab attack, but the real reasons were:;
   - (a) to unite the country;
   - (b) to solve an unemployment problem;
   - (c) to take East Jerusalem and the West Bank from Jordan;
   - (d) to take Sinai from Egypt;
   - (e) to take the Golan Heights from Syria.
2. Once again the Israelis carried out cross-border raids in the hope of provoking a response which they could use as a pretext to launch a war. The worst was the attack on the village of Samu in the West Bank in November 1966. An armoured brigade of 4000 Israeli troops methodically destroyed 125 homes, a school, clinic and workshop, killing 18 Jordanian soldiers.
3. In 1967 Nasser asked the UN to remove the peace-keeping troops policing the strip of land connecting the Gaza strip with Egypt.
4. In May Nasser closed the Gulf of Aquaba to Israeli shipping. The UN Secretary General proposed international arbitration on the Straits of Tiran Question. His offer was rejected.
5. Anticipating possible aggression, Egypt, Jordan and Syria began to concentrate troops on their borders with Israel.

The Course of the Six Day War

1. Without warning, the Israeli Air Force launched a "Pearl Habour-type" attack on the air forces of her Arab neighbours on the ground, largely destroying them. Even the Israeli people were not told about it until afterwards.
2. Jordan sued for peace after three days, Syria and Egypt after six.

3. During the course of the war, the Israelis torpedoed the *USS Liberty* in the Mediterranean Sea, killing 32 and injuring 171. The lack of a response from the US Government demonstrated the power of the Zionist lobby in US politics.
4. The Israelis took the Golan Heights from Syria in violation of the cease-fire, which had already been declared.

Results of the Six-Day War
1. As a result of this war Israel acquired:
    (a) The Gaza Strip and Sinai Peninsula from Egypt;
    (b) East Jerusalem and the West Bank from Jordan;
    (c) The Golan Heights from Syria.
2. On 22nd November the UN Security Council passed resolution 242, which demanded:
    (a) the "withdrawal of Israeli armed forces from territory occupied in the recent conflict."
    (b) the guaranteeing of freedom of navigation through all international waterways in the region;
    (c) a just settlement of the Palestinian refugee problem;
    (d) guarantees of the territorial inviolability of every state in the region.
    The Israelis ignored these demands.
3. The UN sent a force to police the Suez Canal, but it remained blocked.
4. In 1970 a new cease fire had to be arranged.
5. The Arab refugees of the Gaza Strip and the West Bank found themselves under Israeli rule.
6. Palestinian refugees in Lebanon and Jordan effectively destabilized those countries.
7. The Communist bloc broke off diplomatic relations with Israel.
8. Washington became Israel's principal military and diplomatic backer. This is because Egypt and Syria had been champions of the Palestine.

Reasons for the Arab Defeat
1. The Israelis launched a surprise attack.
2. The Egyptian Commander-in-Chief was inefficient.
3. One third of the Egyptian army were reservists.
4. Egyptian communications were faulty.
5. Promised Soviet assistance had not materialised.

The Aftermath
1. Sporadic fighting continued along the borders, e.g. The Israeli gunboat *Eilat* was sunk by Egyptian fire; the Israelis set the oil refineries of Suez on fire.
    In 1968 the Israelis bombed bridges over the Nile and destroyed a power station deep in Egypt.
2. The Israelis began almost immediately to adopt racist attitudes towards the Palestinians, treating them as a source of cheap labour: "hewers of wood and drawers of water."
3. The Palestinians formed the Popular Front for the Liberation of Palestine (PFLP) and Al Fatah, the Palestinian Liberation Organisation (PLO) under Yasser Arafat, to struggle for the return of their homeland. They:
    (a) hijacked aircraft in 1970;
    (b) In 1972 an attack on passengers at Lydda Airport, Tel Aviv;
    (b) attacked the Israeli Olympic team at Munich in 1972.
    These acts were intended to bring the plight of the Palestinians home to world opinion, but in the West, opinion simply resented the threat and inconvenience.

4. Israeli jets attacked the crowded, defenceless refugee camps in revenge.
5. Seeing the PLO as a threat to his own position, King Hussein of Jordan attacked and massacred many refugees in his own country. This in turn led to the formation of **Black September**.

Nasser's Later Years

1. Paradoxically, after the Six-Day War, Nasser's hold upon power in Egypt was strengthened.
2. Showing that Egypt was still a major factor in the region, he conducted what became known as "the **War of Attrition**," in which Egyptian and Israeli gunners traded fire every day, while the Suez Canal remained closed to shipping.
3. Early in 1970 the Israelis began bombing Egypt as far as Cairo, so the USSR supplied Egypt with defensive SAM ground-to-air missiles, forcing the Israelis to stop.
4. In August a ceasefire was arranged.
5. After his nation's military defeat in 1967, Nasser became increasingly dependent on the Soviet Union for military and economic aid.
6. The completion of the Aswan Dam in 1970 was the crowning achievement of his regime. This enabled the Egyptians to:
    (a) better control the available water supply in the Nile;
    (b) extend the cultivated area by 25%;
    (c) export crops;
    (d) generate enough hydro-electric power for the country and some for export.
7. The emergence of the Palestinian resistance inspired a new generation of Arabs. Nasser had sought to control the movement through his backing of the ineffectual Ahmed Shukairy and his opposition to Yasser Arafat. When George Habash's Popular Front for the Liberation of Palestine hi-jacked several Western civilian airliners as a protest at Israeli occupation and Western support for Israel, on **Black September** 1970, King Hussein of Jordan attacked the Palestinian refugees in his country. The Syrians invaded Jordan and forced Hussein to sign a peace treaty with Yassir Arafat. Arab leaders assembled in Cairo for talks.
8. Shortly after the talks ended, Nasser suddenly died.

Assessment of Nasser's Rule

1. Nasser's private life was conservative and austere.
2. No other Arab leader has succeeded in winning the sometimes support of the Arab people throughout the Middle East as Nasser did. Nasser re-established Arab pride, seriously impaired by Western domination and Israeli aggression.
3. Nasser emancipated his people from remnants of colonial rule, restoring national self-esteem.
4. Nasser modernized his country. In 1950 industry formed 10% of the total national output, by 1970 it was 21%.
5. A new middle class began to take the place once held by Italians, Greeks, French, Britons, and other foreigners.
6. He made the community of Arab nations a potent factor in the world.
7. Nasser was, in effect, the first truly modern Arab politician, completely at home the media: the radio, television and all the other means by which leaders speak directly to the people.
8. Arabs everywhere had a leader they could admire, someone whose aims were theirs, and someone whose objectives were the ones they would have chosen.
9. One outstanding achievement was to stay in power for 18 years despite the influence of his many opponents: Islamic fundamentalists, Communists, Copts,* Jews, the old political establishment, rival military cliques, dispossessed landowners, and the remnants of the foreign middle classes.

10. He was never able to deal adequately with the economy. Although progress had been made, it was swallowed up by:

    (a) a fast growing population;

    (b) military spending.

11. Egypt became an authoritarian police state.

Anwar Sadat

The Yom Kippur War

"Everybody has to move; run and grab as many hilltops as they can to enlarge the settlements, because everything we take now will stay ours. Everything we don't grab will go to them." (Ariel Sharon)

The Causes of the Yom Kippur War

1. Egypt and Syria re-equipped their armies with Soviet help. They had created anti-aircraft defences and trained and equipped the Egyptian Army.
2. In February 1971 Egypt offered to sign a peace treaty with Israel in exchange for a full withdrawal of Israeli Forces from Sinai, but was rebuffed.
3. In 1972 Anwar Sadat expelled the Soviet technicians.
4. When the Soviets informed them that the Israelis were about to attack them again, the Egyptians and Syrians chose to pre-empt the attack by launching their attack first on Yom Kippur, a Jewish religious holiday. Iraq also contributed soldiers. Jordan remained neutral.

The Course of the Yom Kippur War

1. They won initial successes on all fronts. The fighting was more evenly balanced than before
2. Moshe Dayan began to speak openly of using weapons of mass destruction against the Arabs.
3. However, after the initial shock of the attack, the Israelis recovered and crossed the Suez Canal. In the north, Israeli forces approached Damascus.
4. The Syrians were supplied with arms by the USSR, while the USA supplied Israel. This made the Yom Kippur War, more than any of the previous wars, an integral part of the Cold War.
5. The Organisation of Oil Producing Countries (OPEC) raised oil prices to pressure the West. This caused oil shortages, inflation and an energy crisis.
6. A cease fire was arranged by the USA and USSR. Brezhnev insisted to Nixon: "I will say it straight, that if you find it impossible to act with us in this matter, we should be faced with the necessity urgently to consider the question of taking the appropriate steps unilaterally. Israel cannot be permitted to get away with the violations."
7. Nixon later claimed that strategic nuclear forces around the world had been put on highest alert, and that this was the biggest international crisis since Cuba. There is considerable doubt about

this, as he had never informed the Allies. He wanted to argue that the Watergate* affair was a dangerous distraction for the president from his "proper duties."

8. The Israelis violated the cease-fire to surround an Egyptian army corps in Sinai.

The Consequences of the Yom Kippur War

1. Israel became the greatest of recipient of US foreign aid.
2. The difficulties in overcoming its enemies led to the secret development of nuclear weapons by Israel, something revealed only in 1986 by Mordechai Vanunu, who was promptly kidnapped by Mossad* and kept in solitary confinement for eighteen years.
3. It became a pariah nation when the Third World countries broke off diplomatic relations with Israel.
4. In October, an Arab summit in Rabat, Morocco recognised the PLO as the official representation of the Palestinian people.
5. In November, the UN General Assembly voted to give the PLO observer status at all meetings. Arafat himself was feted at the UN general Assembly by the representatives of the nations of the world, as a mark of respect for the suffering of the Palestinians.
6. After intensive "shuttle-diplomacy"* by Henry Kissinger, and talks in separate rooms in Geneva, the Israelis agreed to withdraw from the Suez Canal, accepting the peace offer they had rejected in 1971.
7. The Suez Canal was opened in 1975, but not to Israeli ships.
8. In November 1975 the UN General Assembly condemned Zionism as a form of racism.
9. The religious extremists *Gush Emunim* (Bloc of the Faithful), began the practice of deliberately settling Jews on the West Bank territories seized in the Six-Day War. Within twenty years there would be 140,000 settlers there. Again, the Jews were changing the demographics to create a *fait accompli.**

The Significance of the Yom Kippur War

1. More than any of the previous Arab-Israeli wars, the Yom Kippur War was a part of the Cold War, since the two sides were more clearly associated with the rival superpowers.
2. The fighting, more evenly balanced than before, showed the risks for Israel in continuing to defy the entire Arab world.
3. Once again, the Israelis had violated a cease-fire when they saw an advantage to themselves.

Glossary

fait accompli:

Gush Emunim: the Bloc of the Faithful)

Ariel Sharon

The Israeli Invasions of Lebanon

"Its just a bunch of Arabs. Why are you taking it so hard?" (Israeli Army sergeant whose unit had just massacred over a hundred defenceless Palestinian refugees in a UN camp in Lebanon, quoted in an Israeli newspaper)

Background

1. Lebanon is a very mixed and divided society:
   (a) Christian:
       (i) Maronite* Catholics: wealthy, conservative and pro-Western:
       (ii) Orthodox,
       (iii) Armenians,
       (iv) Roman Catholics,
   (b) Muslims:
       (i) Sunni*: composed of generally wealthier Muslims,
       (ii) Shia*: the largest Muslim group, poor, working class,
       (iii) Druze*: poor peasants.
   Lebanon had been deliberately created by the French out of Syria during the mandate, with borders calculated to ensure an area with a Christian majority. However, to ensure that the Christian majority would need French support in the future, they drew its boundaries so that they included only a small Christian majority. The president was always a Maronite Catholic, the prime minister a Sunni, the speaker a Shia and the chief of staff a Druze. The Syrians had never accepted this division of their country.

2. In 1948 Palestinian refugees fleeing Israeli forces settled in Lebanon.

3. Due to differences in the birth-rate, the Christian majority disappeared. In 1957 the National Pact between the Maronite Catholic Christians and the Sunni Muslims, a power-sharing agreement between the two dominant groups, broke down.

4. In 1958 a struggle for power between the right-wing Christians and the left wing Palestinians took place. The Maronite president "invited in" US marines in accordance with the Eisenhower Doctrine, an updated Middle Eastern version of the Truman Doctrine.

5. Although fighting ceased, the central government could not overcome the various conflicts in the

society, between:
    (a) the various religious groups;
    (b) the social classes;
    (c) the clan militias.

6. In 1967, half a million Palestinian refugees fleeing from Israel in the Six-Day War arrived, and were housed in refugee camps.

7. In 1970 the Palestinians were forced out of Jordan by King Hussein. The PLO made its main base in the Lebanon. From here Palestinian partisans sometimes attacked Israel.

8. Lebanon had always been a target of Israeli attacks. These were stepped up during 1974-5. Thousands were killed and hundreds of thousands driven from their homes.

9. The arrival of the Palestinians helped polarize the nation between a Muslim majority which identified with the struggle of the Palestinians and calls for social justice, and the Maronite Catholic Christians, who identified with the West.

10. In 1976 Fighting broke out between:
    (a) Christian militias and the Muslim left, especially the Druze and Palestinians;
    (b) among the Christian militias for dominance.

11. The Israelis sent weapons to the Christian militias:
    (a) to hasten the disintegration of their neighbour;
    (b) to assist in the opposition to the factions which supported the Palestinians.

12. The Syrians intervened to restore order. They occupied all but the far south of the country. Arab League troops followed.

The First Israeli Invasion of Lebanon (1978)

1. In March 1978 Israel invaded Lebanon, ostensibly to prevent cross-border raids. The Israeli Air Force indiscriminately bombed the city of Tyre and South Lebanon, killing one thousand and forcing 750,000 to flee their homes.

2. The Israeli Army occupied the southern part of the country. The Palestinians and other Muslims counterattacked.

3. The USA became impatient and pressured Israel to come to an accommodation with some of its enemies.

4. Before leaving, they installed Major Saad Haddad, a Maronite Christian militia leader as local war lord.

5. Israel was facing economic problems, due to:
    (a) high expenditure on defence;
    (b) the world recession.

6. There was a mutual exchange of visits by leaders, with Sadat of Egypt visiting Jerusalem and Begin of Israel visiting Cairo.

7. In 1978 US President Carter arranged a meeting at Camp David in September 1978, which resulted in a peace treaty in march 1979:
    (a) The Israelis agreed to:
        (i) stop settlements in the West Bank and Gaza;
        (ii) committed themselves to a phased withdrawal from Sinai;
    (b) Egypt agreed:
        (i) not to attack Israel again;
        (ii) to supply Israel with oil from its South Sinai wells.

8. The Israelis continued to plant new settlements in the West Bank and Gaza, seeking to create a new reality on the ground.

The Second Invasion of Lebanon (1982)

The Reasons for the Second Invasion

1. The Israelis intended to drive the PLO from its last remaining land base.
2. In so doing, they would:
    (a) Deprive the Palestinians of all remaining hope of independence, making easier the annexation of the West Bank and Gaza;
    (b) Silence the PLO, and hence the voice of the Palestinian people;
    (c) Deprive the surrounding Arab states of any hope of liberating the Palestinians;
    (d) Defence Minister Israel Sharon wanted to demonstrate Israeli military superiority in the region:
        (i) to drive the Syrians from Lebanon;
        (ii) secure the takeover of the West Bank and Gaza by Jewish settlers;
        (iii) secure a compliant Maronite-dominated Lebanon as a northern neighbour.

The Course of the Second Invasion

1. During 1980-1 cross-border fighting between Israel and the PLO increased. The Israelis launched a series of attacks against Lebanon, the Israeli air force bombing densely populated areas, causing great loss of life.
2. The USA put pressure on the Israelis and PLO to observe a cease-fire. The PLO did so, but the Israelis repeatedly violated it, clearly in order to provoke a response which they could use to justify an invasion.
3. In December 1981 the Israelis declared that the Golan Heights would never be returned to Syria but belonged to Israel.
4. In June 1982 the Israelis invaded Lebanon and advanced, in four days, to the PLO strongholds in the western outskirts of Beirut.
5. For more than a month the Israeli army shelled Beirut, largely destroying the city, in the attempt to annihilate the PLO.
6. On 21st August, after terms had been agreed by which non-combatant Palestinians in the refugee camps would not be harmed, 15,000 male members of the PLO were evacuated by sea under the protection of a multinational force. The leaders went to Tunis, the hard-liners to Iraq.
7. The Israeli army then invaded West Beirut, sealed off the two refugee camps of Sabra and Chatila, and sent in the Christian Falangists to massacre 2,300 Palestinians, mostly women and children.
8. The Israelis were ordered out by the Americans and replaced by a multi-national force, but retained control of the Sheba Farms area.

The Consequences of the Second Invasion

1. 17,000 Lebanese civilians were killed.
2. *Hezbollah* determined that any future Israeli bombardment and invasion of Lebanon would not take place without cost to the Israelis.

Aftermath of the Second Invasion

1. Prime Minister Menachem Begin and Defence Minister Ariel Sharon were criticised by significant numbers of Jews, including many Israelis, who began to:
    (a) Question the nature of their democracy, when the Defence Minister could engage in military adventures independently of the knowledge (as was claimed) of the prime minister;

(b) Find the constant justification of ill-treatment of the Palestinians by appeal to the Holocaust, and equation of the PLO with the Nazis, beginning to wear thin.

2. The Israelis resumed their practice of bombing Lebanon at will.

3. *Hezbollah** (he "party of God"), a Shia Islamist organization comprising
    (a) a political party,
    (b) a political party
    (c) a social organization
   was formed during 1982-5 to fight the Israeli occupation.

4. In 1983 the US Embassy was destroyed by Arab suicide bombers.

5. After US Navy shelled the Muslim parts of Beirut, the US and French military HQs were blown up. The Israeli HQ was also destroyed.

6. The central government of Lebanon was rendered almost totally ineffective by the chaos. In 1984 an alliance of Shia and Druze drove the previously dominant Christian militia out of Beirut, then fought each other for control. Fighting continued until, in 1987, on the invitation of the Lebanese government the Syrians sent in troops again. Civil war continued in Beirut until 1990. The country was gradually brought to order by the Syrians.

7. The Israelis withdrew from the north, but initiated their **Iron Fist Policy** in Southern Lebanon, which included the torture and severe repression of the villagers.

8. In 1987 the Syrians return to northern and central Lebanon, and gradually restored order. By 1990 the fighting was over.

9. The rebuilding of Beirut began in 1993, while the Israelis continue to bombard the villages of the south at will.

10. In *Operation Grapes of Wrath*, a raid on Lebanon, the Israelis killed more than 200 Lebanese civilians.

11. The Israelis finally left South Lebanon in 2000, when Israeli tanks fired at the returning villagers. Many of the prisoners held in Israeli jails without trial for more than a decade were released.

Glossary

Druze: a small Muslim sect

Hezbollah: a Shia Islamist resistance organization comprising:
   (a) a political party,
   (b) a militia
   (c) an extensive social organization providing services for the poor Shiite community which governments of Lebanon had previously failed to do. It runs hospitals, educational facilities, and is responsible for economic and infrastructure development projects.
   It is classified by the USA as a terrorist organization.

Maronites: Syrian Christians who converted to Roman Catholicism during the Crusades, but retain their Syrian customs

Shia: the second largest sect of Muslims

Sunni: members of the largest sect of Muslims

Yassir Arafat

The First Intifada*

"Let us ... say that we have no solution, that you shall continue to live like dogs, and whoever wants to can leave - and we will see where this process leads. In five years we may have 200,000 less people - and that is a matter of enormous importance." (Moshe Dayan)

"Break their bones." (Yitzkak Rabin)

"We plan to eliminate the state of Israel and establish a purely Palestinian state. We will make life unbearable for Jews by psychological warfare and population explosion. We Palestinians will take over everything, including all of Jerusalem." (Yasser Arafat)

Background

1. During the 1980s, the PLO decided to compromise their demands, accepting that nothing could be done about the state of Israel, limiting them to the West Bank, Gaza and East Jerusalem.
2. In December 1988, Yasser Arafat:
   (a) renounced terrorism;
   (b) accepted the right of the state of Israel to exist.
3. Faced with this Palestinian compromise, Israeli prime minister, Yitzak Shamir resisted US pressure to grant some form of autonomy for those regions.
4. The Israeli government offered financial inducements to Jews to settle on the West Bank to increase the settler population there. They lived in armed compounds, deliberately taunting, insulting and sometimes attacking and killing, the local Palestinians, who responded in kind.

The Outbreak of the Revolt

1. Several incidents took place during the last months of 1986.
   (a) Israeli military ambushed and killed seven men from Gaza believed to be members of the Palestinian Islamic Jihad.
   (b) An Israeli settler shot a Palestinian schoolgirl in the back.
   (c) An Israeli plastics salesman, was stabbed to death in Gaza.
   (d) Four Arab workers were run down by an Israeli truck,

2. On December 6, an uprising began in Jabalya Refugee Camp where Israel Defense Forces were attacked by stone-throwing Palestinians.
3. The uprising spread to other Palestinian refugee camps and eventually to Jerusalem,.
   Popular resentment was manifest in many ways:
   (a) by the raising of the Palestinian flag; (This is illegal, and many who did this were shot by Israeli soldiers.)
   (b) by trying to bar entrance to villages to Israeli Army vehicles.
   (c) by hurling stones and abuse at Israeli Army vehicles.
4. The outbreak took the leadership of the PLO in Tunis by surprise.
5. The Israeli Army responded with tear gas, rubber bullets, beatings, and live ammunition and a military curfew. Within two months, over fifty Palestinians had been killed and hundreds injured - many being children. Schools and universities were closed down, to deprive Palestinian students of education. Defense Minister, Yitzhak Rabin, urged Israeli soldiers to break the bones of Palestinian demonstrators

The Causes of the First Intifada

1. The uprising was a spontaneous phenomenon with many causes.
2. There was growing frustration among Palestinians at the lack of progress in finding a resolution for their disinheritance after the establishment of Israel in 1948 and the Six-Day War in 1967.
   (a) The Palestine Liberation Organization had failed to solve the problem, and had even been forced to establish its offices in Tunis since 1982.
   (b) Although all Arab states with the exception of Egypt maintained an official state of war with Israel, they were doing nothing.
3. The brutal Israeli military occupation of the West Bank and Gaza increased Palestinian misery. Israeli occupation was characterised by:
   (a) extra-judicial murders;
   (b) mass detentions;
   (c) house demolitions, often without notifying the people inside;
   (d) routine use of torture;
   (e) deportations;
   (f) daily humiliations It seemed that the Palestinians would spend the rest of their lives as second class citizens, without political rights.
   Israeli practice amounted, and amounts, to the consistent and sustained waging of state terrorism* against the Arabs of Palestine.
4. The limited land available to building or agriculture on what was the poorest land in Palestine, due to increasing Jewish settlement contributed to the increasing density of population.
5. Unemployment was growing in the backward Palestinian economy.
6. Israel was committing war crimes in its military occupation of Southern Lebanon, and getting away with it.

The Course of the Intifada

1. Palestinian teenagers would confront patrols of Israeli soldiers, showering them with rocks. In time, this gave way to Molotov cocktail attacks, over 100 hand grenade attacks and more than 500 attacks with guns or explosives.
2. In 1988, the Palestinians withheld taxes which were collected and used by Israel to pay for the occupations. The Israelis
   (a) imprisoned ringleaders;

(b) imposed heavy fines;

(c) seized equipment, furnishings, and goods from local stores and factories, and even homes.

3. The **Movement of Islamic Resistance (Hamas)** was formed, committed to Islamic rule for all Palestine. It provided social care for the poor and sick.

(a) It rejected:

(i) the PLO as the sole representative organisation of the Palestinian people;

(ii) compromise with Israel over the fate of Palestine.

(b) It proposed a *jihad** against both Israel and corrupt elements within Palestinian society.

4. On April 19, 1988, a leader of the PLO, Abu Jihad, was assassinated in Tunis. During the rioting that followed, about 16 Palestinians were killed.

5. In 1987 and 1988 the Security Council denounced Israeli violence, the US not protecting Israel with its veto, as it usually did.

6. After the Madrid Conference of 1991, the Palestinian Liberation Organisation was able to return from exile in Tunisia.

7. In 1993 Israeli prime minister Yitzak Rabin and Yasser Arafat concluded a deal brokered by the Norwegian Foreign Minister:

(a) The PLO recognised the right of Israel to security, while Israel recognised the PLO as representing the Palestinian people;

(b) Gaza and Jericho were to be handed over to the Palestinians for self rule when details had been worked out.

8. Objections came from:

(a) Hamas, which did not see why the Palestinians should retain only a small portion of their own territory;

(b) The Jewish West Bank settlers, who wanted all the land for the Jews.

9. By this time 1,162 Palestinians (241 of them children), and 160 Israelis (5 of them children) had been killed. These figures suggest the deliberate killing of Palestinian children by the Israeli Army, which was equipped with the most up-to-date protective clothing, arms and equipment by the USA.

10. In 1994, the Palestinians were given limited autonomy in parts of the occupied Palestinian territories. Tension began to ease and the uprising petered out as hopes grew for a better future.

The Results of the First Intifada

1. Israel was successful in containing the uprising militarily. The Palestinians were civilians confronting the very well equipped and trained Israel Defense Forces.

2. The Israeli Information Centre for Human Rights in the Occupied Territories, reported that 1124 Palestinians lost their lives, a high proportion of them being children, and 16,000 were imprisoned, many of these being tortured. Fewer than 50 Israeli civilians were killed

3. Israel did not withdraw from the occupied territories, as they had been agreed at Oslo. Instead:

(a) From 1994-2000, Israeli authorities confiscated 35,000 acres of Arab land.

(b) Settlements were increased at a faster rate, so as to change the facts on the ground. The number of Israeli settlers since Oslo (1993) grew from 110,000 to 195,000 in the West Bank and Gaza. Thirty new settlements were established and more than 18,000 new housing units for settlers were constructed. Palestinians' houses were demolished and their trees uprooted.

(c) Palestinian living in Jerusalem were forced to relinquish their residency rights. In annexed East Jerusalem, the Jewish population rose from 22,000 to 170,000. .31

(d) Palestinian lands were divided into small areas to create easily-controllable and bantustans.*

4. There were some positive results for the Palestinians:

(a) By taking on the Israelis themselves, rather than relying on the assistance of neighbouring states, the Palestinians were able to end the Israeli propaganda technique of denying them an existence by referring to them as "South Syrians".

(b) The brutal Israeli repression drew attention to their plight and the nature of the regime which oppressed them.

(c) The cost of the intifada to the Israeli economy through:

(i) lost exports, largely through Palestinian boycotts

(ii) to the Israeli tourist industry

was notably high.

(d) After the Oslo accords, in 1994, the Palestinians were given limited autonomy in parts of the occupied Palestinian territories, and an independent Palestine first became a distinct possibility.

Glossary

bantustans: a term taken from the racist regime of apartheid South Africa.

Hamas: a resistance movement directed against the Zionist disinheritance of the Palestinians, regarding the Fatah government as corrupt and ineffective. It is:

(a) a political party,

(b) a political party

(c) a social organization. It runs welfare programs, schools, orphanages, and clinics in Gaza and the West Bank.

Intifada: uprising

state terrorism: the practice of terrorism by the agencies of a state against part or all of its own people.

Bibliography

Fisk, Robert, *Pity the Nation: Lebanon at War, 3rd ed*. Oxford University Press (Oxford, 2001)

Gilbert, Martin, *Israel: A History*, Black Swan (London, 1999)

Jones, O., *The Arab World,* Hamish Hamilton, (London, 1969)

Nussbaum, E., *Israel,* Oxford University Press, (Oxford,1968)

Perkins, S. J., *The Arab-Israeli Conflict*, Macmillan (London, 1982)

Rodinson, Maxime, *Israel: A Colonial-Settler State?* Anchor Foundation (New York, 1973)

Scott-Bauman, M., *Israel and the Arabs,* Arnold (London, 1986)

Thomas, H., *The Suez Affair,* Weidenfeld & Nicolson (London, 1967)

The Significance of the Palestinian Problem

"If I were an Arab leader, I would never sign an agreement with Israel. It is normal; we have taken their country. It is true God promised it to us, but how could that interest them? Our God is not theirs. There has been Anti - Semitism, the Nazis, Hitler, Auschwitz, but was that their fault ? They see but one thing: we have come and we have stolen their country. Why would they accept that?" (David Ben-Gurion)

"Even today I am willing to volunteer to do the dirty work for Israel, to kill as many Arabs as necessary, to deport them, to expel and burn them, to have everyone hate us, to pull the rug from underneath the feet of the Diaspora Jews, so that they will be forced to run to us crying. Even if it means blowing up one or two synagogues here and there, I don't care." (Ariel Sharon)

"Israel may have the right to put others on trial, but certainly no one has the right to put the Jewish people and the State of Israel on trial." (Ariel Sharon)

"Anyone who believes you can't change history has never tried to write his memoirs." (David Ben-Gurion)

1. No other claim to the territory of another people, on the basis of having lived there nearly two thousand years previously, would have been entertained for a minute, even in the romantically-inclined nineteenth century, if a large number of Jewish and Christian fundamentalists* had not been disposed to support this claim.
2. It is quite clear that many of the early Zionists always had in mind to dispossess the Palestinian Arabs and take over the entire area of Palestine as an exclusively Jewish state, and were prepared to hide this aim in dealings with other powers in order to establish their foothold in the area and then extend it. The consistency of Zionist aims is apparent in the history of the area since settlement began: whatever the position adopted in negotiations, long-term expansion was always a constant goal.
3. In achieving their aims, the Israelis have frequently:
   (a) achieved advantages by breaking truces;
   (b) engaged as *agents provocateurs* to provoke reactions to employ as pretexts to justify previously planned aggression;
   (c) ignored resolutions of the UN;
   (d) deliberately targeted the UN;
   (e) deliberately targeted civilians
   This is the result of the systematic application of double standards and special pleading* to the Israeli position. "God's Chosen People must not ne judged by the standards used to judge Gentiles* see the third quotation above).
4. The state which the Zionists have created is a racist a state comparable with apartheid South Africa:
   (a) The Palestinians are confined to certain areas;
   (b) They are subjected to arbitrary military authority;
   (c) The attitudes of many of the Israeli population towards the indigenous people is racist, often "sanctified" with a religious justification.
   For such reasons, in 1975 the General Assembly of the United Nations officially declared Zionism to be a form of racism.
5. The aim of the Israelis towards the Palestinians of the West Bank, Gaza and East Jerusalem,

is clearly to make life so intolerable for them that most will emigrate, leaving a depressed and repressed minority living in isolated "Bantustans" on the poorest land as a resource of cheap labour for Jewish immigrants.

6.   The Palestinian Problem from the very beginning compromised the good name of the United Nations Organization, while the use of the US veto to protect Israel continues to undermine its effectiveness.

7. Since the late 1960s, Israel has been a client state of the USA in the region,.

    (a) Since 1976 Israel has been the leading annual recipient of US foreign aid and is the largest cumulative recipient since World War II. The greater portion is military aid.

    (b) The USA consistently uses its veto in the UN to render Israel immune from punitive actions by the world community.

Thus US professions to act as mediator in the Palestinian-Israeli dispute are disingenuous.

8. Israel has been, and remains, a destabilizing influence on all the states around it, rarely losing an opportunity to degrade their infrastructure or incite USA action against them.

9. The determined refusal of the Palestinians, powerless as they are, to accept their total disinheritance from their own land, over almost a century, is almost unique in modern history.

10 Israel has consistently sought to rewrite history to its own advantage, e.g.:

    (a) asserting that Israel was uninhabited before the Jewish immigrants settled there;

    (b) that the Palestinians need not have fled their homes in 1948 (*sic*);

    (c) that whenever they attack a neighbour it is "in self-defence";

    (d) that the only issue over land is the so-called "Occupied Territories" taken in 1967;

    (e) that Israel is a Western-style democracy, and not a racist state;

    (f) that Israel abhors, and has never practised "terrorism".

Glossary

condominium: joint rule by two outside powers

fundamentalists: those who believe in the literal truth of their Scriptures, as understood without benefit of the insights developed by academic historical and sociological studies. Many Jewish and Christian fundamentalists believe that if Isreal rebuilds the Jewish Temple in Jerusalem, it will usher in the Age of the Messiah.

Gentiles: non-Jews

Gush Emunim: "Bloc of the Faithful" an extremist religious Zionist movement which believes in settling the West Bank and the Gaza Strip

mandate: UN authorisation to administer territory

Mossad: the Israeli espionage agency

non-aligned: not favouring either the West or the Eastern blocs

Orthodox Jews: Jews with traditional religious beliefs

veto: the ability to block an action by one's vote against it

Watergate: scandal caused by discovery of attempted break-in of democratic Party HQ by burglars employed by US President Nixon, together with attempted cover-up

9. The Development of Warfare

"Every gun that is made, every warship launched, every rocket fired signifies in the final sense, a theft from those who hunger and are not fed, those who are cold and are not clothed. This world in arms is not spending money alone. It is spending the sweat of its laborers, the genius of its scientists, the hopes of its children." (Dwight D. Eisenhower)

"When the rich wage war, it's the poor who die." (Jean-Paul Sartre)

"If we let people see that kind of thing, there would never again be any war." (A Pentagon official explaining why the U.S. military censored graphic footage from the Gulf War)

"It has never happened in history that a nation that has won a war has been held accountable for atrocities committed in preparing for and waging that war." (Ramsay Clark)

The Nature of Warfare

Wars, Warfare and Weapons

1. Wars may be classified according to the category of weapons used. Normal weapons of war are called **conventional weapons**, and a war fought with such weapons is a **conventional war**.
2. Wars might be fought with non-conventional weapons: chemical weapons (such as poison gas, napalm, agent orange), biological weapons (such as anthrax), or nuclear weapons (nuclear bombs). Today these are sometimes called **weapons of mass destruction (WMDs)**.
3. Along with Germany and Japan, the USA pioneered the use of chemical and biological weapons, granting immunity from prosecution to Japanese and German scientists after the Second World War in return for their knowledge of how to manufacture such weapons.
4. **Chemical weapons** have been used in many wars: poison gas by both sides in the First World War, and by the Italians in the Abyssinian War; phosphorous bombs and napalm were used in Germany by the USA and Britain in the Second World War; and napalm was supplied by the USA to the Greek Royalists in the Greek Civil War, and used by them in the Vietnam War. Agent Orange was used to defoliate the jungle in the Vietnam War.
5. **Biological warfare** was used by North American settlers against native Americans in the seventeenth century, by deliberately supplying them with smallpox-infected clothing; while Alan Watt, head of the Australian Foreign Affairs Department was told that the United States had used biological weapons extensively during the Korean War, "but only on an experimental basis." This was approved by US Secretary of Defence George Marshall on 27 October 1950.

Declassified records show that "research" focused on spreading diseases like botulism (a kind of food poisoning caused by a toxin), cholera, dysentery and typhoid.

6. **Nuclear weapons** have been used twice, each time by the USA, in Japan at the end of the Second World War.

7. Some weapons cut across this classification. Depleted uranium is a chemically toxic substance. Since it is an extremely dense, hard metal, and cheap to produce, it is used by some countries as tank armour, and in armour-piercing shells It is chemically poisoning to the body and radiologically hazardous. It spontaneously burns on impact, creating tiny glass particles small enough to be inhaled. Depleted uranium has a half life of 4.5 billion years, and can pose a long term threat to human health and the environment. Depleted uranium was first used on a large scale by the USA in the 1991 Gulf War, and has since been used in the Balkans in 1995 and 1999

7. It should be noted that both chemical and biological warfare is of limited effectiveness, and liable to rebound against those who employ it; the wind changes and blows the gas in the wrong direction; one's own people could get infected. Thus thousands of US servicemen died premature deaths, suffered illnesses and gave birth to deformed children because of their own use of Agent Orange in the Vietnam War. It is now clear from research using computer models that the use of nuclear weapons would render the entire planet uninhabitable by creating a nuclear winter. For this reason, chemical, biological and nuclear weapons are better described as **terror weapons**.

8. It is important, however, to realise that weapons of mass destruction are not necessary to commit atrocities. Conventional weapons can sometimes inflict greater damage on the enemy than weapons of mass destruction.

   (a) In *A People's History of the United States*, Howard Zinn points out: "The bombing of Japanese cities continued the strategy of saturation bombing to destroy civilian morale; one night time fire-bombing of Tokyo took 80,000 lives." Zinn points out that "night time bombing" was by its very nature indiscriminate, not aimed primarily at military targets.

   (b) In the greatest single massacre of World War Two, which surpassed even the atomic bomb attacks on Hiroshima and Nagasaki combined, as many as half-a-million ordinary German men and women were burned to death on the night of February 13-14, 1945 by two massive firebombing attacks, carried out by the U.S. and British Air Forces. On the next morning a third firebombing attack was carried out, during which American fighter pilots strafed helpless crowds of injured and terrorized refugees as they tried to flee along the banks of the River Elbe.

   (c) Howard Zinn himself took part in the bombing of Royan, in France. Royan was a small town on the Atlantic coast near Bordeaux: "There were a few thousand German soldiers holed up near this town, waiting for the war to end, not doing anything, not bothering anybody. But we were going to destroy them. ... So we destroyed the town, the German soldiers, the French also who were there." Twelve-hundred heavy bombers of the US Air Force dropped napalm on all the people of Royan - men, women and children."

9. A long drawn out war may become a **war of attrition**, in which one side tries to wear down the other. The side wins which is worn down first. Special forms of **static warfare** include the **siege** and the **blockade**. We usually speak of besieging a city or an army, while blockading a port. Economic Warfare involves organising the blockade of a country to bring it to its knees by denying trade, food and medicines.

10. **Psychological warfare** consists of various tricks of deception and propaganda used to deceive or disconcert the enemy during wartime.

11. Economic and psychological warfare is frequently carried out in the absence of a literal war. The USA has conducted such "economic warfare" against Cuba for over fifty years.

12. A new form of warfare is **cyber warfare**, in which one side tries to sabotage the computer systems of the other side. During NATO's undeclared war against Serbia in 1999, Serbian students successfully caused the official NATO website to crash.

13. The word "war" is sometimes used by metaphorical extension to describe campaigns or hostile relations which are not literally warfare. A **propaganda war** is simply the existence of mutually hostile propaganda campaigns. The most famous examples of this kind is the term Cold War, referring to the armed hostility between the USA and its allies/or satellites and the USSR and its allies and/or satellites, and US President George W. Bush's "War Against Terror", designed to replace the Cold War.

When is a War a War?

1. At the beginning of the nineteenth century it was the custom for the so-called "civilised" countries to issue **declarations of war**, formal documents signifying the intent of one ruler or government to order his armed forces to commence hostilities against the recipient of the document. The Japanese attack upon Pearl Harbour, which preceded the declaration of war against the USA was regarded as particularly treacherous precisely for the reason that the declaration of war arrived after the commencement of hostilities, although only by accident. However, such courtesies were not usually extended to those attacked in colonial or imperialist wars.

2. Paradoxically, it is now the normal custom for the US and its Allies not to declare war when hostilities are initiated. To cover this, US-initiated wars are initially described as "police actions," "going to the aid of friendly governments," "peace-keeping operations," "spreading freedom," etc. Thus conflicts such as the Vietnam War and the First Gulf War were called "wars" only by their opponents at the time, and by everyone only safely after the events. This is:
   (a) so that US presidents can bypass the US constitution, and wage war without winning the necessary vote of Congress;
   (b) to disguise aggression by hiding the fact that war is being waged.

When is a War a Single War?

1. This may at first sight seem a simple question, but it may not always be so. It is not always clear when we have one war, or more. The ancient historian Thucydides considered the two ten years wars between Athens and Sparta and their several allies in the fifth century BC, known as the Peloponnesian Wars, to be two parts of a struggle led by Sparta against Athenian hegemony over Greece, even though the two parts were separated by ten years' truce.

2. The First and Second World War were both fought to prevent German dominance of the European Continent, and so could be considered two parts of a single struggle, which might be called the War(s) of German Hegemony.

3. The Vietnamese, under Ho Chi Minh and his successors, successively fought for the independence of their country against the Japanese, the French and the Americans. These are sometimes categorised as:
   (a) a resistance movement against the Japanese;
   (b) a war of national liberation against the French (the Indo-China War);
   (c) a proxy war on behalf of the Communist bloc against the Americans (the Vietnam War).
   There were pauses in the fighting, but from the viewpoint of the Vietnamese they could be thought of as three phases of a single struggle for independence that lasted for thirty years before it was successful.

The Paradox of Modern Warfare

At the beginning of the twenty first century, new developments in weapons technology, particularly computerization of delivery systems, has enabled the production of much more accurate weapons. At the same time, while at the beginning of the twentieth century 90 per cent of war casualties were military men ansd 10% were civilians; at the beginning of the twenty-first, more than 90 % are civilians, of whom some half are children.

The reasons for this must be among the following:

(a) Modern weapons have become more destructive, both in size and ingenuity. Examples of the latter include cluster bombs, shells that eject multiple small bomblets designed to cover an area as large as two or three football fields, many of which do not explode on impact, but present a danger later to civilians.

(b) Increasingly, the traditional laws of war have been ignored. Warfare has become a struggle between peoples, rather than rulers, with the entire nation involved. This is due to the prevalence of nationalism.

(c) The nation most frequently at war, the USA, prefers to use its wealth to wage war by employing very destructive high technology weapons deployed from a distance, and so avoiding risks to US forces (unpopular with the voters) at the cost of civilians on the ground.

This began with the carpet bombing of German cities by the USA and Britain during the Second World War, culminating in the use of the atomic bomb. Other wars in which the US has largely relied upon bombing to achieve its aims include the Vietnam War and recent wars in the Balkans and the Middle East.

(d) Atttacks upon civilians are encouraged by racist attitudes towards the enemy, such as the Nazi attitudes towards Eastern Europeans during the Second World War, American attitudes towards the Vietnamese during the Vietnam War ("If he's dead and Vietnamese, he's Vietcong"), American attitudes towards the Iraqis during the Iraq War (the Pentagon dies not count Iraqi civilian casualties), and Iraeli attitudes towards the Lebanese during their periodic attacks upon Lebanon.

(e) There is sometimes a desire deliberately to terrorize the population on the other side: e.g. in the carpet bombing of German cities by the USA and Britain during the Second World War, and in the aptly named *Operation Shock and Awe* (which gave the game away) which the Americans launched upon Iraq in 2003.

(f) Civilians, and civilian infrastructure, is being deliberately targeted. The bombing of power stations, bridges, hospitals etc. is clearly designed to deny food and medical assistance to the population under attack. The most recent and clear example, at the time of going to press, is the Israeli attack upon Lebanon (2006).

Some moves have been made to counter this trend, of which the most important is probably the establishment of the International Criminal Court (I.C.C.) located in The Hague, The Netherlands, in 2002. Unfortunately, the most likely offenders, e.g. the USA, Russia and Israel, refiuse to accept its jurisdiction.

10. Writing Essays on Wars and Warfare

1. When preparing for examination questions on a war, you should always be aware that the examiner will require answers which display analysis. For this reason, no question will require the simple narration of the events of the course of a war. If you think that it does, you have almost certainly misunderstood it.

   In preparing for the examination, you should, therefore, focus upon those aspects of a war which allow the examiner to ask questions which require analysis. These will usually include:
   - (a) the **causes** of the war;
   - (b) the **nature** of the war;
   - (c) the **quality of the leadership** of the protagonists;
   - (d) **why the winning side won** or the losers lost;
   - (e) the **effects/consequences/results** of the war;
   - (f) the **significance** of the war.

2. You may be asked to choose a war, or wars, of a certain type in order to answer a question, e.g. a civil war or a proxy war.
   - (a) Such descriptions are not exclusive. For example, a single war could be both a civil war and a proxy war, or both a war of decolonization and an asymmetrical war.
   - (b) Such descriptions may be a matter of controversy. The safest thing to do is to begin your essay by defending your choice of a war or wars, by arguing that the war(s) you choose to write about are in fact being appropriately described. e.g. If you are asked to write about a civil war, and you choose the Vietnam War, you must show *why* that conflict can rightly be regarded as a civil war.

3. Questions requiring you to provide the cause(s) of a war should be answered in such a way that you distinguish clearly between the pretext(s) and the causes;
   - (a) show why the pretexts are pretexts;
   - (b) list all the causes, arrayed in a hierarchy of some kind, e.g. standing conditions, long term causes, short term causes, the immediate cause; or as classified by the historiographical controversy;
   - (c) evaluate the comparative importance of the various causes

4. A superficial comparison of the historiography ("There are three main views about the causes of the Second World War..." and a brief summary of each view) will not justify a pass mark.

5. All causes historians have generally considered need to be referred to, even if you think that they were not important. If you think that they were not important, you must explain why.

6. A question asking "to what extent is *X* a cause of the war?" requires a comparison of *X* with all the other causes. Special attention needs to paid to *X*, even if you argue that it is not a cause, or an important cause, of the war. You will need to justify your judgement.

7. Beware of technical questions. A good mark will require specialist technical knowledge. Such technical details are not to be found in ordinary history books, or in this book either. It is simply not enough, to obtain a good grade, when answering a question on technical developments in the Second World War, for example, to mention that there were significant developments in the technology of tanks and rockets, and the introduction of atomic weapons.

8. Questions as to why *Y* won the war or why *Z* lost it usually require reference to the same factors, although they will be explained from a different angle.

9. You should distinguish between the **effects**, **consequences** and **results** of a war. The effects and consequences are the same, they consist of what followed because of the war. By contrast, the results of an action are its *intended* consequences, and come about through intentional actions.

10. Among the effects of any war, the following should be considered:
    (a) casualties: deaths and injuries, including the psychological damage to individuals
    (b) famine and disease
    (c) the displacement of refugees
    (d) the damage to the environment, including the infrastructure of civilised life, works of art, historical remains, etc. with the residue of unexploded bombs, land mines, etc.
    (e) the waste of material resources
    (f) changes in the relative power of the belligerent and non-belligerent states involved, including territorial changes
    (g) the solution of existing problems between states brought about by the outcome of the war, as well as the generation of future conflicts
    (h) the resolution or generation of social conflicts within the belligerent countries occasioned by the war, consequent coups, revolutions, etc.
    (i) advances in science and technology brought about by efforts to win the war
    (j) the effects of the war on the economies of non-belligerent states.

11. If you are asked to compare two wars, without any qualifications, go through your checklist in order to make sure you cover all the relevant points, viz:
    (a) the **causes** of the war;
    (b) the **nature** of the war;
    (c) the **quality of the leadership** of the protagonists;
    (d) **why the winning sides won** or the losers lost;
    (e) the **effects/consequences/results** of the war;
    (f) the **significance** of the war against the background of the larger sweep of history..

Books for the IB from Anagnosis

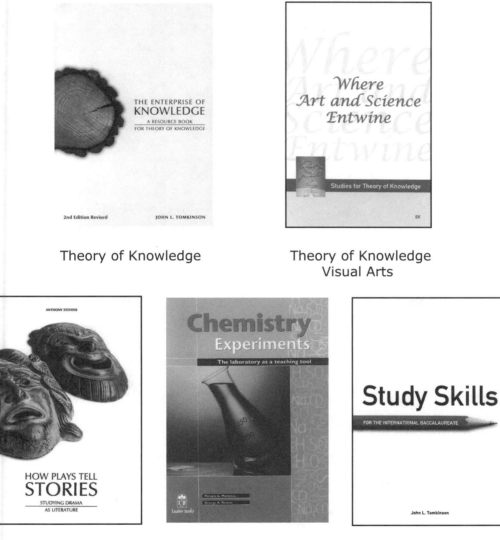

Theory of Knowledge

Theory of Knowledge
Visual Arts

Language A1
Drama

Chemistry

Study Skills

All Anagnosis books can be ordered online by credit card from:

www.anagnosis.gr

For up to date information about Anagnosis books
visit our website: www.anagnosis.gr
email: info@anagnosis.gr

Anagnosis, Deliyianni 3, Maroussi 15122 Greece
telephone: ++30-210-62-54-654
fax: ++30-210-62-54-089
fax: ++30-210-62-54-089